CRICKET'S GLOBAL WARMING

GLENN TURNER

LYNN MCCONNELL

Copyright © 2020 Glenn Turner and Lynn McConnell

The moral right of the authors has been asserted.

All rights reserved. No part of this publication may be produced or transmitted in any form or by any means, electronic or mechanical, including photocopying, recording or information storage and retrieval systems, without permission in writing from the copyright holder.

Published by TurnerMcC Publishing

Contact: TurnerMcCPublishing@gmail.com

Web: fb.me/cricketincrisis

A catalogue record for this book is available from the National Library of New Zealand.

Cover illustration by Garrick Tremain

CONTENTS

Introduction   v

1. The glorious and inglorious uncertainties of cricket   1
2. For starters   15
3. Boundaries   31
4. Building character through sport   59
5. Cricket a reflection of society   69
6. The McCullum myth   83
7. Team cultures in international cricket   111
8. Killing bowlers with kindness   149
9. NZC lost in power struggles   155
10. Cricket just another product — fast food?   169
11. Game plans for ODIs   181
12. The true role of cricket captains   201
13. Another flawed selection system   211
14. The contract system — who wins?   223
15. Neglect leads to power corrupting   227

Afterword   231
About the authors   239
Other books by the authors   241

INTRODUCTION

Having been earnestly involved in cricket since making my first-class debut in 1964, and with 50 subsequent years of involvement in the first-class and the international game in a variety of capacities — playing, captaining, coaching, managing, selecting, writing, television and radio commentary — I have seen cricket undergo significant changes away from the pitch. Pitches are still 22 yards long, the balls are still the same, although their range of colours is increasing in variety. Bats are mostly heavier and players are generally more gymnasium-fit and often less cricket-fit, but the basics of the game remain. It should be recognised that the improvements in technology being applied to cricket are mostly notable as entertainment tools for broadcasters to enhance their product rather than cricketers receiving the same value. Cricketers have not all of a sudden grown wings! It will not surprise anyone that I have my own views on some elements of today's 'modern' game as compared to the 'modern' game when I played. The use of the word modern in this context is a promotional term intended to automatically indicate advancement. Can we assume, therefore, that literally today is the modern game and tomorrow is more modern than yesterday? Yes, I suppose I can be a little pedantic. When thinking of the past, the present and the future, it reminds me of a quote from

Winston Churchill who said 'a nation that forgets its past has no future'.

I hope this book is just as relevant to those in other cricketing countries who may see a lot in common with what I've experienced in New Zealand and beyond. I've attempted to counter, or at least give an alternative view to, what Joe Bennett describes as 'PR propaganda, selling idealism, depicting fantasy, and chipping away at one's sense of actuality'. I can hear the dedicated fans groaning with discontent at anything written that might tarnish their fun and enjoyment. For many people, the protective reaction to uncomfortable knowledge is to suppress it. Unfortunately, these natural human responses are often used by PR machines to mask actuality. I'm prepared to speak out against this deception, because I believe that in the long run, reality comes home to roost and the sooner the better — at the very least, ideas need to be challenged, including my own. Sadly, over many years, there has been a reluctance within the game to probe deeply into the subject areas that matter most. The vast majority of thought and energy appears to go into the survival of individuals retaining their positions and/or securing additional ones. Judging the abilities of players even with the advancement of technology remains astonishingly unexplored, even primitive, which I largely put down to money, boardroom and player distractions caused by conflicts of interest, and accountability issues.

I learnt a long time ago that challenging the status quo or ideas in general was a likely way to become isolated. Surrendering to the concept of working the system to retain employment rather than having the freedom to question it was too much of a price to pay, even at the risk of impotence. It demonstrated USA President Lyndon Baines Johnson's old adage that you need to be 'inside the tent pissing out rather than outside pissing in'. My experience having spent a considerable amount of time inside the tent does not guarantee effectiveness. Inclusiveness in decision-making still needs to apply. As a questioner, I had a distinct sense that being retained was more about a mechanism for controlling and at the same time isolating. This strategy not only stymied my own learning, but others too. The reason I continued as a selector for so long was in the hope that one day the next chief executive would accept that selection panels should be in charge of selection. Eventually, one's patience runs out. Putting forward a contrary view in order to stimulate discussion, no matter how well meaning, is to this day mostly fobbed off as unhelpful, not being a team player or even being disloyal. It is just another example of popularity unanimously favouring those using a system rather than those attempting to improve it. I continue to believe that objectivity and scepticism are helpful and thus important. Once the decision is made to authorise and indulge the wants rather than the needs of those at the rock face, along with their players' associations, the rot sets in. The stage is set for conflicts of interest, a lack of accountability, talented people being sidelined and a whole new wave of internal politicking for parties with vested interests to advantage themselves first and foremost. That's where New Zealand Cricket (NZC) sits to this day.

For a professional player trying to make ends meet in the 1960s and 1970s, NZC administrations could be best described as tormenters (rather than part-time employers) towards any attempts to play as a professional. There was still a quaint, yet frustrating notion that being a professional whether an accountant, lawyer or retailer in business was okay, but in sport it was best to treat you as an amateur with all the subservience that that demanded. Yet the wheel can turn surprisingly quickly. By the time my playing career was completed and full-time employment in administrative positions was available to me, the pendulum had swung 180 degrees. Now we learn ahead of the 2019 Indian Premier League that eight or nine of the prospective New Zealand team for the 2019 World Cup will have six weeks playing that tournament with the prospect of only a week or two back at home before flying out to the World Cup. And why? Because players involved could double the earnings they make from NZC. For the likes of Kane Williamson and Trent Boult, that could make nearly $400,000 difference to their pay packet. Other countries can impose their requirements on their players but it appears NZC can't. The decision-making power connected to the team, had shifted from the board to the players, or at least the senior players. The administration's hierarchy followed the board's path in allowing itself to be dominated by the wants and wishes, rather than the needs, of players and in turn stamping out any actions by any staff that might question or be seen not to follow the often ill-conceived theory of the moment.

Three of my previous four books were largely a chronological order of my playing days and my fourth book about coaching the national team. Hopefully those books (apart from *Century of Centuries*) also provided an insight into some of the ways New Zealand Cricket evolved during the period from 1969 through to 1998.

This book, my fifth, is an attempt to engender discussion and debate about a whole raft of subjects aligned to the game of cricket at international level with some reference to the first-class game. It gives my views on the issues covering what I think works and doesn't work, and the reasoning behind it. Hopefully, it will stimulate conversations that extend beyond the convenience and superficiality of one-liners. Cricket is just about like everything else, there are exceptions to the rule and absolutes are rare.

Nevertheless, it is too easy for detractors to disregard what people of my age have to offer. Ideally, it is the young who need to come forward and challenge the establishment. The inspirational 16-year-old Swedish climate activist Greta Thunberg, surprisingly at such an early age, demonstrates precisely that. One of her quotes that I particularly like is: 'Our civilisation is being sacrificed for the opportunity of a very small number of people to continue making enormous amounts of money ... It is the suffering of the many which pays for the luxuries of the few ... You say you *love* your children above all else, and yet you are stealing their future in front of their very eyes.' I think the game of cricket is also being stolen in front of our very eyes! Too many of the powers that be are showing the same indifference to the damaging changes already affecting the long term future of the game, in the same way that too many politicians and others have shown indifference as global warming affects the world as witnessed by the 2019-20 bushfires in eastern Australia. In addition to the horrific consequences and the devastation caused by these fires, the smoke and unmanageable increase in temperatures at the Australian Open tennis in Melbourne was just another warning of the future that sport as a whole will be facing. It would appear that politicians will continue to pay about as much attention to the catastrophic effects of fossil fuels as ruling bodies in cricket will pay to dealing with the longevity of the game they are responsible for.

Cricket is already talking about reducing Test cricket from five days to four. Unsurprisingly, many players have raised their voice in protest at that. I view this as a strong indicator of where players preferences lie and I'd go so far as to say that most international cricketers would ditch T20 if it wasn't for the money. The amount of time in travel and disruption it causes must surely be revisited.

It is probably too difficult and unrealistic for cricket to come up with someone as young as Greta, but there is the likes of Ed Smith (now 41), who was in his twenties when he began writing some insightful narrative, while being prepared to challenge some of the current norms. We need more like him.

Businesses across the board have had to tighten up on their spending with the financial 'bottom line' being all-important. Cricket, on the other hand, receives an enormous amount of unearned capital from elsewhere, with no requirement to produce any accountability to its shareholders — the supporters of the game. Many would agree that some businesses have put money ahead of service to their customers, even to the extent of dumbing down. Yet, with all its money, NZC has spent extravagantly while still managing to dumb itself down, splashing out aimlessly, seemingly assuming more is better. This mentality has led to a series of actions that can be best described as unqualified, inexplicable and ill-conceived. A preoccupation with following perceptions, assumptions and baseless dreams has replaced common sense, facts, honesty and just plain hard work. Numerous feeble and destructive attempts to come up with novel strategies to outdo, or get the jump on, opposition teams have led to predictable failures. An ongoing 'cargo cult' approach has been applied by an organisation lacking in fundamental practices and an understanding of how international teams function. And one might ask, what is the NZC board doing about it and what about their accountability? A deficit of $9.3 million in 2017 followed by deficits of $3.5 million (2018) and $1.3 million (2019) is surely a strong indication of not only living beyond their means but also enhancing an attitude of entitlement and greed among its players. What a culture to endorse. Looking skyward expecting an Indian cargo plane to turn up with loads of dosh to cover financial shortfalls is perilous to say the least. What if the plane takes a wrong turn? Undoubtedly, player payments needed to substantially increase from the amateur days of the 1970s, but the degree of increase to first team players (and at the expense of others) has created more problems than it has solved, not least the values of the game.

Predictably, the gold rush has caused the roots of cricket across the globe to be over-watered to such an extent that the game and its participants have become more vulnerable and less consistently productive. It has weakened the roots of the game (certainly in New Zealand and elsewhere), reducing the incentive to go searching for more sustainable nourishment. The need to probe deeper is being lost when shallow roots will do. It's much easier when you can stay in one place with your mouth under the tap hooked up to the Indian mains supply, no matter what the risks may bring. No need to do the hard yards to improve, or be fiscally cautious when the money is there (or anticipated) to buy a superficial quick-fix option. Furthermore, it's much easier for players with all their so-called support staff to pass on the blame of failure to someone else for not doing their job while given more time to work out how to keep their heads next to the tap. It all works very nicely for boards too: as long as the free water is flowing, they can continue to hold down their positions, retain their status, lap up the kickbacks, and rev up the propaganda whenever necessary to hide.

These decisions have followed mostly a predictable course of players' and team performances lacking consistency and all those connected generally under-performing beyond the anticipated norms of a game like cricket. The degree of pastoral care and pampering of players is counterproductive for everyone concerned, not least players reaching their full potential. Who among New Zealand's players of the past 20 years can honestly say they achieved their potential? Non-playing staff have been demoted by not being valued to the degree originally anticipated. The lack of trust, respect and cohesion within the organisation has led to a high degree of dysfunction. The powers given to players, and the captain in particular, has resulted in growing egos, entitlement, large amounts of vanity and opened the door, ultimately, for increased levels of self-destruction. The current captain, Kane Williamson, appears to have escaped from most of this stuff compared to some of his more recent predecessors. Having said that, he must share some of the blame of a more recent policy of a body-line approach to bowling, aimed particularly against weaker opposition. Today they call it 'bombing'. The current crop of players seem to be a decent lot, but it is impossible for them to have escaped unscathed by the influences of the many entrenched policy failures of the previous and current system. At least they can't be held responsible for contributing to the unsavoury work of those that came before them.

Having witnessed first-hand the effects this money has had on the players, support staff and administrators, I want to share some of the experiences I have had particularly over the past couple of decades or more. During this period the rhetoric has certainly grown, but money has been recklessly thrown at just about everything imaginable, limiting the areas that really count: cricket knowledge, accountability and avoiding conflicts of interest. The feeding frenzy has been successful in a remarkable growth in jobs at NZC. Around 70 employees sit in their offices plus a number of seasonal contractors across their offices in Auckland and Lincoln and I imagine that doesn't include the eight support staff that accompany the New Zealand Cricket team.

I've endeavoured to back up statements with examples and facts and am conscious in so doing that names, times and places become unavoidable. Does that matter? It will to some, but the stories are incomplete without them. In some instances, there have been too many injustices to ignore and those victimised along the way deserve some truth. It must be galling for them to have witnessed some of the perpetrators walking away blameless, in fact in some cases, applauded while they walked away. NZC states that its core values are: Inclusivity, Respect, Tenacity, Optimism, and Fun. By sharing what I've experienced, just maybe in the future some good may come out of it.

When reading quotes from, in particular, the Greek philosophers, it appears very little has changed over the past 2500 years in terms of human behaviour. It's as though 'modern' young men find it too difficult to comprehend or accept that there's nothing much to be learnt from other than Mr Google or anything that happened more than a few years earlier. What has changed over time is fluctuations in the degree of acceptance of behaviours and the forms of punishment applied to questioning or the challenging of the current norms. About 2500 years ago Socrates' punishment for questioning the status quo was death by hemlock. More serious disagreements requiring more immediate results were dealt with by the sword, dagger or spear. Today, a military drone will do the job. Challenging the status quo today is more likely to be a much slower execution, more by isolation without the requirement for any discussion. Have we really become so much more sophisticated, or just better at selling and disguise?

I find myself constantly challenging and grappling with my egalitarian philosophies applied to everyday life when debating what works best at the international elite level of cricket, where players battle it out for supremacy, no quarter given, and where survival of the fittest is necessary, but not at all costs.

ONE

THE GLORIOUS AND INGLORIOUS UNCERTAINTIES OF CRICKET

The 2019 Cricket World Cup (CWC) final between England and New Zealand was the perfect example of 'the glorious uncertainties of cricket' until a manufactured rule extinguished and dishonoured the whole event.

It's tempting to go through all the instances of luck, fortune and chance that materialised during this contest, but this book is not intended to be the length of Tolstoy's *War and Peace*. As with many games of cricket, the ebbs and flows generated moments to savour and some to forget. The pitch conditions made batting hard work, restricting lengthy periods of bat dominating ball. Nonetheless, keeping the bowlers in the game throughout added intrigue. The status of the event coupled with the closeness and neither team being able to outplay the other was captivating and exhilarating. The resultant tie was a fitting climax to a 600-ball contest.

What a dream result for the game of cricket. Much more had been achieved than just 'the glorious uncertainties of cricket'. It would be hard to find any plausible reasons to manipulate a change in the result if the integrity of the game was to remain undamaged. The players and the supporters of both teams (although they will have preferred their team to have won) would have understood and accepted that justice had been served for both teams to share the title — I would venture to say that the vast majority of the world of cricket would have applauded a shared title.

It beggars belief that the International Cricket Council (ICC) would even contemplate resorting to what could only be regarded as fanciful imaginary rules to alter the result. One of their own Vision Statements refers to 'protecting the integrity of the game, and in their values, fairness and integrity and leading the drive towards meaningful cricket for players and fans'. Accountability also gets a mention, which should open the door for revisiting their decision, which has effectively discredited or even sanctioned bringing the game into disrepute. To have taken place at Lord's, the inner sanctum of world cricket, along with the home team benefiting, sadly adds further speculation. Apart from all else, the members of the so-called winning team (or maybe just some of them) should, on reflection, feel deflated by the hollowness of the result. Ben Stokes, for starters, expressed these very sentiments. ESPNCricinfo recorded a couple of contemplative comments made by Eoin Morgan: 'Nearly a week after leading his side to their maiden World Cup title, England captain Eoin Morgan felt the result was not fair when there was so little to separate England and New Zealand. He went on to say "I'm not sure winning it makes it any easier. A little bit [troubled], because there's no defining moment that you'd say: 'Yes, we thoroughly deserved it.' It's just been crazy."'

In years to come I can predict conversations about this event being more about embarrassment than anything else. I suggest there will be no winners with this devalued result, and the England players that took part don't deserve that either!

It could also be argued that supporting 'meaningful cricket for players and fans' should not include Twenty20 (T20) cricket, but that's another story, which is covered elsewhere in the book. Many of us who have spent a lifetime in and around the game of cricket keep hoping that the game can follow ethical standards and not be drawn into following the latest whim of the moment regardless of the consequences. Why is it deemed necessary that one party must prevail over others? Perpetuating the ethos of domination, even gluttony, is not the answer and reminds me of a shameless adage: 'Those that win can laugh and those that lose can please them bloody selves'.

Let's park for the moment the fanciful, bizarre decision to incorporate a Super Over to decide the result of a tied final and the ensuing embarrassment when that over also resulted in a tie. Just because a Super Over was included in the playing conditions of a previous CWC is not a good reason to excuse its continued presence.

The quoted statement coming from the ICC apex body's general manager of cricket, Geoff Allardice, was that 'the consistent view has been that the World Cup final needs a winner'. Didn't the 2019 CWC beat that by producing two deserving winners? He went on to say that 'the boundary count-back rule was followed as it is in practice in T20 leagues across the world, adding that the tiebreaker after a tied Super Over needed to be derived from something that happened in that particular match'. There's an inconsistency here. What relevance does a Super Over have to do with singling out 'something that happened in the match', other than wanting to find a single winner?

To use T20 rules (a hitter's game at best) as a benchmark to be followed by any other form of cricket is a nonsense — 50-over cricket has little in common with it, has far more skills and deserves better than effectively the toss of a coin to decide the winner of any game let alone a World Cup. I suppose the rationale for rating boundaries above all else is their so-called entertainment value — how superficial, primitive and bogus. Some of the boundaries might have been edges through the slips or inside ones past leg stump or ugly mishits, etc. Compare that to batsmen skilfully manoeuvring the ball into gaps along the ground and chipping over the top of fieldsmen, picking up ones and twos. Presumably the rule makers were convinced of the need rather than the futility of attempting to come up with a fair and just way of rewarding one team over the other.

The criteria applied, when tested, was always likely to be contentious, and the ICC certainly provoked controversy with what they came up with. It has been far more common to regard wickets in hand as a more plausible calculation. After all, when describing results of matches a team is said to have won by X number of wickets or runs. Breaking from these alternatives becomes too circumstantial — not that I'm suggesting any alternatives to a tie and a shared result should have been applied. In the future should we be anticipating that winners must be found in all forms of cricket (Tests included) and therefore draws as well as ties become redundant?

Tied matches are not something that will have entered players' minds prior to, or even during, the match let alone being aware that boundaries would be the deciding factor. I venture to say that neither team would have been influenced or adjusted their game during the 100 overs to advantage themselves in anticipation of a possible tie. As I've already stated, it should have been unnecessary, even demeaning, for the playing conditions to follow this path in the first instance, and to trivialise the importance of a tied result. One could go on hypothesising infinitely on the merits of the various options available in coming up with one winner. It may need to be done during the league phase of a CWC to decide who progresses to the next stage of the tournament. Surely a hard lesson has been learnt this time around that you don't mess with a final. In October 2019 the news came through that finding a winner in a tied CWC in the future would be the playing of a second 'Super Over' if required instead of a count-back on boundaries. At least the boundaries have gone, but ties are still banished.

The detail in the playing conditions that applied during the CWC 2019 is something to behold. Under 'Result', 'Tied Result 16.10.3' refers you to Appendix H where you eventually find the following:

> 13. The team whose batsmen hit the most number of boundaries combined from its two innings in both the main match and the Super Over shall be the winner.

14. If the number of boundaries hit by both teams is equal, the team whose batsmen scored more boundaries during its innings in the main match (ignoring the Super Over) shall be the winner.

15. If still equal, a count-back from the final ball of the Super Over shall be conducted. The team with the higher scoring delivery shall be the winner. If a team loses two wickets during its over, then any unbowled deliveries will be counted as dot balls. Note that for this purpose, the runs scored from a delivery is defined as the total team runs scored since the completion of the previous legitimate ball, i.e. including any runs resulting from wides, no ball or penalty runs.

Phew! The ICC sure wanted a winner at all costs.

The hundredth and final over of the match, and the subsequent Super Over, contained an astonishing range of the glorious uncertainties of cricket. A challenging script for anyone to have ever imagined. How could so much luck, fortune and chance be delivered over the course of a mere six balls? Alas, what could have been a magical just ending to a CWC final after 50 overs per team was about to become inglorious.

The final over had England 8 wickets down requiring 15 runs for victory, with Stokes on 70 and on strike. Trent Boult was given the task of bowling the final over for New Zealand. Could he repeat the deeds of his final over against Australia earlier in the tournament when he was so successful in getting the ball pitched into the blockhole (which is a skill seldom witnessed) and at the same time achieving a hat trick of wickets?

Ball 1 was pitched just outside off-stump but was full enough to force Stokes to dig it out hitting it firmly to an extra cover stationed on the edge of the circle — Stokes decided staying on strike was more important than taking the single offered.

Ball 2 (15 runs still required) was mostly a replay of ball 1 with the same result, no run.

Ball 3 (15 runs still required) was another attempted yorker, but was dragged down sufficiently for Stokes to get under it and slog it over mid-wicket for 6.

Ball 4 (9 runs now required) was a full toss on the line of middle stump at almost bail height — Stokes hit it down to Guptill at wide mid-on, deep enough for Stokes to attempt a second run in order to retain the strike. Guptill's throw was strong and accurate. Recognising the danger, Stokes dived full length in attempting to make his ground. This was the moment when randomness took over to a level of consequences that no one could ever have conceived.

The throw cannoned off the outstretched bat of Stokes travelling all the way to the boundary, triggering a bizarre course of events. The umpire signalled 6 runs when the correct call should have been 5. The law states that the batsmen needed to have crossed for the second run before the ball left the fielder's hand (which was not the case) for the extra run to count. What is more, if the correct call had been made (other than Stokes being given out), Rashid would have been on strike, not Stokes.

ESPNCricinfo reported that umpire Kumar Dharmasena said 'the decision to award England six runs instead of five following the overthrow was a collective one, and was made in consultation with square leg umpire Marais Erasmus'. He went on to say that it was easy for people to comment after seeing TV replays, and told Sri Lankan publication *Sunday Times*: 'I agree that there was a judgmental error when I see it on TV replays now. But we did not have the luxury of TV replays at the ground'. Dharmasena attempted to clarify this statement when he went on to say 'there is no provision in the law to refer this to the third umpire as no dismissal was involved'. Curiously it proves he didn't even consider looking at the possibility of Stokes deliberately obstructing the field. This was further exemplified when he proceeded to explain some of the difficulties of umpiring and precisely what they had to watch out for in this instance. 'He said one must understand that there were too many things on our plate. We had to watch the batsmen complete the first run, the ball being fielded, how it was handled by the fielder and whether the batsmen completed the second run. And where the throw would come from, the striker's end or non-striker's end. In this case, we were all happy that the batsmen had completed the second run because the ball ricocheted off Stokes' bat at the time of him completing the second run.' If he had gone upstairs to the third umpire to check on a possible dismissal, common sense would suggest clarification of awarding the sixth run could have been also checked if they had decided not to give Stokes out. Irrespective of what the laws of the game state regarding what the umpires can and can't refer to the third umpire, common sense needed to prevail under such difficult and critical circumstances. Interestingly, law 2.15 (Correctness of scores) states: 'Consultation between umpires and scorers on doubtful points is essential. The umpires shall, throughout the match, satisfy themselves as to the correctness of the number of runs scored, the wickets that have fallen and, where appropriate, the number of overs bowled. They shall agree these with the scorers at least at every interval, other than a drinks interval, and at the conclusion of the match.' At this point the reader is directed to laws 3.2 (Correctness of scores), 16.8 (Correctness of result) and 16.10 (Result not to be changed).

> 16.8 Correctness of result. Any decision as to the correctness of the scores shall be the responsibility of the umpires. See Law 2.15 (Correctness of scores).
>
> 16.9 Mistakes in scoring. If, after the players and umpires have left the field in the belief that the match has been concluded, the umpires discover that a mistake in scoring has occurred which affects the result then, subject to 16.10, they shall adopt the following procedure.
>
> Once the umpires have agreed with the scorers the correctness of the scores at the conclusion of the match — see Laws 2.15 (Correctness of scores) and 3.2 (Correctness of scores) — the result cannot thereafter be changed.

This added further confusion to the incredulousness that followed when the result of the match was gifted to England. However, had the score been adjusted at the conclusion of the 100 overs and New Zealand awarded victory by one run, England would have also felt justifiably robbed. It would not have been acceptable for England to be told that they needed 3 runs from the final two balls for victory, to be told later that in fact it should have been 4. It would appear that the laws possibly have a loophole that needs closing should circumstances like this materialise again in the future.

Returning to the overthrows situation, the current law allows for any runs accruing to stand as long as no deliberate unlawful act has occurred. Nevertheless, it is an unwritten law and common practice among players not to take advantage of these situations, and had the deflection from Stokes' bat not gone to the boundary, I'm confident Stokes would not have taken any further runs — he indicated that by his immediate apologetic gesture. As it was, the ball only reached the boundary about 4 metres in front of the chaser Colin de Grandhomme — talk about only ifs!

It's hard to fathom why this archaic law still applies today when the obvious call should be 'dead ball'. Curiously, in the playing conditions, the dead ball law does provide an opportunity to make the sensible decision. It states: 'The ball shall be considered to be dead when it is clear to the bowler's end umpire that the fielding side and both batsmen at the wicket have ceased to regard it as in play.' The law also includes intervening in a case of unfair play, when Stokes and the New Zealand captain Williamson made it quite clear that they did not want the ball to remain in play. Their immediate reactions demonstrated and recognised that the spirit of cricket and fair play was about to be contravened.

For me the real clincher that muddied the waters (had it been picked up at the time) was that Stokes had deliberately obstructed the field because he 'did significantly change his direction without probable cause and thereby obstructed a fielder's attempt to effect a run out'.

I had recorded the game on my TV which provided several replay angles providing me with the opportunity to analyse what happened.

As expected the line Stokes took with his first run was on the prepared part of the pitch within the return creases and the obvious shortest route to the other end. The first run presented him with the information he needed because the line of the shot was in front of him. It warned him of the impending danger well in advance and the line he needed to run to give himself the best chance of blocking the throw. On returning for the second run, his partner Adil Rashid continued to run the outside line meaning that Stokes had the inside running closer to the pitch, which would have also been the shortest route to making his ground. However, Stokes was prepared to change/widen his line of direction, manoeuvring Rashid even wider, in order to give himself the best chance of obstructing the throw. When making his dive the reason for so much dust rising was due to his landing in the footmarks of a previous game. And it wasn't the bowlers' footmarks, from that previous game, it was further away where the batsman would have been taking his guard, some 4 feet (1.22 metres) beyond the return crease of the pitch they were playing on.

By not looking over his left shoulder towards the ball, he might have given the appearance of innocence. Stokes' understandable preference so as not to slow him down was to look at the positioning of the wicketkeeper in front of him, automatically warning him of the line of the throw, its accuracy and the threat it presented. The wicketkeeper had remained directly behind the stumps, which indicated the throw was on target. Recognising the danger, Stokes will have sensed the need to dive to give himself the best chance of making his ground. Although he will not have deliberately deflected the ball with his bat, his actions would have already placed himself in the best position to intercept the path of the ball. To add to New Zealand's woes, the replay also indicated that had the ball not been intercepted, Stokes would have likely been short of his ground.

There is an historical influence attached to why Stokes will have possibly believed his innocence and why the New Zealanders' response was bewilderment and frustration rather than a more challenging reaction. Williamson, the New Zealand captain, did respond by extending his arms horizontally with his palms pointing upwards as if to say or ask 'Is this legitimate or lawful?' This reaction could qualify as an inquiry, but was anything verbalised in the form of an appeal? Maybe the umpires weren't cognisant of what occurred either, and unless there was an appeal, it's possible they thought they had nothing to answer.

For as long as I can remember, it became standard practice for batsmen to run a line (when under pressure to make their ground) to block the throw by putting themselves between the thrower and the stumps. It had become viewed as just the smart thing to do. Once normalised, the illegality of it tends to be portrayed as being accidental and is therefore overlooked. The reality is that when batsmen think the danger of being run out is very unlikely, they make every effort to move away from the line of the ball to prevent being hit.

These incidents also tend to be unobserved because batsmen seldom if ever take advantage of any overthrows that might ensue. On the very odd occasion when (as in this case) the ball ends up over the boundary, the consequences are generally minor and treated as such. But when it decides a Cricket World Cup final, the stakes are too high for it to go unnoticed. Maybe it has taken the significance of this event to expose the need to take a closer look at this example in the future.

To the lay person, it may sound unlikely that so many thoughts would be going through a player's mind, but professional cricketers play and practise so often, reactions to innumerable situations become automatic and instinctive. Stokes demonstrated he didn't want to take advantage of the obvious unfairness associated with the additional four overthrows, but that should not be used to confuse his preceding strategy.

Ball 5 (3 runs now required) with Stokes on strike. Boult got it full enough on the line of middle stump for Stokes (who had moved outside leg stump) to hit it down to deep mid-off where Mitchell Santner had come in off the boundary close enough to stop the second run. Stokes in desperation to retain the strike called Rashid through for two resulting in England losing their ninth wicket.

Ball 6 (2 runs required for an England victory) Stokes once again gave himself room outside leg stump, while receiving a knee-high full toss, just perfect for dispatching over the fence or selecting one of a variety of attacking options presented. Bizarrely, he proceeded to pat the ball down to deepish mid-on — this time England's number 11 (Mark Wood) was left well short. Stokes must have predetermined the shot and known that no fieldsman could afford to be so deep as to allow a second run to be taken. Could Stokes have had a bout of conscience from what had happened two balls earlier?

New Zealand's woes had also occurred earlier during England's second-last over (fourth ball) when Stokes had been caught on the long-on boundary by Boult who put a foot back onto the rope before throwing the ball to Guptill who was eagerly poised a few metres away inside the boundary. Boult, when interviewed later, said the noise from the crowd broke the communication between the two, indicating that otherwise Stokes would have been on his way back to the pavilion.

The good fortune that had allowed New Zealand to get beyond the league stage of the tournament had certainly come to a cruel end in the final. During the league stage, Pakistan had finished on the same points as New Zealand and even though they had beaten New Zealand, the playing conditions put New Zealand through on a better net run rate — how the playing conditions' worm can turn! They had also come within a few centimetres of losing to the West Indies when Carlos Brathwaite's attempted 6 to win the game almost cleared Trent Boult on the boundary. The point New Zealand received for a rained-off match against India was at the time viewed as very fortuitous. India had already beaten South Africa and Australia before playing New Zealand and were one of the favourites to win the cup. Earlier in January/February, New Zealand had been dominated by India losing the series 5–1 — New Zealand's one win against them was in the fourth One-Day International (ODI) when India didn't play their strongest team. Additionally, New Zealand had lost three matches in getting to the semi-final but so did England, who needed to win their final round robin game against New Zealand to qualify. It proved to be a one-sided affair with England winning by a margin of 119 runs. Judging form at that time, India and Australia looked to be favourites to meet in the final. The glorious uncertainties of cricket were about to appear when enough of New Zealand's players were able to produce their A game in both the semi and the final. Neither India nor Australia as the top two qualifiers for the semi-finals made the final, even though they had only lost one and two games respectively.

When looking back at the tournament as a whole, the brittleness of teams was evident. Australia had beaten England during the league stage by 64 runs and yet were beaten massively by England in the semi-final by 8 wickets. Australia's other loss was against South Africa who finished a disappointing seventh in the standings, having won only three matches.

Although it is a small sample, when looking back at the past two CWCs played in 2015 and 2011, results appeared to be a bit more predictable. Unlike the 2019 CWC whereby 10 teams played each other in a round robin format, the 2015 World Cup was split into two groups of seven teams, with two qualifying from each group to go forward to the semi-finals. New Zealand and Australia qualified in Group A, with New Zealand having lost no matches and Australia one. India and South Africa qualified in Group B, having lost no games and two respectively.

The 2011 CWC had the same format as 2015 with two groups of seven teams. In Group A, qualifiers Pakistan lost one match and Sri Lanka one. In Group B, South Africa lost one and India one. Australia lost only one also, but didn't qualify.

Looking at history, two other significant ties come to mind. The tied Tests between the West Indies and Australia in Brisbane in 1960 and the one between India and Australia in Madras in 1986. The one most savoured is probably the one involving the West Indies. When people reminisce about the 2019 Cricket World Cup, the same enthusiasm is unlikely to be displayed.

As an aside, some will talk about the New Zealand players having been robbed of at least $US1 million, had the six million prize money been shared equally. The two million they received for being declared the losers would have been an additional hard pill to swallow.

My contention is we are already witnessing the effects of T20 cricket in the longer forms of the game, creating results that become more random. The pros and cons of whether this is good for cricket should reveal some interesting debate. A couple of teams dominating the landscape for extended periods is less likely and is already happening. The very makeup and nature of cricket has always created uncertainties, so it's once again a matter of degrees. It has become more common over time for players to frequently take higher risk options when under pressure, which I believe is mostly responsible for the inconsistent performance of teams. The increased lack of certainty may develop additional interest by keeping up the hopes of more teams' fans. Some spectators will enjoy players' games being less restricted, whereas others will not get the same pleasure out of a sloppier, less consequence-based approach.

TWO
FOR STARTERS

CRICKET WAS THE MAIN SPORT AVAILABLE DURING SUMMER WHEN I WAS growing up in Dunedin. My older brother, Brian, played it and was selected for Otago Under-23s, while my father umpired cricket. For me the game began in the typical New Zealand fashion, in the backyard with my siblings, relatives and, sometimes, my father. We had a strong family affiliation with sport. My paternal grandfather played professional football in the first division for West Bromwich Albion before the First World War. My father was an Otago sprint cycling champion who later umpired first-class cricket. Brother Brian played hockey for New Zealand while my younger brother, Greg, played golf for New Zealand and professionally, mostly on the European Tour, and won 13 professional tournaments. A second cousin, Alan Larkins, competed in the track cycling at the 1956 Olympic Games in Melbourne. During the winter months I had started playing rugby but my school teacher was a hockey man and I changed sports. Just prior to leaving for England as a 19-year-old, I was selected as twelfth man for the South Island team. I was also the junior badminton champion at Otago Boys' High School (OBHS), although they didn't have a significant programme. Hockey continued until I completed my residential qualifying year with

Worcestershire Cricket. I filled in the winter months in England and was selected for the Worcestershire senior hockey side.

I always opened the batting. At primary school, from about the age of nine years, it was with Ronald ('Doc') Murdoch, a liaison we renewed on occasions in Plunket Shield games for Otago later in our lives. Selection in Otago Under-12 and Under-16 teams followed for me. While playing cricket at Otago Boys', any failures were not commented on at home while any successes were met with the comment that I could have done better. The encouragement I did receive was more to do with taking opportunities than from praise. Early influences on my game were Lankford Smith, Bert Sutcliffe and Billy Ibadulla. Lankford was a primary school teacher who was Otago's best all-rounder at that time. He instilled in me the basic batting strokes and I practised them continually, sometimes in front of a mirror to make sure my bat was straight. In my first two years at Otago Boys' High School I attended a few of Bert's coaching sessions. The fact Bert was recognised as New Zealand's best batsman, and was someone my father spoke very highly of, was very inspiring. I was first selected for the First XI in my fourth form year.

Then in my last year at OBHS I came under Billy's wing and that continued through the two years that followed when I was playing for the Otago senior men's team, in the Plunket Shield competition, debuting at aged 17. In those three years Billy probably spent more time with me than any other individual. It included many 6.30 am starts in the nets at Logan Park. Others were invited but they didn't seem to last very long. Billy extended my knowledge beyond the basic skills to the psychological-technique options to be used under various conditions and the like. Billy also proved invaluable in acting as a buffer against criticism at a time when I was most vulnerable to it.

Having been selected to play first-class cricket at such an early age and being criticised very publicly for my stodgy approach was hard to take for a sensitive young lad. On reflection, it must be said that some of that media criticism probably did me some good by hardening me up.

At that stage I was weighing in at only 60.3 kilograms (9½ stone) and stood 1.76 metres (5 feet 9½ inches). Fortunately, batting required skill rather than physical strength and I was selected for representative teams right from the start. What Billy instilled in me was a reinforcement of the work ethic I believe I always had, along with a determination to succeed and hunger for greater success. My family background had given me an understanding that being unpretentiousness was important. This automatically implied that self-praise was no recommendation and you certainly didn't want to be known as a skite. There was an acceptance that others knew a lot more than me and that I should always be open to learning through an inquiring, questioning mind. Much of this wasn't specifically taught; it had more to do with the actions of those around you at home and in the society at that time. It should be remembered that in those days, most contact with people was in person and experiences happened as a result of your own resourcefulness.

In the long run I think the way my career developed is a good example of how influential good coaching and advice can be when received during your developmental years. This was not only from being trained in the fundamentals of the art of batting, but also being indirectly taught to respect age and experience, which automatically opened your mind to learning, through listening and questioning. Building good defensive skills from the outset was routinely considered to be the best system for teaching youngsters. Occupying the crease was the first consideration for your game to progress. Needless to say, you couldn't score any runs back in the dressing room! This approach proved invaluable in constructing a solid foundation from which my game could grow. I wonder if any young player in the future would be persuaded, or view it as necessary, or have the patience or the desire to follow a similar path that was offered to me, when the appeal for longer forms of cricket are waning? Will there be coaches around capable or desirous of coaching the foundation work that I experienced? The question is will the standard of batsmanship (in particular) drop if foundation work is sidelined and the longer forms of cricket markedly reduced, or shelved altogether? Undoubtedly, first-class cricket enhances the opportunities to learn the art of batting and without it, simply training up for the likes of T20 will be like trying to run before you can walk. If this is the future, I would suggest that the standard of players may well decline. The significance of that foundation work comes through strongly when experiencing more game time. That's when the focus should move towards being more about observation, self-examination and learning by doing. This is how it was for me playing county cricket day in and day out in England and I assume it was generally the same for others.

At that time, your only support person was possibly a physiotherapist so there was no one to pamper you and no one to blame for failures other than yourself. It is fair to say that compared to today, there were very few distractions. Ideas of chasing other contracts or being involved in power struggles for contracts and selection were absent. There were not excessive amounts of money involved — when I started in 1968 with Worcestershire, I received 750 pounds for the season and by the time I finished in 1982 it had risen to about 9500 pounds — and there wasn't the same degree of attention and status for players. You were largely left alone to focus on improving your own game. I gained enjoyment from challenging ideas and appreciating that the unexamined is not as rewarding. This also stemmed from an understanding that the more you know, the more you realise you don't know.

In time, I came to appreciate that you had to be your own best critic through self-analysis while appreciating a Plato quote, 'the first and best victory is to conquer self'. From this emerged the ability to cancel negative outside influences such as loss of wickets, sledging around you (although there was very little of it in those days and virtually none in county cricket), pressure to retain your place, domestic problems in your life and so on. Amnesia can become your friend. It was also a case of understanding and using the things that motivate you to greater effort. Everyone has varying degrees of more than one influence but among them there is likely to be a dominant force, possibly the team, self-fulfilment, loved ones, or even the opposition, among others. And behind all of them is the understanding that integrity will automatically take care of doing the right thing for the team situation and the spirit of cricket. Humility, I think, is a strength, as is the understanding that improvement is ongoing. However, the modesty associated with humility need not undermine determination or a strong desire to succeed. At the same time it is more likely to result in the integrity necessary for players to put the team first and play within the spirit of the game. And with that in mind, I think graciousness in defeat is important in accepting that if your opponents outplay you, good luck to them — as long as you've given your best, that's all you can do at that time.

Setting myself a goal of playing for New Zealand was never uppermost in my thoughts. I was not a dreamer, I was more concentrated on trying to sort out the moment, what was happening in my immediate space. Around the time that it became known I had been invited to trial for Warwickshire through Billy Ibadulla's recommendation, I had my first experience of the strong tall poppy syndrome that raises its ugly head from time to time and which I was aware of in New Zealand. I became conscious of an attitude around me that said 'Who do you think you are?' At that time in New Zealand the normal pathway and expectation after leaving school was to get a real job, get married, have kids and stay where you were. That same attitude is less likely to exist today — going on a big OE (overseas experience) has become much more common and is often part of a working holiday. In my case, not so much of the holiday bit. The notion that I was endeavouring to make a career out of playing cricket professionally was always likely to bring out a snide comment or two, particularly from the administration of the New Zealand Cricket Council (NZCC), as it was then known.

The NZCC had always had a Corinthian view of the game. Members of the New Zealand teams to England in 1927, 1931 and 1937 had to sign contracts that they would not return to England to play the game for two years after they completed their tours. When some did go after their contracted time was up, they were effectively barred from playing for the country again. Ces Dacre went back after 1927, while Stewie

Dempster, Roger Blunt, Bill Merritt and Ken James all sought opportunities to play in England once their time was up after the 1931 tour. Only Dempster, after the Second World War, returned to play in New Zealand. It seems crazy that such cricket talent should have been lost to New Zealand at a time when the world was suffering the effects of the worst Depression and the players concerned were only trying to utilise their specific skills. When I decided to carve a professional career a few New Zealanders — Tom Pritchard, Ray Hitchcock and Don Taylor — had been full-time professionals in English county cricket, while Martin Donnelly had played as an amateur, and only Taylor returned to play here. John Reid and some others played some league cricket in England but not full time. NZCC's board of control had a strong belief in the need to retain the perceived wholesomeness of the 'amateur ethos'. Their attitude towards paying the so-called 'dirty dollar' to any New Zealand cricketer at that time was supported by a compliant media and therefore, unsurprisingly, the majority of the public. This would eventually cause me some problems in my determination not to be treated as a second-class citizen. Professional cricket had been around in England for decades, but perhaps what influenced thinking at that time was that rugby union in New Zealand was still an amateur game. It seems unbelievable in today's world where sportspeople come and go at the drop of a hat that such issues should still have existed even then. It was especially ironic that one of my main problems was the chairman of the board, Walter Hadlee, whose son Richard went on to have such a distinguished career for Nottinghamshire, and he wasn't doing it for nothing! Interestingly, both Richard and John Wright received $20,000 from the then Rothmans Sports Foundation. Presumably NZCC had a say in that. Furthermore, Richard received his payment during his English Benefit Year. The most positive conclusion from that is that NZCC had at last opened their minds to learning and that cricket was a legitimate job after all! Talk about bad timing! Yet, Walter Hadlee didn't eschew the opportunity to do some commercial business in England, on behalf of clients of his accounting firm in Christchurch or on his own behalf, when leading the 1949 New Zealand team on tour. Reading through his recently published diary, it is apparent he had many meetings with companies while also managing to buy a car in England, purchased with a loan from NZCC, and having it transported home on the same ship as the team! At one point in the diary Hadlee said, 'There are a few good business opportunities to consider'.

Things improved when Wellington's Bob Vance was appointed chairman of the board, but it came too late in my career — most of the vilification had already been cemented in. But someone has to be first and at least my stance did break new ground and helped to speed up the acceptance that earning a living from playing cricket was not a sin after all. You only have to look at the number of New Zealanders who have played first-class cricket in the last 30 years, and some who didn't achieve that level, who have been able to benefit their careers by playing as club professionals in the England leagues. How much has that helped improve the strength of the New Zealand game? What the whole experience showed me was the inner strength there was to be had from caring more for the truth than surrendering to a submissive void in the public arena. Unfortunately, one hangover from that era and to this day is that questioning the status quo still encourages walls to be put up to keep people out, not to see who cares enough to challenge them. The price of popularity comes at too big a cost for my liking. I've been aware for many years that challenging the status quo too often causes vested interests to develop a gang mentality. I think the busy life of a full-time professional cricketer means largely focusing on a single subject, and this is perhaps truer of cricket than many occupations, which has the side effect of creating a barrenness of wider thinking and knowledge — I should know, I was one of them.

There have been times when I asked myself that if I had my time over again, would I have been better making myself available for England? Memory tells me that at the time there was a four-year qualifying period, which would have been easy for me to achieve in terms of time since I spent 16 seasons there. I'm confident it would have helped my career on the international cricket scene, but I wanted to spend time in the land that I had, and still have, an affection for. I didn't anticipate that NZCC was going to react the way it did. I had other alternatives open to me too. Barry Richards said that I would have had no problem getting an appointment in South Africa and I also had an offer to play for Queensland.

But by the time I was 20, and in my fourth year of first-class cricket while also being in Worcestershire's first team, it seemed logical under the circumstances of the time that New Zealand selection would occur. Being able to play virtually seven days a week for five months of the year in England was the equivalent of attending an Ivy League university for cricket. It telescoped my experience considerably and faster than I would ever achieve playing five first-class matches a season, with no limited-overs cricket, in the amateur game in New Zealand.

When you look at the domestic scene in New Zealand now, the structure is substantially different. Twenty20 has emerged as a significant force on the domestic programme, while there are a lot more 50-overs games. The Plunket Shield is now contested over four days. For a long period of time there were two rounds of first-class play but that has been affected by the introduction of more reduced-overs games. However, it is my observation that the players of today are not putting the amount of time into batting and bowling that occurred during those earlier days and I wonder if, in time, that will have an effect on playing standards. The continuous first-class cricket in England helped bowlers in particular. They built up, and retained, their stamina due to their workloads. By comparison, today's dominance of Twenty20 and One-Day Internationals doesn't help bowlers retain their bowling fitness, nor the extent to which there is a belief that resting players is helpful. A bowler in the Indian Premier League (IPL) might bowl a maximum of 8 overs per week, in possibly four spells, throughout that competition, assuming they play all the games. Then those players, at the end of the tournament, invariably join their respective Test teams having already missed pre-Test warm-up games, expecting to be able to compete at Test level. You have to wonder if the under-prepared bowlers are bowling to batsmen who have been playing the slogging game in the same tournaments and what the consequences are for the quality of

Test cricket. It is the same for batsmen attempting to make the transition from shorter-form cricket to Test match play. Middle-order batsmen might only face a few balls per game in these T20 leagues, none of which will require any semblance of using defensive techniques.

During my time with Worcestershire there was a period when I was unavailable for New Zealand, initially due to suspension by NZCC and then by my own choice. That was when the knives came out fostering misinformation, false rumours, gossip and innuendo. Justifications were rife, and I heard numerous comments of the put-down variety, such as claims that Worcester was largely a batsman-friendly pitch and that's why I scored so many hundreds. Curiosity and the desire to check on the facts encouraged me to do some research. It is a fair statement that it was generally a good surface to bat on, but in the year we won the County Championship it was decided to have lively, green seaming pitches with a lot of pace in them in order to get the results necessary for us to win more games. Teams were being bowled out within 50 overs at Worcester. The theory was that if we won 50% of our games at home, then that should be enough to win the Championship. However, no one foresaw that three of our batsmen would receive broken bones and two would be 'crusted'. As a result of the assumption/theory that I scored most of my County Championship hundreds at Worcester, the facts told a different story. The result: 31 at Worcester and 33 on other grounds. Another claim was that my four double centuries in the West Indies were due to the fact the West Indies attack was very weak and that their best bowler, Vanburn Holder, was well known to me as a team-mate in Worcester. It could be equally argued that his knowledge of me was just as helpful to him. Again, the facts make for interesting reading. Vanburn didn't play in the first Test at Sabina Park where I scored 223 not out. Their bowling attack was Uton Dowe, Grayson Shillingford, Gary Sobers, David Holford and Lance Gibbs. Anecdotally, leading up to that match, there was an old character, 'Sleepy' Williams, who bowled decent leg breaks and googlies in the nets to us. He warned us to 'beware of Dowe, he's not as easy as he looks and watch out for his bouncer, it skids onto you very quickly at 'troat' height — not that I intended to hook anyway. It is pretty standard to assume that short men who were quick bowlers, with their lower trajectory from the hand, get less tennis ball bounce than tall men, which can make their bouncers more effective even though they need to be pitched shorter. My view is the best batsmen are more challenged by late movement, whether it be from the pitch or late swing, than by pace alone. One concedes that the older ball has the potential to reverse swing late for faster bowlers, but that ball doesn't pose the same physical threat and fear factor which most spectators anticipate for all batsmen. Undoubtedly, lower-order batsmen are the ones that have the biggest problems with pace bowling, because of their poorer hand-eye coordination, skills and the associated lack of confidence.

There were even claims that I couldn't play pace bowling and that I was afraid of them. This gained legs once the knives were sharpened and has even been repeated by commentators in New Zealand in recent years — commentators, incidentally, who are not old enough to know. This shouldn't come as any surprise, because if you challenge what others are doing, you should expect them to retaliate whenever they get a sniff of a possible comeback in spite of its legitimacy. Of my 792 first-class innings, 73 Test innings, 40 ODIs and 308 list A innings, I probably opened the batting on more than 1000 occasions. This during a period when county cricket attracted almost all the best opening bowlers in the game. Over my 16 years of county cricket there would be 40–50 opening bowlers many of whom could be classified in the fast or brisk category. At that time two overseas players were permitted to play for each county and most counties used at least one of these spaces for an overseas opening bowler. The West Indians were well represented by the likes of Andy Roberts, Malcolm Marshall, Colin Croft, Wayne Daniel, Sylvester Clarke, Joel Garner, Michael Holding, Vanburn Holder, Keith Boyce, Bernard Julien and Gary Sobers — other overseas players who come to mind included Richard Hadlee, Clive Rice, Mike Procter, Garth Le Roux, Vintcent van der Bijl,

Graham McKenzie, Kapil Dev, Imran Khan and Sarfraz Nawaz. At that time, most players from overseas played for several years, and for the same county. There was also less international cricket being played and, furthermore, those playing for England were also expected to play for their counties in between international duties. Some of those England bowlers were: Freddie Trueman, Brian Statham, Alan Ward, Harold Rhodes, Jeff Jones, Chris Old, Bob Willis, David Brown, Gladstone Small, Peter and John Lever, Geoff Arnold, John Snow, John ('Sport') Price, Robin Jackman, Ken Shuttleworth, Ken Higgs, Tom Cartwright, Mike Hendrick, Graham Dilley, Ian Botham and Neil Mallender. I played against Trueman, Statham and Derek Shackleton at the end of their careers. Outside of county cricket there were bowlers like: Dennis Lillee, Jeff Thomson, Alan Hurst, Geoff Lawson, Max Walker, Geoff Dymock, Allan Frost, Gary Gilmour, Sam Gannon, Alan ('Froggy') Thomson, Tony Dell, Wes Hall, Charlie Griffith, Richard ('Prof') Edwards, Uton Dowe, Grayson Shillingford, Saleem Altaf, Asif Iqbal, Mohinder Amarnath, Abid Ali, Madan Lal, Bob Blair, Dick Motz, Gary Bartlett, Bruce Taylor, Dayle Hadlee, Richard Collinge, Bob Cunis, Ewen Chatfield, Lance Cairns, *et al.*

My response to the suggestion that I had a weakness against the short ball is that if letting bouncers go for most of my career was a weakness, then I was guilty. Interestingly, later in my career, the short ball was sometimes used by opposition bowlers as a ploy to slow my scoring, or to get me off strike. For much of my career, a bouncer would likely become a dot ball and a shortish ball aimed at my hip mostly producing a single to deep fine leg. However, in order to overcome this stalling tactic, instead of hooking I found it more successful to move towards the leg-side, in order to free my arms so that I opened up off-side attacking options. In these instances, by not getting into line, some might assume a fear response and for detractors an opportunity to denigrate. The reality is that by this action there is greater risk of injury, because if the line of the ball follows you, it becomes far more difficult to avoid it. I was prepared to take that risk later in my career, mainly because I wanted to score more quickly for enjoyment purposes all round. I could also answer the claims of critics by saying, if I had been afraid, life must have been hell for 20 years opening the batting against the new ball. Did I ever ask to be put down the order? No, I wanted the challenge.

There were some very useful spinners then too. In county cricket you had bowlers like: Bishan Bedi, Srinivas Venkataraghavan, Lance Gibbs, Dilip Doshi, Mushtaq Mohammad, Intikhab Alam, Javed Miandad, Kerry O'Keefe, Derek Underwood, John Emburey, Pat Pocock, Robin Hobbs, Ray Illingworth, David Allen, John Mortimore, David Ackfield, Ray East, Phil Edmonds, Don Shepherd, Fred Titmus, Jack Birkenshaw, Jack Simmons, David Graveney, Norman Gifford, Vic Marks, Geoff Miller, Eddie Hemmings, Peter Willey, David Hughes, Dipak Patel; while on the international scene there were: Erapalli Prasanna, Bhagwath Chandrasekhar, Pervez Sajjad, Mohammad Nazir, John Gleeson, Ashley Mallett, David Holford, Inshan Ali, Tony Howard, Raphick Jumadeen, Hedley Howarth, Vic Pollard, Bryan Yuile, David O'Sullivan, John McIntyre, Stephen Boock and, surprisingly, Tony Lock after he had moved to Western Australia.

Looking back and asking myself if there was any bowler, or type of bowling, that worried me most, I would say no. This was because I was too preoccupied trying to get my own act together. Obviously, some types of bowling were more difficult to play than others when considering pitch and weather conditions. But my belief was that I needed to overcome myself, not the bowler. My focus and motivation was to be as good as I could be and my attention was never towards an opponent, or being anxious about them. About half of my career involved playing without helmets and even at the end, chest pads and arm guards were only beginning to be worn. When opening the batting day in, day out, one was always confronted with one or two bouncers an over against the new ball. If you couldn't deal with that, you were going to have a lot of sleepless nights and you shouldn't be opening the batting. The analogy I would draw is, when you drive a car you don't think about having a crash, but if you do crash you deal with it. It's the same with being crusted on the head by a cricket ball. Thinking about any dangers would surely undermine confidence and serve to increase the danger.

I copped one bad head knock — it required nine stitches above the eye. Of all people, it was against Bernard Julien, not the quickest of bowlers. At the time I had scored a hundred, but we had reached the point of chasing bonus points and the need to score more quickly dominated my thinking. I had a last-minute change of plan, opting for an attempted hook. I wasn't able to play on, but fortunately my eye had opened up enough for me to play the next game. I was keen to get back 'on the horse' as soon as possible, just in case a delayed reaction might have affected my confidence. The next game was against Northamptonshire and Sarfraz. Like a boxer who had opened up a cut, he zeroed in on my head and bowled as many bouncers as he could get away with. It was perfect for me because it gave me a good workout so soon after the earlier event.

Interestingly, I was able to use this experience when coaching New Zealand. It was during a Test at Lancaster Park in 1986 during which Martin Crowe took a ball from the Australian left-armer Bruce Reid on the chin. Much to board member, and surgeon, John Heslop's annoyance, Crowe's mother, Audrey, turned up in the physio's room causing Martin to go into shock. He was sent for an X-ray. When he returned to the ground I talked him into padding up and going in at the fall of the next wicket. He did and went on to score a fine century.

Some years ago, I read a biography on Donald Bradman, written by a British Labour Peer, Lord Charles Williams. In it Williams covered the criticisms levelled at Bradman during his playing days. One of the accusations against him was that he was suspect against fast bowling. This was the result of an observation made in tricky conditions during his barnstorming 1930 tour of England. Douglas Jardine used that as a catalyst for the bodyline tactics employed during the 1932–33 Ashes tour of Australia. I suppose it partially worked, in that they managed to contain Bradman's average to something just over 50. Williams' book also described the incident in the press box at The Oval in London during Bradman's last Test. The English media were stunned when past team-mates who had moved into the media world, Jack Fingleton and Bill O'Reilly, broke into hysterical laughter when Bradman was bowled by Eric Hollies for 0.

As a guest of Ron Brierley at the New Zealand v Australia Test at the Basin Reserve in 2015–16, I took the opportunity to speak to another of his guests (Neil Harvey) about Bradman and the accusations mentioned in Williams' book. Harvey said he was just a kid in the Australian team with Bradman in 1948 and didn't know much of what was going on. However, he was on the same selection panel as Bradman in later years and got to know him well. I mentioned to Harvey that Williams had attributed much of the Fingleton and O'Reilly animosity towards Bradman in part to Catholic-Protestant issues. Harvey attributed it more to jealousy and envy. I thought if Bradman wasn't exempt from vitriol and false accusations about his batting, why should little old me be immune. Needless to say, the human condition has a lot to answer for.

Given my own views, it was interesting to read what former Hampshire player, and now television host, Mark Nicholas had to say in a Cricinfo article looking at the state of New Zealand cricket in the wake of a disappointing effort during the Test series in 2013 where he described the New Zealand batting as 'feeble'. Nicholas said the New Zealand batsmen needed to 'relearn the art of long-form batting' if they were to ever dominate attacks. This term 'long-form' batting is a neo-liberal expression emanating from the preponderance of reduced-overs cricket in keeping with the instant society and its consequent reduced attention spans of players and fans. But he noted that while the modern New Zealand players were able to pull in good returns in the entertainment-driven IPL, the skills to achieve that were not the same as those needed to succeed against a moving ball in a Test match.

'The art of long-form batting, of making hard-core hundreds that live with you for life, has left the land of the long white cloud in favour of less demanding gratification that comes with innings that last for just over 20 overs,' he said, adding that New Zealand's batsmen looked as if they needed some old-fashioned coaching involving hours in the nets hitting thousands of balls in the orthodox manner.

As will be obvious from other parts of this book, Nicholas's assertion that more ability to indulge in occupying the crease to build an innings in Test match and first-class play finds no fault with me and is something that is central to achieving longevity in the shorter forms of cricket.

THREE
BOUNDARIES

In 2006 at The Oval in London, the Pakistanis' reaction to umpire Darrell Hair accusing them of ball-tampering was a walk-out and forfeiting of the Test match. The laws of the game even then gave the umpire the right to change the ball and impose a 5-run penalty. The outcry emanating from Pakistan itself sent the ICC into what they presumably perceived as damage control. Attempts to appease the moment by sacking Hair had cast aside ethical considerations and sent a clear message to all concerned that political expediency came first. On this occasion the anticipated convenience of their decision backfired, because Hair challenged the decision and an out-of-court settlement followed for a sum allegedly around three to four hundred thousand pounds. This episode raised a whole host of issues and discussion around acceptable boundaries, definitions, and who is responsible for what, but to this day they still remain as muddled as ever. They remain muddled or unattended, largely because of the unwillingness for all concerned to enforce or accept what is now written into the laws of the game.

Since 2006 stronger measures have been written into the spirit of cricket in general, but the application of the penalties still has its challenges, not only to the spirit of the game but also what constitutes fair and unfair play. Curiously, in South Africa in 2018, a bolt out of the blue. Following a sandpaper ball-tampering incident, Cricket Australia (CA) imposed their own punishment of a one-year ban on the perpetrators, Steve Smith and David Warner, and a nine-month ban on the new boy Cameron Bancroft who had been cajoled into doing their dirty work. The penalties were excessive to say the least, particularly when considering CA's past record of consistently ignoring their players' on-field behaviour. CA's actions on this occasion looked suspiciously like attempts to preserve and recover their own credibility and positions.

Perhaps it was the reaction of Australia's Prime Minister Malcolm Turnbull to the ball-tampering saga that influenced CA's decision. He was quoted as saying: 'I am shocked and bitterly disappointed by the news from South Africa. It seems beyond belief the Australian cricket team have been involved in cheating. Our cricketers are role models and cricket is synonymous with fair play. How can our team be engaged in cheating like this? It beggars belief.' Turnbull later added: 'I have spoken with David Peever, the chairman of Cricket Australia, and I have expressed to him very clearly and unequivocally my disappointment and concern. He has said to me that Cricket Australia will be responding decisively, as they should. It's their responsibility to deal with it, but I have to say that [to] the whole nation, who holds those who wear the baggy green up on a pedestal — about as high as you can get in Australia, certainly higher than any politician, that's for sure — this is a shocking disappointment.'

There were also suggestions that it was a very un-Australian act, even though there is copious evidence to suggest it was very Australian. To mention just a few that come to mind from the 1970s onward.

Ian Chappell's behaviour during the Australian Test against New Zealand at Lancaster Park in 1974. It was triggered by a trivial set of circumstances following the umpire mistakenly signalling a six when a four should have been the call. The fact that the ball had bounced up into the stand, along with the crowd signalling six, must have created the confusion for umpire Bob Monteith. I was at the non-striker's end, so I was in a position to help sort out the correct call with him, which I did. As Monteith was about to change his signal, having thanked me for helping him make the right call, Chappell arrived on the scene and the abuse of the umpire began. He started off by suggesting he was blind and used foul language in doing so. I quietly went to say to Ian that it was okay, that things had been sorted out, that Bob was about to signal four, but before I got halfway through this he blew his top completely and wasn't prepared to wait and listen to what I was trying to say. At this point he began abusing me, telling me to mind my own business and his language was extremely abusive. He carried it on for an unacceptable period and continued when I got down to the other end. As a participant in the game it was as much my business as his. It was all a bit rich, since I was in fact supporting their cause, not ours. Maybe his conduct had a lot to do with the fact that we were 177/4, needing only 51 runs for a first Test-match victory against Australia.

An Australian website, The Roar, some 44 years later (2018) decided to revisit this ugly incident. Presumably the ball-tampering episode in 2018 in South Africa prompted their decision to raise it again. By now, the 74-year-old Chappell still couldn't let the ball go through to the wicketkeeper without attempting another wild hack to justify the unjustifiable. He even managed some further abuse by referring to me as a liar. I'm not sure what I was supposed to be lying about? Perhaps his definition of verbal abuse is different to most of us. Graciousness in impending defeat was also not an emotion high on his priority list.

There seems to be a brashness in the attitude of many Australians towards the spirit of cricket, even from unexpected quarters. I finally came to this conclusion after a discussion I had with two mild-mannered, intelligent Australian friends of mine on two separate occasions. Both were in their mid to late forties. The first topic of discussion centred on what was hitting cricket headlines at the time. Mitchell Johnson, the Australian fast bowler, was being talked about for his obvious mouthing off towards opposition batsmen. My friend defended his countryman by saying 'but that's what fast bowlers do.' The second person's discussion focused on whether the Aussie cricketers were generally the biggest 'sledgers' in world cricket. His automatic response and assumption was that 'getting under the batsman's skin' was part and parcel of the game. I pointed out that verbal attempts to do so were not permitted under the laws of cricket. But suggested there were several ways it could still be achieved legitimately, by the bowler repeatedly outplaying the batsman by often beating the outside edge of his bat, or by intelligent field placements *et cetera*.

I suppose, over time different practices exist in every country, and become normalised, but that doesn't mean their habits should be automatically accepted by a sport played internationally. One practice that springs to mind, although not cricket related, was when I was in Peshawar (Pakistan). I was approached by a local well-dressed man in the foyer of our hotel, whose sales pitch for his Kashmiri carpets was that they had been stolen from palaces in the Middle East.

Maybe New Zealanders do live up to sometimes being referred to as 'South Pacific Poms' and the Aussies 'South Pacific Yanks', appearing to use America as their mentor. I wouldn't normally bother to respond to regurgitating the Chappell incident, except in this instance, this event is a good example of an attitude that too often features with some in Australian cricket to this day. They just don't seem to get it, or they don't want to. In fact, there has been a steady decline in ethical standards and sportsmanship right across the world of cricket. Chappell can attempt to defend his behaviour on that day as much as he likes, but the bottom line is that he was arrogant, abusive, and showed no respect for the umpire, an opponent, and the traditional values of the game.

I imagine the significance of traditional values will be irrelevant to some? Maybe discussions on this subject need to be revisited, particularly if it's agreed that a new set needs to be established. The current set is frequently being broken and the game dragged through the mud. With countries becoming more self-centred, it appears to be more difficult for rules to be accepted universally.

In an ODI at the Melbourne Cricket Ground (MCG) in 1981 there was the infamous underarm incident, when Trevor Chappell (apparently under orders from captain and brother Greg) delivered the last ball of the match to Brian McKechnie with New Zealand requiring 6 runs, not to win the match, but to tie it. Apart from the obvious lack of sportsmanship, I don't think there had been a six hit in the entire match. Furthermore, the MCG is well known for its long boundaries, and McKechnie was not a six hitter. To be fair, it was not a popular move with most of their team members, but it only takes a couple (the captain included) in a team to lower the tone for everyone. In typical fashion New Zealand's Prime Minister Rob Muldoon quipped that the Australians were like the colour of their shirts — yellow!

Having not played for New Zealand since the end of Australia's tour here in 1977, I was selected to play in the 1982–83 World Series Cup competition with England as the third team. It didn't take long before I renewed my acquaintance with Australia's attitude to the game. The first ball I faced was a welcoming bouncer, delivered by the military medium pace of Greg Chappell, which flagged an attitude that would soon return them to type. It had been almost 10 years since my Christchurch run-in with his brother Ian. On this occasion it was their objection to me being replaced in the field at Melbourne. The situation arose as the result of an injury to a quadriceps muscle batting against England. I wasn't able to field in the second innings of that game. Before our next game, against Australia, I received plenty of physiotherapy and was declared fit to play. We batted first and I was able to bat without any hindrance, including running between the wickets. But when in the field, halfway through the Australian innings, I chased a ball to the boundary, quite a long run on the wide expanse of outfield at the MCG. My thigh went into spasm and while I stayed on for a few balls hoping to run it off, I couldn't and I left the field. As I was leaving Greg Chappell was coming out to bat. He proceeded to talk with the umpires protesting that I had come into the match unfit and therefore I shouldn't be allowed to be replaced. I knew nothing of these claims at the time because I was on Graham Alison's table receiving treatment. Unwisely, the umpire decided to go along with this puerile, indignant request and we were refused a substitute fielder. It caught all of us off guard, so on the spur of the moment, I felt obligated to return to the field. I proceeded to just stand at mid-off or mid-on and be a spectator. It soon became obvious to everyone that the situation was farcical. It took a message to be sent out to the umpires at the drinks break for the decision to be reversed, allowing me to return to the dressing room. In those days I don't believe an English umpire would have been influenced by such a cantankerous request from a player. I did receive an apology from one of the officials afterwards. On reflection, we should have fielded with just 10 men to make the point stronger. It might have been a first if we had done so. The reality is that if this procedure was followed, no player would ever be allowed to have a replacement if they broke down after coming back from injury. When summing up this episode, one word comes to mind: pathetic!

In many ways it's a pity that sportsmen appear to hold such a significant place in the minds of young people. I tend to agree with what Michael Henderson had to say in *The Spectator* in July 2012 where he wrote: 'Sport, in its best moments, is a wonderful distraction but it is essentially trivial, and trivial things do not translate into genius. The great contests may illuminate our lives. The great players may live in our memories. They do not alter the way we see the world.'

When researching 'Monkeygate', the incident in 2008 when Harbhajan Singh was charged with racism after allegedly calling Andrew Symonds a monkey, I came across a report whereby Singh claimed that he'd been relentlessly sledged in the same game by Darren Lehmann. In typical Sikh fashion, Singh was not prepared to take the abuse lying down and responded by asking the rotund Lehmann whether he was pregnant. Lehmann went on to become the Australian coach and was still in that position during the ball-tampering fiasco in South Africa in 2018. However, back to the infamous spat with Symonds. Singh was quoted as saying: 'I didn't say monkey. It was their allegation. I only told him — "teri maa ki … haath ki roti khaane ko bada dil kar raha hai". He did not listen at all. Anyway, he did not know Hindi, and I don't know English.' Translating the Hindi into

English, he alleges he said, 'at the moment I would very much like to eat the food made by your mother's hand'. My Indian friends tell me that the word 'haath', in the Hindi quote above, has been used as a replacement word for another that is sometimes used in a similar context, with a very different meaning. If this is so, in his own language Singh has been as sexually abusive as possible in referring to Symonds' mother. It is common in Hindi/Punjabi and no doubt other languages to use mothers and sisters when using crude language. This explanation is more plausible and does remove the possible racist insult of monkey, but Singh's language was still highly offensive. Singh admits to trying to give back more abuse than he receives and it is reasonable to assume that he was provoked. Even an Ocker would have struggled to top this one. Incidentally, the Hindi word for monkey is 'bundar'.

What interests me about this episode is that every so often the Aussie cricketers are up in arms about someone else's behaviour and yet they seem to be oblivious to their own. In 'Monkeygate' you had a mixed-race player accusing an Asian player of racism and the white South African match referee Mike Procter being accused of racism for handing out a penalty to the Asian player. Once a breach of the code had occurred, Procter should have been safe from being accused of racism because neither player was of European origin, but alas no. Sure the ethnicity of both non-white players is different, but they are both coloured, so the accusation of colour prejudice is partly removed except that Symonds may regard himself as black, since one of his parents is West Indian. Deciding on the ethnicity of mixed race complicates matters more, because even with DNA testing, individuals may not want to be identified with their strongest bloodline. So for political expediency to be fully met it would require the match referee to be ethnically a combination of both the players in question, plus being from a neutral country. Just imagine how many match referees there would need to be on hand, and that doesn't account for the variety of white ethnicities. Yes all of this is ridiculous and it's meant to be. It's a roundabout way of saying that unless governing bodies make decisions on ethical grounds, they surrender to countless pathways fostering prejudicial decisions, right across the board.

Cricket has experienced many instances when accusations of racism have occurred. In this book I've also referred to a couple more. The Darrell Hair affair at The Oval involving the Pakistan team, and the West Indies in New Zealand during their tour in 1980 when Colin Croft assaulted Fred Goodall by deliberately putting his shoulder into Goodall during his delivery stride. I had been told much later that the West Indians believed they had reason to believe Goodall was a racist. Although it is impossible to totally eliminate the race card being played from time to time, if the laws were consistently applied, the focus is more likely to be diverted towards judging each decision on its merits free from prejudice. Once the laws are applied more consistently, there is far less likelihood of protests and outcries of indignation.

In the lead-up to the last Ashes series in Australia (2017), the Australian vice-captain David Warner was widely publicised extending indirectly a welcoming announcement to the England team, stating that the Australians should gain motivation by 'hating the Poms'. He compared the Ashes with war and went on to say: 'You try and get into a battle as quick as you can. I try and look in the opposition's eye and work out how can I dislike this player, how can I get on top of him. You've got to find that spark in yourself to really take it to the opposition. You have to delve and dig deep into yourself to get some sort of hatred about them. At the moment I'm not going to put any vibes out there or get into a verbal stoush … but come day one when we walk out there, there will definitely be some words exchanged. I think the subtle approach these days is how it is and how it goes.' I think Warner must have confused the word subtle with its antonym, blatant!

Back to Malcolm Turnbull's (the then Prime Minister of Australia) quote after the sandpaper ball-tampering episode, which comes to mind, when he said 'the whole nation, who holds those who wear the baggy green up on a pedestal'. With that degree of status comes power and responsibility. Instead of it serving as a badge of honour, what we see is something closer to a badge of dishonour. It's as though honour is seen as a weakness.

Cricket Australia's muteness over this matter, and numerous others including those leading up to the sandpaper ball-tampering in South Africa, demonstrated support, even encouragement for effectively bringing the game into disrepute. The South Africa-Australia series followed the Ashes, and was described by match referee Jeff Crowe as the most ill-tempered he has seen in cricket. 'Never in my 14 years of refereeing have I seen such animosity between two teams that was mainly a result of the debacle in the previous Test in Durban,' said Crowe's report to the ICC. The debacle that Crowe is referring to was the verbal confrontation on the field of play between David Warner and Quinton de Kock that spilled over into the stairwell at the tea break on the fourth day of the first Test. Warner had to be held back by teammates as he abused Quinton de Kock.

The following are extracts from a *Guardian* report on that first Test in Durban.

> Here we go again. A better than decent Test match concluded on Monday in Durban but will never stand a chance of capturing the attention it deserves. Events of the previous afternoon made sure of that. Press conferences came and went where the participants argued their corner in the usual way. Match officials will try to unpick it all from narrators unlikely to give an inch. Will anything change? Almost certainly not.
>
> That David Warner was front and centre was all the spice the tale required. Of course he has form, most of it some years ago, but he'll forever be known as a crosser of the line. Oh, that bloody line. The one the Australians routinely talk about headbutting (their chosen word) but not stepping over. This time, there is no disputing that it has been breached.
>
> But the twist. When Warner went after Quinton de Kock at the tea interval on Sunday — revealed in leaked CCTV footage that both

sides woke up to on the final morning of the Test — Steve Smith said it was due to an attack levelled at his deputy. 'Quinton got quite personal and provoked an emotional response from Davey,' he said. 'Those things aren't on and you can't be getting into somebody's personal life like that.'

Specifically, de Kock is alleged to have made derogatory comments about Warner's wife. This wasn't refuted by Faf du Plessis, who like his opposite number expressed regret at the episode, but did raise that 'both parties' had been rolling around in the personal mud. 'Who started it?' he continued, 'I don't know.' Smith returned serve: 'Faf can say what he likes.' As far as he was aware, his charges had not (sigh) crossed that line.

The hosts didn't much care for this. Within minutes of Smith leaving, the long-term South African team manager Mohammed Moosajee popped his head up to say that de Kock had 'most definitely' been provoked. The South Africans have also briefed that Warner called de Kock a 'bush pig', would you believe.

Sick of this yet? The skippers acknowledge that they are. Both forwarded the argument that there is an inevitability of situations like this in elite, intense sport. For du Plessis' part, he said he relishes it, while Smith believes his side are at their best when 'hunting as a pack.' But that doesn't mean they enjoy the associated nonsense.

By logical extension, this is where the umpires — the pair paid to control the game in a dispassionate fashion — can do more to help protect players from themselves. As du Plessis said, this whole sorry saga would never have made it into the stairwell had it been dealt with in the middle. 'The fact that it spilled over off the field shouldn't have happened.'

It was a view shared by the former Australia opener Simon Katich.

'If it is allowed to keep going on, then things are going to get out of control,' he told Cricinfo. 'This is where the umpires need to step in as soon as they start. We have all heard about the stump mics being turned up and everything being heard, but initially, the umpires have got to be the ones to put it to rest straight away; give the warnings to the skippers and get the skippers to control it. That obviously hasn't happened.'

If that doesn't work, Katich continued, then some heavy-handed intervention might result in welcome self-regulation: 'If they start rubbing blokes out for this sort of behaviour and miss a Test then it is going to cost a team at some point and if that happens the team-mates are going to clamp down on that behaviour and probably police it themselves.'

PRIOR TO THE first Test in Durban, the Aussies asked the local broadcaster and match officials to keep the on-field microphones' sound down when the ball is dead. Their argument being that in Australia, Channel 9's microphone fader is generally turned up and down by an operator as each ball is bowled, capturing sound effects as a delivery is sent down, and immediately before and after. The fader is usually turned down during the period between deliveries and overs. However, in South Africa the microphones tend to be left on more often. Since then it seems that the standard practice of broadcasters is to leave the on-field microphones live most of the time. The mute button has become my friend so that I don't have to listen to the inane on-field kindergarten chatter coming from all and sundry. In particular, it has become standardised for wicketkeepers to relentlessly regurgitate the same lines of encouragement under the pretence of motivation.

Just in case you needed any further evidence of the Aussies wanting a free licence to verbally break the fair play laws, the microphone request is a full-on confession of guilt. It's not surprising when spurious arguments in defence of sledging are likely to follow. Sure enough, on this occasion Nathan Lyon represented the age-old excuse when asked about the prospect of a verbal battle over the next five days. 'What happens on the field stays on the field.' He followed it up with: 'We're all grown men. We compete hard. We know where the line is. We head-butt it probably, but we are not going to go over the line.' Grown men indeed — more like spoilt children in gangs having been given the keys to the city. Masking verbal abuse with words like banter and gamesmanship is just plain attempts at deception.

From what their new coach Justin Langer was quoted as saying after his appointment in May 2018, it sounded like nothing substantive was likely to change. He declared sledging still has its place after being tasked with reforming Australia's cricket culture as national coach. Langer said: 'I think some of the best banter is among each other to get the opposition thinking about other things. Mental toughness is simply about being 100 per cent focused on the next ball. If you're worrying about what you've just said to me, then there's a distraction. But we all know what the acceptable behaviours are. There's a difference between competitiveness and aggression and we've got to be careful with that.'

Moeen Ali, England's cricket all-rounder, had a few things to say to Mike Atherton writing for *The Times* in September 2018. Moeen Ali has hit out at Australia as 'rude' and the only team he has disliked, yet says they have been 'humbled' by the sandpaper ball-tampering scandal.

Ali told *The Times* he wanted to be dropped during the 2017 Ashes series in Australia where he averaged 19.88 with the bat and 115 with the ball.

Australia was an abusive side that disrespected people and players, he told former captain Mike Atherton, a columnist for *The Times*: 'Everyone you speak to ... they are the only team I've played against my whole life that I've actually disliked. Not because it's Australia and they are the old enemy but because of the way they carry on and [their] disrespect of people and players. I'm someone who generally feels sorry for people when things go wrong but it's difficult to feel sorry for them. This ODI series they were very good actually; they'd been humbled.'

Tim Paine led Australia to England in 2018 after captain Steve Smith and vice-captain David Warner were banned for one year.

Ali told *The Times* his lack of respect stretched back to his first meeting with Australia at the 2015 World Cup, where England lost by 111 runs in Sydney.

'They were not just going hard at you, they were almost abusing you. That was the first time it hit me. I gave them the benefit of the doubt but the more I played against them they were just as bad, the Ashes here [in 2015] they were worse actually. Not intimidating, just rude. Individually they are fine and the Aussies we've had at Worcester have been fantastic, lovely guys.'

All of that aside, is it possible that finally the Australia-South African series has exposed enough disorder from both these teams and others, to prove that the integrity of the game requires a complete overhaul? For much to change, the focus must follow ethical standards right across the board from the top down, from the ICC to the grass-roots level. The Marylebone Cricket Club (MCC)/ICC have provided the laws of the game to be followed, but unless the ICC, the International Umpires Association, and the member countries are prepared to be united in their support, the game of cricket will not rise above the depths to which it has sunk.

Cricket Australia might appear to have shown some leadership in response to what happened in South Africa, but its problems appear to run too deep to feel confident that this ethical gesture will be sustained over the medium to longer term. Redefining what playing hard means and changing engrained attitudes will not come easily. Nor will the necessity to accept, promote and enforce the laws of the game as written, particularly covering the traditional values of cricket, the spirit of cricket and what constitutes fair and unfair play. Enforcement by others would help.

None of the cricketing countries is exempt from guilt or in a position to cast the first stone. New Zealand Cricket, for instance, only needs to go back to when Stephen Fleming was captain and the Australian Steve Rixon was coach. At that time the Australians were probably correct when they accused the New Zealand team of being the biggest sledgers in world cricket. Although the current New Zealand team has recovered from its behaviour at that time, there is nothing in place to convince me that preventive measures have been established by NZC to avoid a repeat performance.

What are the differences between cheating, dishonesty, lying, deception, conning, sledging and gamesmanship etc. and what weighting and label is put on each offence? The degrees of offending in some instances may vary, but in essence the laws of the game are there to prevent attempts to gain an unfair advantage. No matter how you want to dress it up, cheating is cheating. Nevertheless, how would you classify the following? Verbal abuse (sledging), questioning umpiring decisions, trying to con the umpire through verbal and/or physical actions, claiming a catch when you know you haven't caught it, distracting the batsman with verbal abuse, standing your ground when you know you're out (not walking), refusing to signal boundaries when you are in the best position to do so, changing the condition of the ball (ball-tampering), actually changing the ball during an innings, appealing to the umpire to give a batsman out when you know he/she isn't out, batsmen and bowlers running on the pitch, bowling beamers, deliberately overstepping (bowling big no balls) and so on. All cricketing countries, or at least individual players, try it on one way or another from time to time. There are differences between each country/culture as to how it categorises or views the seriousness of the various offences, but so what? Laws have been agreed through a democratic process, so take your medicine and move on!

When I look back over the past 53 years (since I first started playing first-class cricket), as long as I can remember, teams when fielding have endeavoured to change the condition of the ball to advantage them. New Zealand players along with others would use lotions of various types to get a better shine on the ball. It's intriguing, even contradictory, when the law states that you can't alter the condition of the ball. Polishing the ball has been permissible, although the execution of it has not always won favour. I remember when a piece of cloth attached to your trousers was not regarded as appropriate. I assume the concern may have been the assumption that the cloth was more likely to contain some form of lubricant. Frankly, if a player wanted to play that game, there were other options such as applying the likes of suntan lotion to your face, arms or wherever. I recall the intention of cloth attached to your trousers was more about saving your trousers from marking and wear and tear. As an aside, most players rubbed the ball on the inside of the upper thigh, but curiously in South Africa it was more prevalent under the armpit — perhaps that was more about accessing more moisture. A piece of loose cloth was often used and accepted to dry the ball, but not acceptable for polishing it. Although polishing the ball has become an accepted norm, how a player goes about it is still judged with caution, because in reality it is altering the condition of the ball.

In the '70s, when touring India, I recall complaining to the umpires about the Indians deliberately trying to take the shine off the new ball by throwing it along the ground from first slip to mid-off. At that stage the umpires hadn't worked it out that there was more than one way to change the condition of the ball, other than by rubbing it in the dirt. In those days the Indians played three world-class spinners who generally bowled throughout the innings from about the fourth over onwards. Picking (lifting) the seam was standard practice for everyone for many years. Even to this day, it is accepted practice for spinners to rub their fingers in the dirt around the crease area, which can then be transferred either deliberately or inadvertently onto the ball. Presumably the assumption is that the bowler is merely drying perspiration from his fingers, but there are various other more legitimate options available to achieve the same thing.

The condition of pitches on the subcontinent over the years encouraged seam and swing bowlers to work out ways to overcome the rapid deterioration of balls. The abrasive nature of their surfaces caused the ball to scuff up and lose its shine more quickly. Obviously, this became more of an issue for the Pakistan attack than for the Indian spinners. Around the period of the '70s and '80s, damping down one side of the ball with saliva became common practice in order to gain some movement. When Imran Khan first arrived at Worcester as a young lad, he was very happy to share this knowledge. In more recent times it became known that by scarring one side of the ball, considerable reverse swing and often late swing could be achieved by the faster bowlers. If executed well, instead of the rougher, unpolished side of the ball providing more drag, the air breaks up over a more scarred surface producing less drag than the polished side. The label of 'reverse swing' comes about because the ball in this condition reacts diametrically differently to when it is newer and less disfigured.

There was a time when some Pakistanis prided themselves in being better at it than anyone else. Sharp objects like bottle tops were carried in pockets to secure the best results. I recall the England captain Mike Atherton being caught with dirt in his pocket which he was illegally applying to the ball. Chris Pringle preferred bottle tops, whereas Shahid Afridi just took a really good bite of the ball. Faf du Plessis is a multiple offender. He used the zip on his pants to rough the ball up and more recently mint to help shine the ball. Come 2018, Cameron Bancroft used sandpaper.

For a period teams were deliberately throwing the ball back to the wicketkeeper on the bounce. The aim was to throw the ball into a scuffed-up area around the region of the crease, landing it on the selected side to damage it further. The umpires caught on to this one fairly quickly and put a stop to it. In an attempt to prevent the escalation of deliberately changing the condition of the ball, legislation was passed instructing the umpires to receive the ball at every stoppage in play (at drinks, fall of wickets, end of a session), and intermittently at the end of an over. Today, with two white balls being used in ODIs, the umpires receive and retain their ball at the end of each over. In Tests, teams batting last on wearing pitches are very wary and concerned about what the fielding side might be doing to the ball. How dare you do to me what I might do to you? How dare I do to you what you have just done to me?

I've already given my opinion on why I think the Australians have been so heavily punished and criticised for ball-tampering in 2018 in South Africa. What is more interesting is the lack of sympathy for the Aussies throughout the cricketing world as a whole, particularly when considering the number of instances of ball-tampering over such a long period by other nations. I think it has much more to do with their unrelenting Ocker behaviour, and their interpretation of fair play, than a desire to put down a strong cricketing nation. Bringing out the box of tissues when they're caught doesn't help their cause much either.

A further breach of the ball-tampering ICC code of conduct allegedly took place in June 2018 by the Sri Lankan captain Dinesh Chandimal during a series in the West Indies. On this occasion it was some form of sweet presumably mixed in with Chandimal's saliva. Umpires Aleem Dar and Ian Gould had raised concerns about the condition of the ball towards the end of day two. In protest, Sri Lanka then took to the field two hours late on the third day. The tourists eventually decided to play following lengthy discussions between match referee Javagal Srinath and Sri Lanka's coaching staff. Sri Lanka were told play could not continue with the existing ball. In the end, the West Indies were awarded 5 penalty runs, the ball was changed and the tourists grudgingly agreed to continue. Sri Lanka Cricket (SLC) later released a statement denying any wrongdoing by its players. I'm sure match referee Mike Procter would have been relieved not to have been on duty and mixed up in this fiasco.

What a mess! At least the ICC backed up the umpires and the match referee, but surely in the future it should be made clear to teams that they must immediately continue the game, or it results in a forfeiture and a weighty fine. From a player's point of view, it would be unreasonable to ban them from putting anything in their mouths to suck on. Chewing gum has long been the preferred option, but I'm unfamiliar with what effect other sweets can achieve. The application of unadulterated saliva is currently still regarded as acceptable, but any hint of it being otherwise may not be, particularly if the umpires detect an obvious change in the condition of the ball. It is possible that Chandimal and numerous others may have got into the habit of contravening a law that umpires have probably been asked to tighten up on. Nevertheless, you would think that the amount of publicity given to the subject of ball-tampering around the world of cricket at that time would have been warning enough for players to have reassessed their actions, even if they think they have the key to the cities they play in! The contradictions that exist in and around what is and isn't changing the condition of the ball does need to be more clearly understood. When some practices have become normalised by players, those accused of wrongdoing are likely to feel aggrieved, but the indignation expressed by their administrations and the country they represent is unwarranted. If the game is not careful, in a worst-case scenario, teams could be tempted to use protest 'sit-ins' as a tactic to save a game.

It appears that cricket has been very slow compared to other sports in putting in place laws to control player conduct, fair and unfair play. The reluctance to do so stems from an assumed ethos in cricket ('it's just not cricket'), whereby everything will be played in the true spirit of sportsmanship. In the 1970s, those on boards governing the game in their respective countries backpedalled on doing anything substantive — they wouldn't even encourage it to be written into the laws. In the past it was assumed that the implicit Spirit of the Game was understood and accepted by all those involved. It wasn't until the year 2000 the Marylebone Cricket Club (MCC) finally felt it right to put into words some clear guidelines on 'the spirit of cricket'. But administrations and umpires have been extremely reluctant to enforce them. The change in behavioural norms and the increase in player power have contributed to inaction. The Aussies have appeared at the top of the list of paying lip service to the 'spirit of cricket' for as long as I can remember. It's not as if the MCC has been autocratic. It has consulted widely with all the Full Member Countries of the International Cricket Council, the governing body of the game. There was close consultation with the Association of Cricket Umpires and Scorers. The Club also brought in umpires and players from all round the world. The more recent version includes several necessary amendments arising from experience and practical application of the Code around the world since October 2000. In 1788, the MCC took responsibility for the Laws of Cricket, although changes to the laws are now determined by the International Cricket Council — the copyright is still owned by MCC.

The Aussies have defiantly favoured following the 'Australian way' and at one point, their players chose to draw up their own set of rules. When commenting on the Smith/Bancroft/Warner ball-tampering episode, Steve Waugh, while strongly condemning their actions, suggested the Australian team return to the modifications he and the team agreed to implement in 2003. Their modifications were 'to empower our players to set their own standards and commit to play the Australian way — respect for team-mates, opposing teams, match officials and the game.' Sounds plausible, because those headings largely follow what had already been written into the laws. The difference lies in their interpretation, because after all, actions speak louder than words. It reminds me of indigenous societies wanting to introduce their own set of laws. Could it be that the Aussie cricketers and their administration see themselves as the original people of cricket and that the MCC/ICC shouldn't interfere? Playing with themselves appears to be favoured. It needs to be remembered that the ICC board has representation from the 12 full member countries, three associate member countries plus a deputy chairman and independent female director.

The ICC has allowed T20 cricket to swamp Test and ODI cricket, so what is in place to prevent countries from establishing their own set of rules? At one point, Australia followed by New Zealand introduced eight-ball overs. It would not be easy for countries to change fundamentally the laws of cricket and still expect to remain in the game globally. However, it would not be so difficult for countries to insist on drawing up their own set of expectations of the 'spirit of cricket', particularly when cricket is played in their own country. It could be argued that this is already happening because of the reluctance to enforce what is already written.

Going further back in time, the unwillingness of administrators to look ahead and be proactive let alone reactive became evident to me and others at an end-of-year county captains' meeting at Lord's in 1980 that I attended as captain of Worcestershire. The purpose of these Test and County Cricket Board (TCCB) meetings was largely to hear if the captains had any suggestions for law changes and the like.

During the West Indies tour of New Zealand earlier that year I had witnessed the physical assault of New Zealand umpire Fred Goodall when Colin Croft deliberately elbowed Goodall during his approach to the bowling crease. I had suggested that it was time to write something appropriate into the laws of cricket to cover for such eventualities and be generally stronger in dealing with unfair play, let alone assaults. The chairman Doug Insole responded by saying that a physical assault would not happen in England and words to the effect that it would be very unfortunate to write something that covered that sort of thing into the Laws of Cricket. Even though people running cricket then were mostly ex-cricketers (unlike today), some of their decisions appeared to be overly anxious and timid towards protecting the integrity of the game, when a firmer hand was needed. It has been very hard and distasteful for the old school of thought at that time to come to terms with the reality that rules needed to be formally written into the Laws of Cricket to protect the integrity of the game whether they liked it or not. This reluctance has resulted in a half-hearted attempt, to a level that invokes degrees of penalties equivalent to a slap on the hand. They perished the thought of yellow and red cards, although just recently red cards have appeared on the list of penalties, but don't expect to see any issued any time soon. Although there are now several offences which have 5-run penalties attached to them, hardly any of them are applied and on the very odd occasion that one is, it creates major controversy and indignation. They can be applied for offences such as: time wasting, damaging the pitch, deliberate attempts to distract the striker, deliberate distraction or obstruction of batsmen, a player returning without permission, tampering with the ball. The legacy of the old culture is so hard to shake off that just about everyone involved appears to be offended and/or hurt by these decisions. Umpires and match referees are made to feel like villains for merely applying the laws and often they don't find the courage to do it because of the probable consequences.

As an aside, Doug Insole was an interesting character with a high profile in the English and world game. Insole was embroiled in his own controversy as an England selector when, in 1968, the selectors, of whom he was chairman, left South African-born Cape Coloured player Basil D'Oliveira out of the England team to tour the apartheid republic. D'Oliveira had left South Africa to play cricket in England and was a colleague of mine at Worcestershire. The correctness or otherwise of D'Oliveira's omission was not helped by the fact that he had just scored 158 against Australia in the final Test at The Oval in the 1968 Ashes. Insole's response to questioning on the matter was, 'We've got rather better than him in the side'. However, cynicism among anti-apartheid ranks suggested D'Oliveira's omission was to show that appeasement, in spite of the lessons associated with Prime Minister Neville Chamberlain's policies before the outbreak of the Second World War, still lived in British society with the South African Government unlikely to accept his selection. Insole was one of five selectors who chose the team while another five MCC 'advisors' were also involved in the process. Following the original selection, bowling all-rounder Tom Cartwright was forced to pull out of the tour. At this point D'Oliveira, a batting all-rounder, was named as his replacement and, as suspected, the South African Government reacted accordingly by calling off the tour — how times have changed. Insole was left to carry the can for the episode and he wasn't helped that the minutes of the selection meeting went missing — or maybe it was helpful! However, the impression remained that the selectors had originally bowed to behind-the-scenes pressure not to select D'Oliveira. The alleged truth of the matter is that tour captain, and selector, Colin Cowdrey had not wanted D'Oliveira in the side because of his commonly acknowledged issues with alcohol.

Another costly example of administrative convenience which in this instance had total disregard for truth or ethical standards took place following New Zealand's tour of the West Indies in 1996. During that tour, two players, Chris Cairns and Adam Parore, faked injuries and proceeded, without discussion, to head for the hills deserting the team, presumably to satisfy their own level of dysfunction and selfish interest. Cairns left before the first of the two Test-match series and Parore at the end of the first Test. Parore had earlier tried to persuade management that there was no need for him to continue onto Bermuda following the West Indies tour, because he preferred to get back to his job in New Zealand. It wasn't as though Bermuda was an add-on at the last minute. It was in the players' contracts which they all signed (including Parore) before leaving New Zealand.

Chris Doig, the chief executive of NZC, following his arrival in Barbados described the two's behaviour, among other things, as miscreant and petulant. In an interview with Kim Hill on her Nine to Noon show on National Radio back in New Zealand, Doig said: 'There was nothing new when it came to Adam's behaviour and as for Cairns, he had chosen a collision course with management that was wholly inappropriate. He's part of a team structure and the style that the team was going to use both on and off the field was discussed and accepted by the players prior to the tour, and therefore neither he nor Parore has a right to contravene.' Doig could have also added that I had flown to England to meet with some selected players who were playing county cricket (Cairns, Nash and Twose) to get their buy-in to what had been discussed and agreed by those back in New Zealand. It received their approval, so you can't get much more consultative and democratic than that. Furthermore I'd toured New Zealand meeting with a selection of former players to pick their brains. Doig went on to say he'd met with all the players and found all of them focused, contented and ready to do battle in the second Test. In fact most of the players were pissed off with Cairns pulling the plug just before the Test series started. Some of his peers had actually forecast his withdrawal. Hardly anyone bothered to see him off; he simply disappeared. Interestingly it was only a year later (1997) when Cairns wanted to come home from Australia when New Zealand had been knocked out of the one-day series there. The difference this time around was that he was advised, if he left he'd never play for New Zealand again. My contacts at Nottinghamshire (the county Cairns played for in England) told me he was not prepared to follow instructions. For example, slogging out when the team needed him to occupy the crease. This just adds to New Zealand Cricket's record of negligent treatment of its staff as a whole. Not just those that might have been sacked wrongly over time, but also by supporting and therefore encouraging the bad behaviour of offenders that needed reining in, for everyone's good including their own.

The selfish, destructive personality often uses the argument 'keep me happy, I'll play better and that will be good for the team'. Cairns' main publicised gripe was that he didn't receive enough praise. It reminds me of a quote from Noel Coward who said 'I love criticism just as long as it's unqualified praise.' I'm also reminded when it is said that the difficult player is very likely to return to type, particularly when it goes unquestioned.

What followed at the conclusion of the West Indies tour was in retrospect a decision which would rapidly promote a major shift towards a disproportionate amount of power being reserved for the players. Doig refused a tour debrief and instead set about convincing the board that the two players, by his own words 'miscreant players', would be supported and the coach, manager and physio would be sent packing. What a message to give cricket in New Zealand. What a message to give employees of NZC. The back-stabbing and lack of process that went into this decision behind the scene begs the question, who were the biggest miscreants? Predictably, the spin-doctoring of lies and deception had to follow to justify their decision — out came the predictable one-liner to extinguish the need for further discussion: 'A lack of man management hit centre stage as it often does when people want to discredit someone to secure the survival of the unfittest.' One-liners are commonly used to dismiss any investigation of the facts.

What was intriguing about this episode in the ongoing saga of NZC was what motivated Doig to go down this path. Over time you get to hear a variety of opinions as to why, and naturally some more plausible than others. A couple of the most likely are that prior to becoming CEO of NZC, Doig at one time was a school teacher and later an opera singer, who had run the Wellington Arts Festival, with ostensibly promotion and fundraising as his two biggest strengths. He had purportedly been heard to say 'NZC needs Cairns more than they need Turner.' I suppose he had money in mind. Actually, neither of us was essential, but what should have been indispensable was integrity and ethical decisions. Another possibility was that Doig admitted to being a very good supporter of Cairns and said he understood what makes him tick. Maybe Doig thought he was an expert in the psychology of how cricket teams operate. By accident, a couple of years later, I came across Doig in the restaurant bar at the Clearwater Golf Club. For some inexplicable reason he stood up from his chair, walked briskly across the room to me, proceeded to shake my hand enthusiastically and immediately rejoined his group. I still don't know what to make of that.

Everyone involved needs to be held accountable for their actions, if it is accepted that 'The Game' and its intrinsic values should remain bigger than the individual. This should apply equally to administrators and players. The issue then becomes a question of appropriate timing for accountability. During the course of a match, the Laws of Cricket state that the umpires are the sole judges of fair and unfair play, indicating that in most cases they should apply penalties at the time of the infringement. Sadly, if at all, most of these are applied later by match referees when they are less likely to be effective. What we are seeing far too often are players and teams wanting to take over the umpiring duties and behaving more like a gang than a responsible team. The next step might be closer than we think, players deciding on who umpires their matches. If that were the case, both teams will naturally want umpires they can manipulate to advantage themselves, so logically they will end up selecting one each fighting over who chooses the third umpire.

Generally, the reaction of players to decisions will depend on the state of the game, their mood at the time and their relationship with the umpire. A convenient excuse used in defence of just about any form of errant behaviour is to complain that the situation wasn't handled with due care and sensitivity. If the umpires at The Oval had allowed the Pakistan team to have their protest sit-in and tried to negotiate to get them to continue playing, how much of a time delay is acceptable and what precedent does this set for future protests when a team doesn't get their own way?

A more recent protest sit-in by the Sri Lankans following another ball-tampering episode in July 2018 occupied a whole morning session of two hours. To try to cover up for bad behaviour by blaming the umpire for a lack of man management is very convenient and irresponsible. Red herrings and downright preciousness come to mind! The days of accepting rules or authority when it is obviously necessary to do so seem to have been put on hold for at least the foreseeable future. Instead, blame, greed and entitlement has taken centre stage.

Another example was when bodyline bowling reared its ugly head once again and it appears to be largely going unchallenged. In the Boxing Day Test 2019 it turned into its ugliest form. Mitchell Starc, Australia's fastest and tallest bowler decided to cynically resort to deliberately targeting the hands, upper body, and head of New Zealand's number 11 batsman Trent Boult. Boult bats at number 11 for good reason and his brief visits to the crease are often accentuated by extravagant sideways movements in order to get himself as far away from the assumed line of the ball as possible, particularly when the faster bowlers are 'bombing him'. Starc was being offered all three stumps to aim at on several occasions, but that didn't seem to satisfy his thirst for blood. He preferred to line up Boult ignoring the stumps until eventually he couldn't resist aiming at them. In the meantime he had fractured a bone in Boult's right hand. Boult continued and even bowled a few overs later in the day before heading back to New Zealand for an anticipated four week recovery. The fact that New Zealand had already been played out of the game by this stage (319 runs behind at half time) added fuel to the fire, yet the whole incident appeared to go unnoticed. An unanswered question remains: where were the umpires in all of this? Was there not enough convincing evidence for them to apply the spirit of the game or the laws of cricket?

41.6 Bowling of dangerous and unfair short pitched deliveries

41.6.1 The bowling of short pitched deliveries is dangerous if the bowler's end umpire considers that, taking into consideration the skill of the striker, by their speed, length, height and direction they are likely to inflict physical injury on him/her. The fact that the striker is wearing protective equipment shall be disregarded.

This incident reminded me of a four-day interprovincial final in New Zealand between Canterbury and Otago. The Otago number 11, Peter Petherick, who couldn't bat his eyelids, was being bounced/bombed by the Canterbury quick. As captain of Otago, I declared the innings closed at 9 down. I made the call for two additional reasons other than the obvious one. We had been played out of the game by this stage and Petherick had just been selected to go on his first tour with New Zealand. Referring back to the Boxing Day incident, this memory prompted me to think that Kane Williamson could have also declared the innings closed at 9 down. I suppose he had the complication that as captain it appears that he is supportive of bodyline bowling through the actions of Neil Wagner.

When I was growing up as a kid, if a policeman said 'Jump', I/we said 'How high?' Maybe this was excessive too, but at least it resulted in a more workable outcome. We were also more respectful of age. One can understand young minds having a narrower perspective on life and less awareness of the consequences of their actions. But I was brought up through an era in New Zealand when there was less pampering and an expectation of the importance of personal responsibility. However, it is of concern that the administrations of countries are showing scant regard for upholding the laws of the game, or its codes of conduct. Maybe less of this will be necessary with the preponderance of T20 cricket. The shorter the game, the less likelihood of players having the time or opportunities to infringe. To continue running the game down its current path is a sure way of ending Test cricket in its present form. Does that matter? Ask classical music buffs if they think symphonies should be shortened. As with Test matches, some symphonies may drag on a bit, but the time frame in both provides for the opportunity of something more.

For long-term sustainability, initiatives need to be put in place to resolve problems, not just manage them, and where the difference between a principle and a compromise are established instead of alternatives where money alone rules. In the meantime, surely cricket's management can at least make a better fist of retaining what values are left.

If anyone has doubts about the game suffering, just go along to club cricket and listen to the verbal exchanges. Within your own circle of friends, ask around what parents and grandparents think about the game of cricket and what alternative activities they would prefer their kids to be involved in. T20 leagues might have softened some opinions, but if introducing your kids to desirable values, I doubt if cricket would be high on the list. As an example, the following is an extract of what Dr Farah Palmer, a former captain of the New Zealand women's rugby team, the Black Ferns, thought about cricket in an opinion piece she wrote back in 2012 in the *Otago Daily Times*: 'Traditionalists often refer to cricket as the gentleman's sport but that label is well and truly dead: gentlemen do not sledge, cheat, use bodyline bowling tactics, have temper tantrums or appeal excessively. These days sportsmanship (the essence of behaving like a gentleman) has been replaced by gamesmanship: the art or practice of winning games by questionable measures: intimidating the opposition physically and verbally is encouraged.'

International Cricket Council chief executive David Richardson says, 'The public has spoken on cheating in the game and ball-tampering will not be tolerated.'

Richardson addressed the ball-tampering scandal in the South Africa-Australia Test series in 2018 when delivering the MCC Spirit of Cricket Cowdrey Lecture at Lord's: 'Cricket's DNA is based on integrity, but we have seen too much behaviour of late that puts that in jeopardy and this has to stop … Sledging that amounts to no more than personal abuse, fielders giving send-offs to batsmen who have been dismissed, unnecessary physical contact, players threatening not to play in protest against an umpire's decision and ball-tampering. This isn't the version of our game that we want to project to the world. The public reaction around the world to the incidents in the recent Australia-South Africa series was an eye-opener. The message was loud and clear, cheating is cheating and it's not what we signed up for.'

FOUR

BUILDING CHARACTER THROUGH SPORT

IN AUGUST 2006, I WROTE A PIECE HEADED 'BUILDING CHARACTER through Sport' that I think is still relevant today. It largely gives some of my thoughts on alternative thinking, other than gaining motivation through hate, more commonly referred to as sledging.

The sports field and battlefield are often linked as locations for the demonstration of legitimate patriotic aggression. Throughout history they have been places for moral commitment to defend the society and its core values against all odds. Heroes of sport are viewed as symbols of national prowess, quality and virtue. Do we fundamentally agree with these statements and if so are we happy with the direction our respective sports are taking in terms of the messages they are sending right across society? These statements relate mainly to the elite level, which tends to set the example for their respective sports as a whole. More significantly, though, are the millions of others who play at a far less public level. They make the most of what their sport can do to help them become responsible citizens by developing positive values and attitudes. If all is not well, what systemic changes are needed to heal rather than just trying to manage the problems?

There is a portion of society that watches elite level sport and may well have a preferred winner, but their focus is not hero related. Their interest is on the skills and the physical, mental and competitive struggle. Although they may prefer that the performers behave like good role models, few of this group of enthusiasts appear to expect the performers will live up to such expectations. Nevertheless, there is still widespread passion for sport and whether sportsmen and women like it or not, their conduct does affect their supporters, relationships between groups of people and even nations. The behaviour of two players in particular (the Zidane/Materazzi head-butting incident) during the 2006 World Cup football final between Italy and France will have created a great deal of animosity between many of the people in both those countries.

The record numbers of red and yellow cards handed out during this world cup proved once again that trying to manage a problem like this with a card system is very short term and in this instance didn't appear to deter the players from continuing to offend even in the short term. Recognising that problems exist and trying to manage them like this is a form of acceptance and is therefore unsustainable. For systemic problems to be resolved they need to be reconciled and that requires a long-term approach. The attempts to uphold the 'Spirit of Cricket' (codes of conduct) in our provincial cricket within New Zealand, although well meaning, is having limited success because the problem is only being managed. A systemic change is needed to get to the root of the problem.

In more recent times, the so-called professional era has allowed players to be turned into products, destroying the very essence of their being. Competition needs to retain humane, humanitarian qualities allowing for what some call character moments, opportunities to show honesty, respect, responsibility and sportsmanship. Sport can be used as an ideal vehicle to develop a sense of community through an emphasis on the social virtues of loyalty, cooperation, discipline and being winners in life. None of this prevents participants being highly competitive, aggressive, determined while striving to be as successful as they can be. Understanding that you can win on a variety of fronts and that being ahead of your opponent is only one winning possibility. There are times when you may have played poorly yet ended up winning on the score board and other occasions when you have played very well and lost.

Cricket by its very nature, more than most sports, provides many opportunities for character moments to be expressed. When a game is played over such a long period of time it automatically allows for the ebbs and flows of fortune. It encapsulates the challenges of an individual and team sport with personal and shared ecstasy, despair, happiness, sadness, pleasure and pain.

When I was asked recently what were my reasons for playing cricket, my answers were:

I played for enjoyment, in other words I liked playing, at least most of the time.

I enjoyed considering the tactics and applying the practical skills of the game, and challenging myself to see how good I could become.

I played because I found the game gave me opportunities to test and apply personal integrity and doing well gave me confidence in life.

I saw playing as a means of strengthening my character and ability to cope with adversity.

There was enjoyment in a group feeling of success.

Cricket provided opportunities to travel, visit new places, meet new people and cultures, explore new ideas.

From time to time I was able to give others pleasure.

On reflection, my answers probably reflect the era before players came to be seen as products, a time when society was less exposed to commercialism and consumerism. Obviously I needed to make enough money to be able to play, but money was never the priority. I'm not suggesting it is wrong to be well paid for playing a sport or wanting recognition for doing so. However, if these and a win-at-all-costs attitude becomes the primary reasons for playing, then the cost is likely to be too high. The intrinsic values of sport are put at risk and so too is the greater prize of winning in life.

It is interesting to observe that even at the lower levels of sport, where money and recognition are not at stake, a win-at-all-costs attitude appears to have permeated through. This is a pity, for sport could still play a vital role in being used as a vehicle to build character and maturity in the development of its people. If the erosion is to be cured, work will need to occur on many fronts. The toughest groups to influence would be those in the more senior categories where personalities are more likely to be firmly set.

Has society moved too far in another direction to believe that a significant change is possible? We may be pleasantly surprised to see just how many administrators, coaches, teachers and players have been waiting for the opportunity to support a more values-orientated movement. I'd like to think there are still many parents and grandparents who would be delighted to support a move in this direction. A long-term sustainable approach calls for a systemic change to take place (in particular) at the junior levels where core values are taught, or should be at a time when a young person's character is being developed and set for life. With some encouragement, I'm sure there are also lots of people of retirement age, not currently involved, who would see it as an opportunity to contribute to society.

To those sceptics who are worried about competitiveness being taken out of sport, think again. The suggestion is not about reducing competitiveness, it's about retaining it in a healthy manner by adding winning values.

Preface to The Laws of Cricket

These Codes have been subject to additions and alterations recommended by the governing authorities of the time. Since its formation in 1787, the Marylebone Cricket Club (MCC) has been recognised as the sole authority for drawing up the Code and for all subsequent amendments. The Club also holds the World copyright. The basic Laws of Cricket have stood remarkably well the test of well over 250 years of playing the game. It is thought the real reason for this is that cricketers have traditionally been prepared to play in the Spirit of the Game as well as in accordance with the Laws. In 2000, MCC revised and rewrote the Laws for the new Millennium. In this Code, the major innovation was the introduction of the Spirit of Cricket as a Preamble to the Laws. Whereas in the past it was assumed that the implicit Spirit of the Game was understood and accepted by all those involved. Finally the MCC felt it right to put into words some clear guidelines, which help to maintain the unique character and enjoyment of the game. The other aims were to dispense with the Notes, to incorporate all the points into the Laws and to remove, where possible, any ambiguities, so that captains, players and umpires could continue to enjoy the game at whatever level they might be playing. MCC consulted widely with all the Full Member Countries of the International Cricket Council, the Governing Body of the game. There was close consultation with the Association of Cricket Umpires and Scorers. The Club also brought in umpires and players from all round the world. This latest version, *The Laws of Cricket* (2000 Code 6th Edition — 2015) includes several necessary amendments arising from experience and practical application of the Code around the world since October, 2000.

Preamble — The Spirit of Cricket

Cricket is a game that owes much of its unique appeal to the fact that it should be played not only within its Laws but also within the Spirit of the Game. Any action which is seen to abuse this spirit causes injury to the game itself. The major responsibility for ensuring the spirit of fair play rests with the captains.

1. There are two Laws which place responsibility for the team's conduct firmly on the captain.

Responsibility of captains

The captains are responsible at all times for ensuring that play is conducted within the Spirit of the Game as well as within the Laws.

Player's conduct

In the event of a player failing to comply with instructions by an umpire, or criticising by word or action the decision of an umpire, or showing dissent, or generally behaving in a manner which might bring the game into disrepute, the umpire concerned shall in the first place report the matter to the other umpire and to the player's captain, and instruct the latter to take action.

2. Fair and unfair play

According to the Laws the umpires are the sole judges of fair and unfair play. The umpires may intervene at any time and it is the responsibility of the captain to take action where required.

3. The umpires are authorised to intervene in cases of:

Time wasting

Damaging the pitch

Dangerous or unfair bowling

Tampering with the ball

Any other action that they consider to be unfair

4. The Spirit of the Game involves RESPECT for:

Your opponents

Your own captain

The roles of the umpires

The game's traditional values

5. It is against the Spirit of the Game:

To dispute an umpire's decision by word, action or gesture

To direct abusive language towards an opponent or umpire

To indulge in cheating or any sharp practice, for instance:

(a) to appeal knowing that the batsman is not out

(b) to advance towards an umpire in an aggressive manner when appealing

(c) to seek to distract an opponent either verbally or by harassment with persistent clapping or unnecessary noise under the guise of enthusiasm and motivation of one's own side

6. Violence

There is no place for any act of violence on the field of play.

7. Players

Captains and umpires together set the tone for the conduct of a cricket match. Every player is expected to make an important contribution towards this.

Ball Tampering penalties

Some acts that may alter the ball are permitted. A fielder may polish the ball as long as no artificial substance is used, remove mud from the ball under the supervision of the umpire and dry a wet ball on a towel. But no-one may rub the ball on the ground for any reason, interfere with any of the seams or the surface of the ball, use any implement, or take any other action whatsoever which is likely to alter the condition of the ball.

If a player illegally changes the condition of the ball, the umpires replace the ball with another one with similar wear to the old ball before the ball tampering. The umpires also award five runs to the opposing team and report the incident to the authorities to which the player is responsible. These authorities are then expected to take further disciplinary action against the player as appropriate. If there is a further incidence of ball tampering in the innings the same procedure is followed, but the bowler of the immediately preceding ball is banned from bowling further in that inning too if the tampering was committed by the fielding side.

Distracting the opposition

If a member of the fielding side deliberately distracts or attempts to distract the batsman on strike while he is preparing to receive or receiving a delivery, the umpire immediately declares the ball to be dead. The umpire also informs the fielding captain of the incident and awards five penalty runs to the batting side. The batsman may not be dismissed from the delivery, which must be repeated.

It is also unfair for a member of the fielding side to deliberately attempt to distract or obstruct either batsman after the striker has received the ball by word or action. If this happens a procedure similar to the procedure for the first instance of ball tampering occurs, although the batting side also scores any runs that they have scored before the attempted (or actual) distraction or obstruction.

Unfair bowling

The bowling of fast short pitched balls and of high full pitched balls is dangerous and is also considered unfair. Where the umpire considers that there are regular fast short pitched balls, that by their length, height and direction, coupled with the relative skill of the batsman is dangerous, the umpire calls no-ball and cautions the bowler. If this happens a second time in an innings, the bowler is barred from bowling again in that innings, also is reported to the authorities he is responsible to for further disciplinary action. Where a delivery, after pitching, passes over the head of the striker, the umpire calls no-ball and includes it in his consideration of whether fast short pitched bowling is unfair, even though such a delivery is not dangerous.

High full pitched balls that pass or would have passed on the full above waist height of the striker are deemed dangerously unfair, except for slow deliveries, where the rule is above shoulder height. The same sanctions apply to high full pitched balls as apply to fast short pitched balls. Such deliveries, which are called beamers, can be incredibly dangerous. Usually they only occur by mistake, when a ball slips in the bowler's hand at the point of delivery and bowlers usually immediately apologise to the batsman for their mistake. If they are bowled deliberately, no-ball is immediately called, the bowler is removed and is reported to the authority to which he is responsible for further disciplinary action.

If the umpire considers a bowler has deliberately bowled a front-foot no-ball then the bowler is immediately suspended from bowling in that innings and reported to the authorities for further action.

MARYLEBONE CRICKET CLUB (MCC) is a cricket club founded in 1787 and based since 1814 at Lord's cricket ground, which it owns, in St John's Wood, London, England.

The club's own teams are essentially *ad hoc* because they have never taken part in any formal competition. MCC teams have always held first-class status depending on the quality of the opposition. To mark the beginning of each English season, MCC plays the reigning county champions. In 1788, the MCC took responsibility for the Laws of Cricket, issuing a revised version that year. Although changes to the laws are now determined by the International Cricket Council (ICC), the copyright is still owned by MCC. The club was formerly the governing body of cricket in England and Wales and, as the sport's legislator, held considerable global influence.

For much of the twentieth century, commencing with the 1903–04 tour of Australia and ending with the 1976–77 tour of India, MCC organised international tours in which the England cricket team played Test matches. On these tours, the England team was called MCC in non-international matches. In 1993, its administrative and governance functions were transferred to the ICC and the Test and County Cricket Board (TCCB).

FIVE
CRICKET A REFLECTION OF SOCIETY

THE PLAYING AND RUNNING OF SPORT IS OFTEN REFERRED TO AS A reflection of the society of the moment. Society's effect on cricket has been written about by historians since at least the beginning of the 1700s, but the speed of change over the past five decades or so may well have exceeded anything previously experienced. I rather liked what Sam Neill said in an introductory line when fronting a documentary series called *Uncharted* (about James Cook's voyages through the Pacific). He said, 'History is more than just the past, it lives with us in the present. History makes us what we are' — I would add to that by saying who we are, are the values we practise. It succeeded in getting me to ask myself how much importance I placed on the history of cricket when I was growing up. The short answer is not much, but I was very keen to learn from those that had a successful history in cricket. At that time there were far fewer former players (other than those playing county cricket in England) with the same degree of experience as we have today. Over time we all become part of history and the opportunity to experience and learn as we go.

I don't easily fall into the trap of saying everything was better in my day, unless it can be qualified. Unsurprisingly, nothing is all good or all bad at any one time, but it is unwise not to recognise and filter out the good stuff from the past and continue to apply it to the present and possibly the future. We seemed to be more time rich. It's certainly very different today and for good reason, because we are confronted with many more distractions and considerations. When I was growing up, and even throughout my playing days, the lack of available money created a very different approach and attitude to cricket and life itself. It forced greater self-reliance and resourcefulness, presenting a platform for hastening maturity for those willing to grasp the message. The distraction and scourge of entitlement didn't come into consideration, because there wasn't much around to be entitled to. In some ways this upbringing created an attitude of being thankful for what you had and the associated humility attached to that. There was an absence of much of the technology that exists today and even travel was more restricted. Today's improvements and access to a wide range of technology has real advantages for those that use it wisely and are serious about learning, but some of it has not improved the overall wellbeing for many. Social media has hooked vast numbers of our young into what is referred to as 'snacking'. The effects on cricket have been a noticeable increase in the numbers of paid cricketers and a decrease overall in the numbers playing cricket.

When I was learning to drive a car you needed to be able to double-declutch to change gears, then automatics came along and now driverless cars. There are many examples right across society including cricket that pamper and coddle us. But what are these developments doing to stimulate our thinking and ability to problem-solve if we don't use what's available wisely? The dumbing down trap is too often a more convenient path to follow. Surely the most beneficial decisions for the present and the future are to select and add the best of the past to the pick of the present. This won't happen unless we embrace those with that knowledge, instead of persisting with those locked into only the present. This adds further weight for the need to capture the attention of the young and create a wider educational platform, encouraging a broader perspective. They would then be in a better position to contribute and work alongside others in addition to their peers.

The drug scene in the 1960s and '70s was very different. Alcohol was the accepted drug, but all this other stuff was largely absent or not easily available — I'm told marijuana was around, but not within my consciousness. We never used anti-inflammatories as standard practice after a day's play either. We were products of the environment of the time. It's reasonable to assume that had we been brought up in the current setting, our behaviours might well have been similar to the current crop — me included.

I can only speak from personal experience about cricket from the time I started playing first-class cricket in (1964) 55 years ago. As with the rapid changes in climate and human degradation of our planet, cricket also appears to be charging towards a tipping point. Some, or similar, symptoms can be applied to both. Sooner rather than later, another financial crisis might also put the cat among the pigeons and force a rethink.

Parallels can be drawn with the greater influence of big business and money, unsustainable growth, greed and corruption and the increasing gap between the advantaged and the disadvantaged. The avalanche of images disseminated by mass media also fuels narcissism and the need for instant gratification. Sure, much of this has always existed to varying degrees, but nowhere near the levels we are experiencing in more recent times.

The spirit of cricket is not at the top of big corporations' priority lists. The electronic media's sole goal is to attract viewers and advertising dollars by delivering unwarranted amounts of positive spin. The sensory assault of emotionalism and sensationalism obliterates reality and truth. Highly paid pundits parrot back the official description full of easily digestible clichés. Sober examinations are dismissed as too complicated and boring. Instead, we are fed an insatiable appetite for the celebration of entertainment, celebrity, and self-aggrandisement. It has attracted many newcomers to watch and follow T20 matches and optimists are telling us that it is/will have a flow-on effect to supporting ODIs and Test matches — but is/has it? It doesn't appear to be the case.

An analogy might be to say that those who support fast-food outlets are being groomed to attend fine-dining restaurants. From what I'm experiencing, numerous people around my age have been turned off by the so-called progress of cricket and for that matter sport in general. Adding fuel to that fire is often the promoted belief that humbleness and modesty are signs of weakness, not promotional sellers let alone performance enhancers. From ball one, the openly extravagant degree of celebration by players immediately following even the smallest of successes rankles with my generation, because we see it as over the top, unnecessary and disrespectful of your opponent. 'Skiting' and self-praise is still frowned upon. For example, the first wicket taken by a team is celebrated to the magnitude of a match-winning tenth wicket. The job is far from complete when 9 more wickets still need to be attended to. Premature ejaculating comes to mind! The dictates of the time certainly have a bearing on human responses, and these traits can become normalised very quickly. Sadly, the pressure to conform to the current norms has encouraged cloning, suppressing individuals' natural responses.

The unsustainable growth of T20 is surely servicing instant gratification, feeding social narcissism and manufacturing illusions. My description of T20 is a soulless, primitive game of light entertainment. An adjunct to that could be, from what I'm told, likened to Bollywood films, predictable and shallow. The Indian Premier League (IPL) is at the top of the T20 list, largely because it gifts exorbitant amounts of money to a number of players made possible by a few loaded Indians.

Spectators often take the opportunity to costume up, with one eye on the stadium video screen (in the hope of a few seconds of self-aggrandisement), half an eye on mates and the other half on their favourite player or even perhaps the game itself — snack chatting by texting a mate to share your moment of fame is an added bonus.

The players are up for it too, with plenty of high-fives, glove love (batsmen touching gloves) and constant displays of affection towards team-mates (responding to successes and failures) all part and parcel of demonstrating the illusion of team unity. The player huddle (or is it cuddle?) at the beginning of a session (on the field of play for all to see) has become standard practice in all forms of cricket, adding further weight to the illusion. Cricket is not alone in this; similar cloning behaviour has spread like wildfire across many sports. Doubles in tennis must take the cake — there is touching between partners after every rally.

Breaks for drinks were supplied once per session, but today players are delivered whatever they want as often as they want, as long as it doesn't hold up play. Just about any pause in play is used as an opportunity to deliver refreshments. Even a 75-minute innings, as with T20, is considered to be too long to survive with only one official drinks break. The incessant amount of on-field chatter, particularly by wicket-keepers, often only reaches school playground level. The objective appears to be aimed at encouraging greater effort and demonstrating team unity and how much you care.

Today, cricket boards are dominated by business people who have been, presumably, attracted to these positions by the increased status and perks that cricket holds. Their lack of cricket knowledge severely inhibits their ability to govern and predictably they routinely pass decisions onto others. This has allowed the players' associations to extend their influence beyond what most would consider appropriate, such as with who should receive player contracts and where each player is positioned on the list of 20. The employment of consultants such as Sheffield is engaged to assist with screening applicants for jobs within cricket, but where is their cricket knowledge to qualify them for that work? How is it possible for the significant majority of the people on the New Zealand Cricket Board to assess the performance of their CEOs when it comes to cricket-specific matters? Even though judging conflicts of interest should be straightforward, even they continue to be largely glossed over. Following the last financial crisis it has not been uncommon to read about judges commenting on the need for boards in various walks of life to contain people with more knowledge about what they are governing.

Players for too long have been endorsed to greatly influence selection, contracts, hiring and firing of support personnel and have been encouraged to sign contracts with whomever, while still grabbing annual contracts from NZC. It's been admitted to me by a board member that they don't want to have to deal with agents, nor risk losing the availability of first team players. Well, hello, it's already been happening for several years.

In November 2011, I made some notes of some examples of this already happening.

- Those New Zealand players in the IPL in 2009 (Daniel Vettori, Brendon McCullum, Ross Taylor, Jacob Oram, Kyle Mills, Scott Styris, Luke Ronchi, Jesse Ryder) delayed signing their annual contracts for three weeks until they were successful in getting NZC to drop a Test match from the home series against Australia (2009–10 season) so that they could go to India earlier in order to earn more IPL money. I don't know how many of these players delayed signing or whether it was just a collective decision. Since then the Board has passed a motion that the New Zealand team does not play any cricket in April to further appease the wishes of those playing in the IPL. The possible ramifications of this move could jeopardize future tours of England in the first half of their season or result in the late arrival of players. *It did result in the late arrival of players.* England usually has New Zealand touring in the first half because they are not the season's main event. Tours to the West Indies usually involve the month of April too.
- In relation to bowlers' workloads [of which there is more later in the book], rest time and matches off, Daniel Vettori played a hit and giggle one-day match in Fort Lauderdale (USA) on the 23rd May 2010 and didn't play again until the 5th October

2010, an ODI against Bangladesh. A stand-down period of 73 days. It should be noted that in the players' contract they are also entitled to six weeks' annual leave. McCullum had keyhole surgery after playing T20 cricket in England thereby missing New Zealand's tour of Sri Lanka. All decided by the NZC performance director. Taylor played in the Australian T20 competition during his holiday break. Vettori did the same.

- A statement from the Cricket Players Association that it is unfair to put the players in a position whereby they have to make a choice between two playing opportunities.

These decisions are nothing short of self-serving, short-term, politically expedient policies, feeding the illusion of first team player entitlement. Much fluff is talked about the importance of having the right team culture. What sort of team culture is this encouraging other than greed and a stronger sense of entitlement? Among other things, it is another example of market-driven folly, increasing the gap and opportunity between the advantaged and disadvantaged cricketer. Furthermore, it undermines the player depth and future strength of the national team. The ever-increasing money going into first team contracts could be more wisely spent going into the A programme (they are in fact the Bs), and emerging talent budgets. These actions may have made more sense if the growth of T20 leagues had not been endorsed. This has effectively undermined the preservation of the international game. The way forward is going to be very interesting. The question is, should attempts be made to repair the traditional game or not, and if so, how and to what extent is it possible?

Mike Atherton writing in his column for *The Times* on 7 January 2019 had a view on this subject. The headline read 'Lessons for all in Australia's batting decay':

> '4 Sleeps Till the Return of Warner and Smith' wailed the headline in a daily newspaper down under late last week. Never mind that

Australia had just conceded 600 — and effectively the series to India — it is their batting that is causing angst among the locals with the Ashes and World Cup looming, a problem given more acute focus when they were made to follow on in Sydney this weekend for the first time at home in three decades. The match ended in a draw today with no play possible because of rain, giving India their first Test series win on Australian soil.

The *Courier Mail* in Brisbane trained its fire inwards last week, calling Australia's lack of batting depth 'a national sporting embarrassment'. Former greats concurred: Mark Waugh tweeted that the batting against spin in the Big Bash League (BBL) was, well, 'embarrassing'. Simon Katich turned on Cricket Australia for prioritising 'the business of entertainment, not cricket', a reference, no doubt, to the hiatus of first-class cricket in the schedule as a result of the expansion of the BBL this year. He noted that 58 new Test caps had been awarded in the past decade or so, as against 15 in the seven years before that.

That in itself is saying that something is not right with the system.

If an argument can be made that Australia's selectors are overlooking some of those in the best form in domestic cricket, it is undeniable that batting stocks are thinner than for generations.

Outlining the problem may be straightforward, analysing the reasons for the decline is more problematic. There are echoes of the kind of navel-gazing — it's the system, it's cyclical, it's the players, the attitude, the coaches, technique etc etc — amplified now by the rapid expansion of voices contributing to the debate through social media. It can feel a little overwhelming keeping up with opinion, even for someone whose job it is to do so.

One common theme has emerged, though, which is the reduction of the Sheffield Shield as the breeding ground for greatness. A lesson from afar is that you tamper with your premier competition at your peril.

Countries put so much time effort and expense into attempting to train and educate their players to a higher level, making them more marketable for others, and yet they are receiving less and less in return. One might think that transfer fees, as with other sports, might be one way of getting some money back into their coffers, but may not increase the availability of more players. I imagine for this to have any chance of working, the ICC would need to be in the forefront producing the detail and securing buy-in from at least all the full member countries. In a worst-case scenario, NZC may find itself providing many more players full time to teams beyond their shores. Policies and market forces are already happening with the older players departing, but don't count on age becoming a barrier in the future. The problem with this scenario is a weakened national team that may not be competitive at the international level, therefore compromising the ability to fund the infrastructure necessary to develop players in the first instance. As with any organisation within a country, presumably its first responsibility is to look after its own people. The problem facing NZC in this regard is the magnitude of its reliance on receiving overseas funds for its survival. Building a sizeable contingency fund and operating within its means is surely a priority.

NZC's policy with its 20 contracted players is to pay them annual retainers and match money and yet they allow them to sign contracts with other teams and take time off during New Zealand's programme to rest and attend to injuries. I can't foresee this being sustainable for the wellbeing of the game in the longer term. Compounding this problem for NZC is that some of their best players can acquire more money in the IPL in six weeks than they can receive in 52 weeks with NZC. Add in the potential to collect money from some of the other T20 leagues being played around the world, plus a possible stint in English county cricket, means retaining players becomes even more difficult.

In the IPL contracts for 2018, Kane Williamson was signed up for $NZ641,000, Trent Boult $470,000, Colin de Grandhomme $470,000, Colin Munro $406,000, Tim Southee $214,000 and Adam Milne

$US104,359. All of these players were retained by their franchises in 2019 with the addition of Lockie Ferguson $NZ330,000 and Martin Guptill $NZ200,000. Previously in 2017, Boult's contract was $1.07 million. There is a fickleness about contracts in the IPL, because players' records don't always result in a contract. Furthermore, the money offered to those that do receive one doesn't necessarily reflect their true value. For instance, Ben Stokes' contract in 2018 was for $NZ2.67 million, whereas Corey Anderson and Martin Guptill were not offered contracts.

The following outlines what NZC is offering.

New Zealand Cricket men's player payments for 2018–19 under the new Master Agreement:

Black Caps contracted players (1 August – 31 July):

Retainer for top-ranked player: $236,000 (retainers for No. 2–17 each drop by about $8000)

Retainer for No. 18–20: $100,000

Match fees: Tests $9000, one-day internationals $4000, T20 internationals $2500

Domestic contracted players (1 September – 15 April):

Retainer for top-ranked player: $53,000

Retainer for No. 16: $27,000

Match fees: Plunket Shield $1650, one-dayers $800, T20 $575

Captain Kane Williamson could have topped $450,000 in New Zealand Cricket remunerations in the 2018–19 season while all 20 Black Caps contracted players could have banked six-figure retainers for the first time. New Zealand Cricket finally announced the completion of the new four-year Master Agreement with the players nearly nine months after the parties first sat around a table. Both sides trumpeted a return to a fixed-revenue share model, through which the country's 116 contracted men's cricketers receive 26.5% of revenue generated from professional cricket. Over the four-year term this was forecast to be $65.3 million, an increase of around 16% on the past four years. On top of that, the player payment pool will receive 30% of professional revenue over and above the forecast amount.

For the 2018–19 season, the Black Caps' annual retainers will be $236,000 for the top-ranked player — understood to be Williamson — dropping in increments to $100,000 for those ranked 18 to 20. Match fees will be $9000 per Test, $4000 per one-day international and $2500 per Twenty20 international. It means a potential $181,500 in match fees alone if a player was to play in all of New Zealand's scheduled eight Tests, 23 ODIs (including nine World Cup preliminary matches) and seven T20s in the following 12 months. With top earner Williamson's $50,000 captain's bonus thrown in, he would bank close to $450,000 from NZC, depending on injuries and how many home limited-overs matches he sat out.

In order to save Test cricket from the ravages of T20 cricket, a number of recommendations are being put forward. One that caught my attention was that England and Australia were the only two countries that paid their players enough for their Test programme not to suffer from the T20 leagues. The recommendation is that the ICC further subsidise the remaining full member countries so that they can retain their playing strength. I suppose the next question is should they do it and if so, does the ICC have enough spare cash and does anyone really know how much is going to be enough? I suspect it's a bottomless pit.

During the 1970s and '80s, New Zealand teams travelled overseas with the only additional staff of a manager and a physiotherapist. In more recent times, international agreements have been formalised whereby the host nation pays for the expenses of the visitors' eight support staff in addition to 15 players. For some countries, eight support staff has become a minimum number, rather than a maximum. I think of all these additional people justifying their presence by standing in front of players with a water hose, encouraging them to drink from their fountain.

I like to draw upon the analogy of successfully growing plants and people (in this instance, cricketers). When a plant is in its infancy, it is important to assist it in establishing itself, by supplying nourishment and generous amounts of water. There comes a point, quite quickly, whereby a plant needs to be weaned off copious quantities of water so as to encourage it to search for its own supply and nourishment. Its search will encourage and develop its roots to go deeper and wider, making it stronger in its ability to cope with challenging conditions. To continue to oversupply water not only limits the root structure, but also increases the risk of disease.

Today, international cricketers are flooded by water coming in from all directions. Throwing more money at some things might increase numbers, knowledge and productivity, but in international cricket I have observed an overall decline in some standards and many of the skills that defined the character of the game before the gold rush of T20. How the game was shaped, its identity, its distinctiveness, its values, its history and where it came from is increasingly viewed as irrelevant, replaced by spectacle and seductive elusions. One can compare it to a diet of fast food that may satisfy immediate hunger, but its health and nutritional value is very limited and short-lived.

Perhaps a comparison can be formed for those that believe T20 cricket is doing more harm than good, and those that might feel similarly in the classical music world, if the following suggestion was introduced into their concert halls. The suggestion is an 'Orchestral 6', to include works from six different composers on a 1 hour 15 minute programme. The programmes could be designed to include six 10-minute pieces, one from the works of a different composer whether it be from a symphony, concerto, sonata or opera. They could include a complete movement or just rearranged selections. The objective would be to draw in a similar audience demographic to T20 cricket. Dynamic sections of music would ideally be presented — a good example being Tchaikovsky's 1812 Overture with the cannons featuring.

A one-minute break between each piece would accommodate time for members of the orchestra to interchange when necessary and those remaining to receive refreshments. The contents of chilly bins positioned near the stage could be operated by those musicians sitting out a section of the programme. An entertainment package of clips showing major sporting events could be presented on a big screen during these breaks and at a 10-minute interval midway through the programme.

Those in the orchestra could dress in the national costume of one of the composers represented on the night, to add colour to the occasion. More than one concert per evening is a possibility and the product as a whole may draw in wider commercial opportunities, such as TV rights, sponsorships and perhaps a well-heeled owner. The musicians are unlikely to be required to learn as much music as in the past and could receive significantly increased salaries if the orchestra is owned by an affluent individual. Musicians could put their names forward to an annual auction and anxiously wait for the bidding to start. I imagine in this instance, a conductor would be of considerable value!

Just imagine, 'modern concerts' could become the order of the day. A possible reduction in the number of traditional orchestral concerts or at least their form could be reduced in length and composition to meet today's 'modern society'!

SIX
THE MCCULLUM MYTH

THE UNANSWERED QUESTION ABOUT BRENDON MCCULLUM'S REIGN AS captain is, was his captaincy an asset or a liability? As far as I know no one's asked it publicly, just as no one's asked, is his legacy likely to be enduring or short-lived, and what repercussions will there be, if any? But one way or another, it sure was a fascinating, often perplexing and sometimes bumpy ride. Many found it 'exciting', predictably unpredictable on the one hand and entirely predictable on the other.

And alongside it all — on the periphery, one might say — a lot of fascinating other stuff went on. For instance, arranging for an injunction to be put on the *Sunday Star-Times* preventing them from printing a story about him. Take the Chris Cairns trial in London where McCullum's professional neuro-human performance specialist, 'spin doctor cum mental skills coach' Kerry Schwalger was willing to appear in court and challenge the reliability of him as a prosecution witness when McCullum went to the extent of having his lawyer accompany him in London, to protect his interests. Schwalger's Statement of Witness was not accepted into evidence by the judge. It's an indication of changing times when a player is flush enough with dosh to be able to protect his own interests and when cash-strapped newspapers are unwilling to spend the money necessary to do their job. When they cease to apply public enlightenment and act as watchdogs you have to ask, sport is big business now, so why should it escape scrutiny? How much well-informed critical and insightful analysis are we getting when unquestioning, 'talk-it-up' media coverage and promotion at all costs is so prevalent? And once it was decided that McCullum was a brilliant tactician, from then on, this rolling stone was unlikely to gather any moss.

At the conclusion of the 2016 second Test against Australia, McCullum's last, he was quoted in the *Otago Daily Times* as saying what the vast majority of the media failed to accept, that 'New Zealand will be better, and more professional, without him.' I would agree with him that New Zealand would be more professional without him, particularly as captain. But his playing abilities would be missed. He went on to say that he does not believe he leaves a particularly large hole to fill — I suspect these words could be best described as transparent, a *volte-face* in order to cripple argument. He then referred to the playing and leadership depth that has been developed in recent seasons. I suppose he was indirectly referring to the fact that he did his own thing and, therefore, he assumed others felt free to do likewise. But were they, and did they? Being encouraged to loosen up, to play more aggressively, may be helpful for some players, but any possible influence in this regard still needs to be serving responsibility.

Generally, the term 'leadership' refers to players taking responsibility for their own game and actions. Taking personal responsibility is fundamental, but leadership becomes somewhat blurred and possibly intrusive when a smaller selected group of players is formed, referred to as 'the leadership group'. When there is also the positions of captain, vice-captain, coaches (times three), the manager and all the support staff who are all leaders in their own right.

Looking for the moment at McCullum's on-field batting and captaincy, I think it's fair to say that his batting style was a fair representation of the nature of his tenure both on and off the field: entertaining, fearless, carefree, reckless, ostentatious and self-absorbed. Some of those aspects were acknowledged and admired.

Prior to becoming captain, his name had often featured at management meetings as a disruptive influence. I experienced this first-hand when I was invited to speak to the team's leadership group in 2010. Roger Mortimer, who had been employed as the performance director of the team, had read a paper that I had largely put together in 2006, expressing my views on 'Game plans for ODIs'. It was his attempt to get the leadership group to open their minds to debate and engagement. He had become frustrated by their lack of interest in doing so and was hoping that this meeting would stimulate their interest.

Following my presentation, I remember being somewhat disappointed/frustrated at no one being interested enough to ask a single question. My main objective at that meeting was to encourage some discussion so that everyone could advance their thinking, including myself. Their lack of any response led me to the conclusion that from the outset they were not interested in what I had to say. Following my presentation, they immediately moved on to discussing which members of their support staff should be fired next. To be more accurate, McCullum (remembering that Vettori was captain at this point) led the way on this, although there didn't appear to be anyone objecting to what he was saying. He targeted two people, the physiotherapist and the manager. He said in some colourful language, the physio (Kate Stalker) was no good because she couldn't take a glove at practice and the manager (Lindsay Crocker) was too old. At the time, I couldn't help but question his statements since others appeared less inclined. I asked if the physio was good at her job, because that didn't seem to be important — no response. As for the manager, I wondered whether McCullum was conscious of the fact that I was 11 years older than Crocker. I suppose that, as much as anything else, was expressing his contempt for age and experience.

The tsunami of hype arrived with the introduction of a scallywag captain and the imminent staging of a home Cricket World Cup. The timing was perfect. Satisfying the thirst for instant gratification was under way.

It wasn't long before the majority of the public appeared to accept the fluff that the team's success should be attributed mainly to the captain's 'leadership' and inventiveness. The stage was set for the arrival of a cult personality. Cult personalities are known for using some of the techniques of mass media, propaganda, the big lie, spectacle, patriotism, creating an idealised heroic and worshipful image of themselves, often through unquestioning flattery and praise — concealing records that might reveal the truth also fits the character. As with any cult figure, they appeal mostly to those open to forms of celebrity worship syndrome.

Many spectators loved the occasions when New Zealand's batting brawler flogged opposition bowlers to all parts of the ground regardless of the game's circumstances. Putting it 'up' the opposition was what really mattered. The captain's batting, particularly in his last year, could be compared to a quick fix or a brief downer. To the trained or aesthetic eye, that sort of batting fails to allow for the pleasures to be had from witnessing artistic expression of elegance, prudent flair and accurate shot selection.

It never ceased to amaze me how few opposition bowlers avoided brawling with him. Bowlers with oversized egos couldn't resist slugging it out. I could understand the faster bowlers, in particular, feeling that by bowling more of a variety, McCullum's contemptuous approach wouldn't last. The problem that they needed and failed to recognise was that within a matter of very few balls, considerable damage could occur to their bowling stats if they were not prepared to retrench.

How many repeats does it take before many bowlers and captains 'get it', when the bloke facing you has cut himself free from any semblance of caution, consequence or accountability? It was as though discipline and *nous* had been erased from bowlers' minds. The best way to retrench is to get a batsman in this mood, off strike early in the over, by getting the ball into the blockhole with as many fieldsmen as possible defending the boundary. By losing most of the strike and largely being restricted to singles will most likely frustrate the batsman into becoming even more reckless.

Does a scrapper's approach to batting inspire others to follow him? One of the catchcries that appeared to gain a significant degree of support was that the captain led by example. But what were some of these examples and did they justify admiration or were they foolish? One that stood out (even when he was batting against the new ball) was a habit of moving outside leg stump and charging down the pitch towards the bowler. Although this is not an original approach, totally committing to attacking the ball no matter what is flaunting with excessive danger.

Although McCullum had some attacking alternatives, he appeared not to have, or failed to entertain, any bail-out defensive options. For him, consequences didn't appear to be part of the equation. It's all very well for players to use their own style to deliver a result, but sound decision-making, good technique and rational dash are still vital if longevity is a consideration. This approach bore little resemblance to the touted 'Team First' mantra, leaning rather more towards self-indulgence.

But does any of this really matter if the figures stack up and the popularity of this approach is deemed entertaining and exciting enough to draw more interest from beyond the boundary fence? It depends on who's playing that way. I think it can be more than acceptable if such licence is given to, say, a player from the ranks, although I wouldn't be making overly-optimistic claims for its merits on more than one count. That said, the rest of the squad and its management should be strong enough to accommodate it. But claims of McCullum leading by example as captain is fabrication.

In his book *Declared*, McCullum said on one occasion he told the whole team that he was prepared to drop any team member who was not prepared to follow his formulated tactics. In particular, he was referring to Martin Guptill scoring only 5 from his first 13 balls when opening in a Twenty20 match against Sri Lanka. He followed this up by telling them 'this isn't my team, it's not Mike Hesson's team, it's New Zealand's team'. Yes, but where was the evidence that he meant it? What also comes to my mind is what would have happened to McCullum if the selectors were prepared to drop any team member who frequently 'fired his stick' recklessly when the team needed a responsible approach? There was no fear of that happening when the captain monopolised the power of selection and its accountability. His monopoly didn't finish there; he was also convinced a big clean-out was needed in New Zealand cricket, and saw himself as the man to do it, New Zealand's saviour. In his book he appears to believe that the boys were crying out for him, and 'Hess', to rescue them and, by inference, New Zealand cricket from Ross Taylor and many others' inadequacies. New Zealand's team eh! In the next breath, he says that the younger players seemed happy enough under Taylor, but that they didn't know any better. So what was the for and against split in the ranks? I suspect that any senior players who were feeling insecure about their selection would push for a captain who was more likely to look after their interests. This is just another example of the damage that can be created by conflicts of interest coming into play.

Some say that McCullum's successes at the batting crease inspired his team to greater effort. Maybe occasionally, as with any player in the team that is having a good day. Logic suggests that anyone who might have been emotionally stimulated by McCullum's successes might just as likely have been deflated by the greater number of his failures and the nature of many of them. For example, during his last 13 months, from 3 January 2015 to 20 February 2016, his 19 Test match innings produced only one hundred and four fifties. Of his 14 scores under 50, three were ducks.

In One-Day Internationals in the year leading up to his last 50-over match on 8 February 2016, his 27 innings produced no hundreds and seven fifties. Unquestionably his very high strike rate produced some rollicking starts to the team's innings but still left much to be done by others. Further scrutiny of his stats show that in Test matches

McCullum averaged a hundred every 13.9 innings, compared to, at the time, Williamson's 6.3 and Taylor's 8.8. There were occasions during McCullum's 176 Test innings when he applied himself admirably and scored three double hundreds and one triple, while batting lengthy periods of time and therefore showing caution and concern for the team's situation.

It was noticeable that in the final year of his three as captain, his work ethic and willingness to occupy the crease declined. It appeared as though accountability for his game went further out the window, encouraged, possibly, by the security of his dominance over all and sundry.

Much has been made of his approach to batting, the inference being that his was an example to be followed internationally. I venture to say that, certainly in Test cricket, such an approach is unlikely to be repeated or tolerated by the hierarchy running other international teams, unless they have also lost much of their influence.

I'm sure that many players at international level could match McCullum's hitting if given the same licence. Much of the batting in T20 cricket today is evidence of that. McCullum was apt to 'take it to the opposition' without an arm guard (and I suspect any chest padding either). This blithe approach continued at the 50-over Cricket World Cup following a serious blow to his forearm during the pool match against Australia. This and any future blows could have ended his tournament.

One of his team-mates was quoted as saying that in the field the captain was prepared to dive into the boundary fence, even when there was little or no chance of preventing a boundary. What about 'risk versus reward' when at best one run might be saved? It was only a matter of time before the boundary fence got even and it did. Were these actions commendable or irresponsible or just laddish bravado?

His decision to pull the plug on playing for New Zealand and continue to play for others was his to make, a decision he is entitled to make.

The reasons he gave were that it was in his and his family's best interests, not least financially. Whatever people thought of that, they can be certain he's not been treated roughly by New Zealand Cricket's administration, the media or the public at large. To the contrary, his support and popularity was unprecedented, although to pull out just prior to the T20 World Cup was odd. Interestingly, in his book he doesn't seem to have a positive view of how things worked out for him. There is an opinion that when Taylor was sacked as captain, NZC was guilty of deflecting attention away from itself onto McCullum by encouraging him to threaten court action against John Parker for defamation of character. At the time, because I knew Mike Hesson well, I phoned him to try to convince him to advise McCullum, for a variety of reasons, not to follow through on the defamation suit. Lo and behold, the very next day, Hesson declared publicly he would do the same. There is much about the whole 'Taylorgate' episode that doesn't add up. Whether the true story will ever unfold remains to be seen but there is a healthy weight of opinion among those who have been around the cricket scene long enough to know, that there is more to be told in this whole situation. Was McCullum involved in the coup? He has denied that, but in today's world in which truth can become 'alternative facts', and let's not forget that NZC itself wasn't too bad at this even long before the captaincy issue arose, what can be believed? It's the same as when New Zealand beat Pakistan in Abu Dhabi after a dramatic Pakistan collapse and the manner of it, in November 2018. Given all the controversy that has occurred over results in games, sceptics were more than entitled to ask if everything was above board in the result. It may have been entirely innocent, but the players themselves have allowed grounds for these types of thoughts. The fact that McCullum took out an injunction suggests something was rotten in the state of Denmark. Given his claims of innocence in the whole affair, it begs the question of why it was necessary to take out an injunction and what he was attempting to keep from the cricket public. Will he ever be tempted to clear the air by lifting the injunction? Because that is the only way the situation will ever be resolved. Questions could also be asked of how much the administration of NZC knew or should have known about what was going on and whose bests interests were being served by changing the leadership. Given the change in coaching leadership that occurred soon after with John Buchanan returning to Australia, was there a power play in action? Certainly NZC emerged with egg all over its face in the incident and the only victims appeared to be Taylor and the chairman of the board at the time, Chris Moller, who departed soon after. Try as NZC and McCullum might like to spin their way out of the situation and believe it is all behind them, it remains an indelible stain on the administration of the game in New Zealand.

Let's go back and look at more aspects of McCullum's on-field captaincy. Take the 2015 semi-final of the Cricket World Cup between New Zealand and South Africa at Eden Park. It was described as one of the most memorable World Cup ODIs in recent times. That game has been tagged as an example of McCullum's captaincy at his tactical best. Furthermore, the PR machine was working overtime after the match, convincing us (the public) that there was far more to the victory than on-field brilliance. We were fed the 'total team unity' (TTU) line. TTU was touted as being one of the key elements responsible for the team's success. Where was the evidence that this was true? And to what extent is so-called unity necessary for a cricket team to be successful? Some in the team were prepared to convey the 'happy family' line in interviews, but believe me, words are often chosen to keep up appearances. Furthermore, why would any player be silly enough to gripe publicly at a time when the team was winning and the public support was on such a high?

Players will do the right thing by the team if they have personal integrity or when knowing that if they don't, they are putting their selection on the line. Some will have more or less integrity than others, as is the case with any group of people. To believe that it's possible to get everyone in a team — especially cricket — to pull in the one direction is to ignore enforced fraternisation, character differences, the nature of human beings and the length and nature of cricket.

Captaincy changes (as with 'Taylorgate') don't happen as quickly as that one did without significant fallout among the ranks where players take sides and where respect and trust is lost. In *Declared*, McCullum will not leave the reader in any doubt what he thought of Ross Taylor not only as a captain, but also as a person, and yet he said he was a good vice-captain. Replacing Taylor as captain didn't appear to have satisfied his scorn towards him, and Taylor would not have been in any doubt what he thought of McCullum or Hesson for that matter. McCullum admitted Guptill sided with Taylor and there will have been others. In his own words, McCullum admitted to a 'continuing division in the ranks'. That's not the line we were being constantly fed! Time often heals, but I suspect this issue is unlikely to be readily forgotten. Sadly, in his book McCullum has chosen to reignite these flames. Perhaps more truth will emerge if Taylor decides to expose his side of the story or if anyone is prepared to front up with the money to break the infamous injunction. There is much scepticism, even within the legal fraternity, as to whether the injunction was justified in the first place. And where was the Players Association in all of this? Taylor must have been asking the same question, although he would have obviously been aware that a senior player within the ranks of the team, Kyle Mills, just happened to be the brother of Heath Mills, the chief executive of the Players Association.

Where is the reality in believing that every player is happy even when their performances are below their usual standards? The team winning only goes partway to cushioning individuals' disappointment. For example, as the tournament progressed, it's reasonable to assume that New Zealand's two best batsmen, Taylor and Williamson, would not have been happy with their overall Cricket World Cup performances. From 9 innings (although both had two not outs), each only passed 50 once. And I don't think Adam Milne would have been happy with his six appearances taking only 5 wickets at a cost of 40 per wicket and an economy rate of just over 5. All of this and the fact that Guptill was so successful and yet very unhappy with McCullum and Hesson's treatment of Taylor is hardly supporting the view that McCullum's TTU influence was the determining factor!

It's hard to believe that either Kyle Mills or Mitchell McClenaghan was happy sitting out the CWC on the sideline (McClenaghan played one game). Worse still, after Milne was injured, another pace bowler was brought in from outside the squad to play ahead of them. A decision like that is sure to 'put the cat among the pigeons'. Mills and McClenaghan will have known that this decision had come from the captain and coach, the two people who they expected would believe in their playing abilities and with whom they are meant to work closely, with confidence and trust.

And yet McCullum was quick to tell us in his book the success and importance of creating the right culture and environment, getting buy-in, building a team-first attitude. It's all about the 'ethos', pressing the right buttons. As with any group of 11 people, the variety of personalities would be challenging enough for a group of sports psychologists/psychiatrists to press the so-called right buttons, let alone a couple of novices attempting to instil their version of behavioural compliance.

There are quite sufficient buttons being pushed by opposition batsmen and bowlers that require an instantaneous response. These responses have long since been programmed into players' subconscious minds through the practised repetition of these skills over a significant period of time. It is nonsense to think that versions of someone else's theories can be called up on demand and suddenly applied. Certainly I agree that players should be able to call on more than one approach to their game, such as going into attacking or defensive mode. But it's important to recognise that the makeup of New Zealand's team for the 2015 CWC contained players who had already developed an aggressive approach to their limited-over game.

Thankfully the only team talks I recall during my 16 years at Worcester were not much more than a sentence long, such as 'Yes, we are going for the target set by the opposition' or 'No, we are attempting to save the match' or with time running out, maybe 'We need to up our tempo with the bat in order to set a target' and so on. That was quite sufficient information, thank you very much!

At the beginning of a session in the field, captains had their own cue calls so that teams didn't enter the playing area in dribs and drabs. Don Kenyon's cue, for instance, was 'Come on, let's go and do these Yorkshire twats' (or whomever we were playing against at the time) and Tom Graveney's words were 'Come on, you bastards, let's have ya.' Nowadays, when teams enter the field of play, public demonstrations of team unity are performed in front of the spectators. The widely-cloned practised procedure is to form a huddle and receive presumably some last-minute words of wisdom, possibly along the lines of those in-depth utterances delivered by Don Kenyon in the privacy of the dressing room.

It's often assumed that captains in winning teams must be good. I disagree. It's far more accurate to say that captaincy, although important, is only one of very many — and possibly 11 — reasons behind a team's success. The truth is, losing teams can sometimes have a very good captain, conversely winning teams can get by with a very poor captain. Judging the performance of captains needs a far more refined analysis than simply taking the credit or blame for others' performances. The very same could be said about coaches.

So let's balance the inconclusive ledger when captaincy is judged on team results alone, by adding some recent information. In Pakistan's *Daily Times* (dated 5 November 2018) it was reported that Brendon McCullum had lost his Pakistan Super League (PSL) deal. The Lahore Qalandars had decided not to retain McCullum for the next edition of the tournament. McCullum had an unusually tough time in the PSL, captaining the Qalandars for two seasons where they finished bottom both times. The former New Zealand skipper played 18 games for Qalandars with his best score being 44. He scored 311 runs at an average of 20.73 with a strike rate of 114.33.

The 2015 CWC was a good example of New Zealand's successes being attributed to a number of players, playing their already well-established games. One of the major indicators can be recognised by Man of the Match awards. Boult received two, one against Scotland (2/21) and the other against Australia (5/27). Guptill for his 105/100 balls versus Bangladesh and 237/163b against the West Indies, Anderson 75/46b and 2/18 with the ball v Sri Lanka, Southee 7/33 v England, Vettori 4/18 v Afghanistan and Elliott 84*/73 v South Africa (SA).

Any Cricket World Cup is a very small sample from which to draw substantive conclusions, but since many people appeared to be persuaded that New Zealand excelled beyond any previous performances, and that the captain in particular had shone a new light for all to follow in the game of limited-overs cricket, I've additionally looked at a few statistics from the 2015 Cup to see if there were any persuasive reasons for others to hold this view.

New Zealand's game figures below do give an indication of some less-than-convincing results during the sectional play. There are three sectional games that add weight to this argument, those against Australia and two of the less significant teams in the competition, namely Scotland and Bangladesh.

Scotland 142 (36.2 overs), NZ 146/7 (24.5 overs). A high-risk, unconvincing run chase when considering NZ were down to batsmen number 8 and 9 at the crease.

Bangladesh 288/7 (50 overs), NZ 290/7 (48.5 overs). Once again batsmen 8 and 9 at the crease — not a convincing win against a mediocre team.

Australia 151 (32.2 overs), NZ 152/9 (23.1 overs). NZ's number 11 Trent Boult survived two balls from Mitchell Starc before Williamson, who had come in at number 3, saved the game with a 6 to be 45 not out.

In the final, New Zealand got rolled batting first for an uncompetitive total of 183. McCullum had set the tone at the top of the order with a swashbuckling three-ball blonger.

It should be noted that New Zealand played the most games (nine) of any teams in the tournament because they played in the final, whereas the other finalist, Australia, had one fewer game since their match against Bangladesh in section play was abandoned without a ball being bowled. Of the other leading teams, South Africa played eight, Sri Lanka seven, India eight. The teams with the highest number of runs in the tournament were: SA 2293; SL 2184; Australia 2149; NZ 2107; India 1979. SA scored more than 300 four times of which two exceeded 400, Australia also passed 300 four times of which one was in excess of 400, SL passed 300 four times of which two were scored when batting second, India passed 300 three times and NZ twice. It should be recognised that when teams bat first, they have the opportunity to score bigger totals than the possibility of chasing small totals when batting second. In this regard, NZ batted first on three occasions, Australia four, SA five, SL three, India three.

Perhaps a more relevant statistic is the batting average per wicket lost by each of those teams. SA 50.95 per wicket lost, India 46.02, Australia 42.13, SL 39.00 and NZ 36.96.

With regard to bowling, Australia averaged 20.20 per wicket, India 22.75, NZ and SA practically the same to a second decimal place at 24.53 and 24.57 respectively. SL were 35.32.

A QUOTE from Ed Smith's book *Luck* about captaincy comes to mind, particularly when the short sample of a CWC is applied: 'Fooled by randomness touched another raw nerve. The idea that we dress up luck as judgment or skill was a painful one to contemplate. When things are going well, it's not easy to say you've just been lucky. Why does it matter if we often mistake judgment for luck, if we are fooled by randomness, if the world is steered more by the winds and the weather than it is by the captain's sagacity'?

Although there is some value in considering specific statistical data, we also know its limitations. A more studied approach is crucial. For example, in the World Cup semi-final, the New Zealand captain's on-field decision-making abilities were of concern. He showed a lack of understanding or acceptance that in limited-overs cricket the fielding team can apply more pressure, and therefore be more attacking, by denying batsmen additional opportunities to score runs easily. His lengthy retention of slip fielders was more likely to gift the opposition runs than succeed as a wicket-taking attacking strategy. When setting fields you need to be looking for the best odds, for those that are more likely to work for you. It's also necessary to be astute with one's timing of when to make changes. Gambling and persisting with certain field placements when their value has significantly diminished is not smart.

As long as the timing is right in relocating these fieldsmen, they are far more likely to create more pressure, save runs, take more catches and have more opportunities for run-outs. A better and more accurate wider approach to pressuring the batsmen is also more likely to encourage rash shots. Any batsman worth his salt would not see the retention of, or addition to, the slip cordon as more intimidating or challenging, but rather more helpful in the pursuit of runs. The same could be said about the so-called in-your-face positions in front of the wicket in the 'sillies': mid-off, cover, mid-on and mid-wicket.

Incidentally, in the semi-final, no batsman was dismissed caught in the slips. All of this reminded me of inter-school matches when bravado and posturing were often prevalent. The New Zealand captain's approach followed this pattern of fantasy under the guise of creative leadership throughout the tournament and most of his tenure. His obsession with slip fielders was evident in the World Cup semi-final when he retained three slips and a gully right through until the fifteenth over when South Africa was 58/2 with both batsmen, du Plessis and Rossouw, established at the crease. After 20 overs (SA 77/2), he still had two slips and a gully in place. He persisted with two slips right up until the twenty-seventh over (SA 122/3), and even when South Africa had decided it was time to hit out, he retained a slip right to the end of the thirty-fifth over (SA 184/3) when the batting powerplay came into force, restricting the opportunity to defend.

His organisation of New Zealand's bowling attack was shambolic, with little if any regard for the medium- to longer-term consequences. It should be recognised that over time some norms are set and often for good reason. It's all very well to work on so-called instinct, but it needs to be backed up with some logic and planning. (Instinct is a term often used by those who are struggling to come up with logical answers.) There will still be numerous opportunities throughout a game to respond strategically to changing situations without continually gambling, or having knee-jerk responses. Without pondering on the whole of the South Africa innings in the World Cup semi-final, the following is a small example of what emerged during their final few overs.

By the time 35 overs had been completed, and the mandatory batting powerplay came into force, of the 15 overs remaining, New Zealand's four main bowlers (Boult, Southee, Henry and Vettori) had only 9 overs left between them. Furthermore, Vettori had completed 9 overs at the 32-over mark. That meant the captain needed to find 6 overs from either Anderson, Elliott or Williamson at the most vulnerable stage of the innings. It's not as if South Africa were being bowled out. They were 184/3 with du Plessis and de Villiers in full cry. By the end of the thirty-eighth over when rain stopped play (SA 216/3), New Zealand's bowling situation had become even more desperate. Of the 12 overs remaining, New Zealand's four main bowlers only had 6 overs left between them.

By the time they returned, the rain delay had reduced the game to 43 overs per team. This reduction saved the New Zealand captain from his blunder, because now he only had to find a total of 5 more overs. The requirement from his lesser bowlers had been reduced from 6 to 2 overs. It still came at a cost because Anderson went for 72 from 6 overs, and New Zealand leaked 65 runs from those last 5 overs. The rain delay was a major blow to South Africa because of the speed at which they were scoring leading up to the break for rain, and the fact that they still had 7 wickets in hand. Furthermore, du Plessis and de

Villiers had just posted a 100-run partnership and were making seriously rapid progress.

In *Declared*, McCullum said that his response to du Plessis and de Villiers was 'I can feel the complexion of the game changing and pull what levers I can'. He doesn't describe what those 'levers' were, but I think any guess will do. Then he goes on to say 'we're haemorrhaging runs and I'm not sure how the hell we get to apply a tourniquet'. Hardly the words of someone who knew what he was doing.

Even though New Zealand won the game, the weather, the Duckworth-Lewis system and the poor decision by South Africa to bat first significantly aided New Zealand's cause. Undoubtedly, the semi-final had been great entertainment, was full of drama, and its closeness held everyone's full attention right to the end. But this match had more than its share of luck, randomness and absurdity. The closeness of the game could also be attributed to significant bungling from both captains.

In short, de Villiers' decision to bat first after the covers had been kept on the pitch longer than normal due to overnight and morning rain was taking an unnecessary risk for his batsmen. His two openers Amla and de Kock's response to these circumstances were likely to be more cautious than normal. As it transpired, they were both back in the pavilion with SA 31/2, putting South Africa on the back foot. Knowing that further rain was forecast along with Auckland's humidity, it was no surprise that his bowlers were likely to be majorly disadvantaged by having to bowl with a wet ball later in the evening when trying to defend 298.

During McCullum's term as captain of New Zealand, I wasn't alone in finding his approach to numerous matches inconsistent and illogical. The following two examples are, perhaps for some, at opposite ends of the attacking and defensive scales. A summation of the third Test at Eden Park against England in 2013 is an example of an extremely defensive approach. With rain looming, New Zealand batted on unnecessarily long, leaving England to score 455 to win the match. The most any side anywhere had made in the fourth innings to win a Test was 418. England's fourth-innings record score was 332. As predicted, rain did arrive and only 29 overs were possible on day four, with England having received 13 of them *and* ending the day on 44 without loss. On day five, England just managed to hang on ending the match on 315/9, hence being able to draw the series nil-all.

The following is a more detailed assessment of the final two days of this Test match when New Zealand were in a very strong position to dictate the outcome of the game, at a time when the captain's decisions and influence on the result were to play a major part. There is enough information to work with during days four and five without the need to go into the pros and cons of whether New Zealand should have enforced (or not) the follow-on with a first innings lead of 239.

New Zealand started day four at 35/3, giving them a lead of 274, with a possible 180 overs left in the game. To their credit, in the morning session they scored at an exceptional rate, clocking up 141/1 from 26 overs, reaching 176/4 at lunch, giving them an overall lead of 415. New Zealand had not only played England out of the game, they had also secured enough overs to make it extremely difficult for England to save the match.

A declaration at this point appeared logical, when considering that the biggest total chased down in a fourth innings in the long history of Test cricket was 418. Furthermore, the slowness of the pitch and the likely number of overs needed to dislodge a side digging in to save a game should have been the main consideration.

No declaration was made at lunch, so was the captain waiting until Fulton reached his hundred? It took Fulton only another three overs, by which time New Zealand were 195/4, a lead of 434 with 149 overs left in the game. New Zealand proceeded to bat on for another 6 overs, adding a further 46 runs (241/6 dec), setting England a massive 481 to win in what had become a possible 143 overs.

Exactly how the captain was about to handle his bowling attack and the fields he would set were about to be tested. There could be no good reason for other than an all-out attack, particularly with the new ball. Astonishingly, the captain started with only four close catchers (three slips and a gully), with two on either side of the wicket saving the single.

It was reasonable to assume that the captain was afraid of England getting away to a flying start, but was it possible that he was fearful of losing the match? How could taking wickets not be the priority with the new ball? My assumptions were supported later when more attacking fields were set when it was recognised that England had no intention of chasing the total.

When the second new ball arrived, the New Zealand captain had four slips and two gullies and at one point a short leg was added into the mix. It wasn't as though New Zealand had got through to the English tail. Bell and Root were at the crease with Bairstow and Prior to follow.

Fundamentally, to get the best results with the new ball, three seam/swing bowlers should be rotated so as to allow each bowler to have opportunities with a new or newish ball while at the same time keeping them as fresh as possible. For example, as a rule of thumb, one of the openers bowls, say, 4 overs and is replaced by the third seamer/swing bowler while the more likely of the two opening bowlers on the day bowls, say, 6/7 overs from the other end. If he is making inroads into the opposition batting he may be given an extra couple of overs. He is then replaced by his opening partner and the result is the first 20 overs have provided the best opportunities for success.

The New Zealand captain had opened with Southee and Boult, replacing Boult with Bruce Martin (left-arm spinner) after a total of only 10 overs had been bowled. New Zealand's third seamer/swing bowler Wagner didn't get the ball until the twenty-second over. It wasn't as though Wagner was bowling poorly; he did, after all, proceed to take 1/6 off 7 overs. Martin, on the other hand, continued bowling 16 overs straight, without taking a wicket and looking less likely to do so than any of the other four bowlers used. Martin was to end up with innings figures of 39-18-74-0, having bowled 10 overs more than any of the other four bowlers.

The decisions made by the captain on day five went from bad to worse. England was 90/4 overnight with 52.1 of the 143 overs having been completed. Any bowling plans for day five had to take into account that the second new ball was due in 28 overs' time.

However, at the start of any day's cricket (subject to extenuating circumstances) you want your two best bowlers opening up, simply because batsmen are at their most vulnerable when they are starting afresh. Both considerations (getting wickets early and largely conserving your opening bowlers for the new ball in 28 overs' time) could have been served by Southee and Boult opening up with, say, 4 overs each. Instead, Williamson added 2 further overs to the five balls he needed to bowl to complete the over he started the night before. Astonishingly, Martin immediately replaced Williamson and apart from a change of end, Martin proceeded to bowl 10 overs straight through to the second new ball.

Boult did, belatedly, bowl 3 overs during the period prior to the new ball being taken, but not at the most opportune time. Another opportunity to improving New Zealand's chances of taking wickets had been lost during those 28 overs.

The tactics adopted by the captain followed a similar pattern with the second new ball in that Martin was bowled ahead of Wagner and Wagner didn't start his spell until the ball was 19 overs old. Although Southee and Boult took a wicket each with the second new ball, Prior and Bell were still at the crease when Boult finished his spell of 7 overs and when Southee finally ended his spell of 9 overs straight. The captain's bowling plan once again failed to get good use out of the new ball, or keep the pressure on the English batsmen. It didn't help to conserve the strength of his two main bowlers either, in view of what had to come. By the time Southee and Boult had finished their bowling spells with the new ball, there was still a possible 45 overs left in the game and 4 wickets still to be taken.

The fact that England finished 165 runs short and were 9 down is testament to the argument that the declaration was also misguided. After the match, the New Zealand captain was quoted in the *Dominion Post* (26 March 2013) stating, 'You can't have regrets in this game. You can't doubt your decisions; they were made with sound judgment'. My response at that time was that this captain requires a lot more education, an improved attitude, an open mind to learning and sounder self-analysis, or we can expect more winning opportunities to be lost.

The prevailing wisdom then was that the captain was an attacking captain. Perhaps this view stems from his aggressiveness with the bat and the assumption that it will automatically be transferred to his captaincy. I would sooner look at the evidence rather than assumptions. On this occasion I was not alone critiquing McCullum's performance.

Ed Smith, who was writing for an English newspaper as well as commentating on the match, wrote a piece largely dedicated to an analysis of England's captain, Alastair Cook. In his article, he made brief but telling references to McCullum's captaincy when he said: 'Let me give two examples to balance the ledger. On the last morning of the final Test, in Auckland, McCullum, searching for a victory, opened the bowling with the part-time off spin of Kane Williamson rather than his best bowler, Trent Boult. The batsmen at the crease were Ian Bell and Joe Root, both accomplished players of spin. By that point in the series, however, it had already been decided that McCullum was 'a brilliant tactician', so the mistake slipped by mostly without criticism.

Smith's second example came in the over before the second-last one of the match. After the fourth ball, McCullum seemed undecided about whether to bring up the field or leave it out. It seemed to Smith that everyone in the New Zealand team had an opinion and McCullum was finding it difficult to navigate events. Finally, watch again the last over of the match. Many arms were waving around in the field, not all of them belonging to McCullum. Had it been Cook, this would have been taken as evidence that he was insufficiently 'in charge'.

My reply would be that on a number of occasions in other matches, when the pressure went on in the field and success hadn't followed, McCullum commonly stated that he had 'pretty much tried everything'. This response could be more accurately assessed as McCullum lacking in his own substance to call on. This sounds more like an occasion when persevering with the best percentage odds is wiser than dishing up an assortment of postulant attempts.

The next example relates to throwing caution to the wind. It was the two-match Test series against England in England in May 2015. To summarise, in the first Test at Lord's, during the final innings of the match, the New Zealanders got themselves into a position at 61/5, whereby they needed to put every effort into saving the match and, furthermore, in order to keep the series alive. Instead, they handed the game to England by continuing their run chase regardless of the situation falling 124 runs short with only 9 overs left in the match. In the second Test at Headingly, New Zealand won easily by 199 runs, which meant a drawn series instead of one that should have been won 1-nil.

A significant question that needs asking is, does a compulsive gambler make a good captain? Gamblers are known for seldom considering the consequences of their actions. Some may see it as strong leadership, but is it intelligent, level-headed and enduring? Being reckless with your own game is one thing, but the risk of dragging others down with you is another matter. From what I've studied and assessed, this captain's reputation was greatly enhanced by the successes of other players around him. Having four players (Taylor, Williamson, Boult and Southee) of genuine international class was a big help. How much influence did his approach have on others? He inherited naturally aggressive batsmen in Taylor and Williamson, both of whom have developed their own style of game. Guptill and Anderson were already in the category of hitters. It could be argued that these two felt even more comfortable in playing their natural game, because it would be difficult for others to hold them accountable for possible reckless failures. Encouraging players to play their 'A' game is not a new discovery or invention!

McCullum's final Test and the World Cup (ODI) final, both of which were against Australia, summed him up as a player and a captain. In the first innings of the Test, he came to the crease with New Zealand at 32/3. Once again he decided the situation was irrelevant and he would throw the bat at the ball regardless of the consequences. Early in his innings, he looked like getting out every other ball and was caught from a no ball at 39, but it was about to become his day. I suppose the theory is you have to gamble big to have a chance of starring big. He went on to post a world record for the fastest hundred in Test cricket — from 54 balls — ending up with 145 from 79 balls. The team had bashed its way to 370 from a mere 65 overs. Big problem: New Zealand had scored too few in too short a period of time. Why is that? Because it was a five-day Test match. Australia cruised to a 7-wicket win but that didn't seem to matter. The impressionable celebrity worshippers, the media and the captain had got their fix and the four remaining days of downers were probably erased from memory.

In the World Cup final, in an attempt to take it to the Australian left-arm quick Mitchell Starc from ball one, McCullum's innings ended abruptly in an aggressive three-ball duck — incidentally, these were the first balls of the match. This aptly demonstrated, once again, the folly of a negligent approach that came home to roost when it mattered most —inspirational, leading by example eh! New Zealand went on to be bowled out in 45 overs for an uncompetitive 183. The Aussies needed only 33.1 overs, winning by 7 wickets.

There is no denying it, McCullum's hand-eye abilities are up there with the best. His approach to batting and execution of many of his shots sparkled in the eyes of many and was often ugly to the eyes of others. Then there's McCullum's wicket-keeping, which shouldn't be overlooked. In the era of batsman wicketkeepers, he stood out as probably up there with the best of them. Had he not been captain, would he have played with the same freedom? Hard to say. Would he have been more successful in terms of greater consistency and bigger tallies? Again, hard to say. Was he genuinely influential in improving the ability of others to perform? You would need to ask the players concerned and by now, the dust should have settled enough, so that fear or favour has subsided. Has he encouraged more kids to take up the game? Possibly so, but you wouldn't advise them to follow his example. There has been an influx of young Indians into the game in recent times in New Zealand, but I suspect the Indian Premier League has been the main influence. Do I think that his on-field captaincy was up to standard? I hope I've more than qualified the answer to that. Do I believe in the presumed importance of togetherness, feeling comfortable and the speculation of 'pushing the right buttons' as crucial performance enhancers? Hopefully, I've also put that theory into its rightful place. I can't resist adding that these beliefs are a very comfortable, convenient replacement for dodging and applying the knowledge that really counts.

McCullum's captaincy philosophy was diametrically opposite to Taylor's. McCullum condemns Taylor for going to his room rather than the bar to chat with the boys — interestingly, Don Bradman wasn't much of a drinker either and preferred to go up to his room. What would Taylor and Bradman be missing and what would other players be missing? It shouldn't be difficult to work out the main topics of conversation among a group of above-average-testosterone-driven young males. The suggestion that joining in socially to chat to the boys would make all the difference to them performing better, appears to ignore the significant motivations that should already be present. Playing international cricket for New Zealand, self-fulfilment, the team's success, family and money will to varying degrees play a part in every player's makeup. Sure, alcohol can be a truth drug, but McCullum does mention that Taylor stated that his door was always open.

Another gripe from McCullum was that the senior players wanted more direction from Taylor. What are some of the directions that could be of value, remembering that much is said about the need for individuals to show leadership and personal responsibility for their own game? McCullum says under Taylor the players had got to the stage where they didn't care any more. So is he trying to convince us that by getting the 'pip', New Zealand's best cricketers are prepared to take their bat and ball and go home? How much of this stuff are we expected to believe? What is more believable is what McCullum says about the reason for Taylor's silences at some meetings: 'someone must have been telling him to watch his back'. Indeed!

Unpredictably, McCullum's field settings (for a short period) became very much more orthodox following New Zealand's thrashing by Australia in the Brisbane Test in November 2015. It followed some very pointed criticism from Channel 9. Although there had been some critical analysis done by a few earlier, mostly beyond the shores of New Zealand, this work seemed to help destroy the fallacy — or perhaps the illusion — that McCullum's field settings were smart, effective and ahead of his time. But none of this seemed to filter through to a revering media in this country. Much easier, I suppose, for them to become advocates, to jump on their own bandwagon than to probe deeper. Perhaps the pie had become just too humble to eat, or was it more to do with the pressure from editors and produces to hype up the promotion? At one point, I sent through some copy to the *New Zealand Herald*, the *Dominion Post* and a longer piece to Cricinfo along the lines of this chapter, in order to give another perspective. For whatever reason, none was prepared to publish my work.

The best thing to come out of this period was the national team's exemplary approach to the 'spirit of cricket', curiously lead by the captain. Initially, being the nice guys was to be used against the Aussies as a strategy to 'get up their nose'. The positive feedback must have encouraged its continuation. This story reminded me of what the CIA had to say about David Lange having cashed in on the 'no nukes' policy. According to them he wasn't initially in favour of it. There was even talk within the New Zealand camp of how to mentally unsettle and destabilise the South Africans in the field, not through sledging, but a more subtle approach, by appearing to be disorganised. Williamson's captaincy tends to exhibit a more convincing approach to the spirit of cricket. However, it is worth remembering that during the New Zealand tour of England in 2013 at the beginning of McCullum's captaincy, Neil Wagner took on the 'sledger-in-chief' role and could provide a list of the English batsmen he had hit. He was quoted by stuff.co.nz: 'It's more about getting into a guy's face. It's about irritating them, making them very angry. Make them look at you and think I really do want to hit this guy for four. You have just got to get them to the point where they really hate you. When you get to that point you sometimes make them think about something else in a split second of concentration lapse that could give you a wicket.'

If anyone had any doubts about conflicts of interest within New Zealand Cricket, player power and what it can lead to and the damage it can cause, McCullum's book inadvertently (I presume) produces precisely that.

McCullum's attack on John Parker and the people who were concerned about NZC's handling of Taylor's dismissal as captain totally misses the point. His assumptions failed to understand or accept that the 'Taylorgate' saga wasn't about him at that time, it was about another example of the deficiencies demonstrated by NZC. The board is, after all, responsible for any change in the captaincy. The so-called mafia (bad people) that were supposed to sit in behind Ross Taylor were not, in most cases, known to, or friends with, Taylor. In fact, Parker had come across Taylor on only one occasion and that was only for a few moments (not long enough to get beyond saying hello and wishing him all the best), when he bumped into him in the foyer of a hotel.

Over the course of several years I'd had some brief chats with Taylor. I did send him an email when I was managing the selection panel, asking him for his views on captaincy, as I had also done with McCullum. Since then I've had no contact with Taylor other than sending through an email in July 2018 asking him a few questions (assuring him he wouldn't be quoted), in an effort to clarify a few points and test my thinking for this book — he chose not to reply. I should have anticipated this reaction, because he has more reason than most to be suspicious of engagement with anyone in New Zealand's world of cricket, past or present. A further indication of his mistrust in more recent times is his notable absence from captaining the team in the absence of the incumbent. It's not as though a new young player has appeared on the scene who is being groomed for the future or an older established player is more deserving.

Some believe that all the shenanigans were worth it because Taylor had to go. It's become standard practice for national sports bodies to employ a spin doctor to promote the workings of their organisation's good and bad decisions. In the case of Taylorgate, some people were persuaded that the right decision was made, due largely to both a concerted selling effort from NZC and the work behind the scenes on behalf of McCullum by his 'neuro-human performance specialist Kerry Schwalger', spin doctor cum mental skills coach.

I didn't go to the same lengths of studying Taylor's on-field performance as I had done with McCullum, simply because Taylor's approach was far less questionable. McCullum's captaincy caught my interest, largely because of all the hype surrounding it. I wanted to test the validity of his work and see what he might have to offer. The game of cricket and, I suspect, many sports are crying out for more refined assessments when judging the performance of their players, captains and even to what extent support staff are needed. We will never know if Taylor was good captaincy material, because his tenure was not only short-lived, but vested interests undermining him were dishonourably supported by his employers and his union.

If captains of international cricket teams are to be viewed as important role models, it should be understood by all concerned that players and captains are merely servants of the game, not given licence to be bigger than the game. Those driven to judging the abilities of captains solely by team results might want to ponder these statistics. The fact that Taylor was given such a short period to prove himself meant that any sample to judge him by team results alone would be too small to have much meaning. He was only captain for a period of 12 months, captaining in 13 Tests from November 2011 to November 2012 and one Test in 2016 — McCullum, on the other hand, was given 31 Tests.

If you take both players' first 10 Tests, Taylor's stats read 5 losses, 2 draws and 3 wins (2 wins were away from home); McCullum's stats read 4 losses, 6 draws and 1 win (1 win at home and none away from home).

This recent period, in the annals of NZC, is just one small sample (some might say inconsequential since it's only a sport) of how cricket and so-called modern-day society can be dumbed down and destabilised in so many areas even with access to much more money and improved technology. What an interesting sociological case study Taylorgate could be for those willing to evaluate the workings of so many organisations and the part they have played. The NZC board, their CEOs, the Players Association, the captain, the head coach, the media, and even the judiciary. Should any of them justifiably be satisfied with their contribution to the integrity and ethical standards of cricket in New Zealand? Sadly, I see no discernible signs that much has changed since then.

I think we deserve better.

SEVEN
TEAM CULTURES IN INTERNATIONAL CRICKET

AN ENORMOUS AMOUNT OF TIME, ENERGY AND MONEY CONTINUES TO go into attempting to develop a winning team culture. Over the years systems have come and gone, some less successful than others depending on who you talk to. Opinions on this subject are about as diverse as they are when it comes to trying to get people to agree on what constitutes a good pitch. During my playing days with New Zealand there were virtually no attempts made to develop a team culture. The administration was totally autocratic (at times bullies) and there was no support personnel for the team, other than a manager and, sometimes, a physiotherapist. New Zealand provincial teams had just a manager and English county teams had no additional personnel, other than a physiotherapist who was usually home-based. Pendulums have a habit of swinging violently one way or the other, before hopefully settling somewhere in the middle or where it makes more sense. At present, my observations are that we are well short of finding either.

With teams, the assumption appears to be that a happy team will be a successful team. My experiences are that a team need not be happy or unhappy, but they are more likely to be successful if they have a professional approach and some good players. With unprofessional teams, more often than not, a team is a happy collective after winning and a happy player is one who has performed well. The most successful teams and players I have been associated with were less likely to be fazed by the result, win or lose. Their professional approach to the game and their peers, irrespective of how they felt about each other, gave them greater consistency and allowed them to play closer to their full potential. In these teams a number of the players had little in common and some even disliked each other. After all, that's what happens with enforced fraternisation. Players focused on their own performance, knowing that getting that right would be the greatest contribution they could make to the team and themselves. There have been some well-known examples of that in the New Zealand game. Probably the most obvious was the differences Richard Hadlee and Jeremy Coney had in the third Test against the West Indies in 1987 in Christchurch, a game that was Coney's last. Before the Test Hadlee had used his newspaper column to criticise a lack of discipline exhibited by New Zealand during the second Test, a game New Zealand lost by 10 wickets. Coney took issue with Hadlee before the game about his column, also blaming Hadlee for leaking a story that Coney, having already announced his retirement once the series was over, wouldn't play in the third Test. It was subsequently found to have been passed on by a physiotherapist who overheard a discussion. Hadlee asked for an apology from Coney but he said he wouldn't give him one. I happened to be the coach at the time and although I knew nothing about the reason for the stand-off between the two, I arranged for John Wright to be the intermediary in terms of passing on necessary messages between the pair. After all, it's essential for your opening bowler and captain to converse. Fortunately, Hadlee, after an indifferent bowling start, helped New Zealand claim a series-levelling win. It was also well known later that Martin Crowe and Ken Rutherford were hardly bosom buddies. There was controversy during the 1992 Test series against England which preceded the World Cup. They were hardly talking. Crowe had been portrayed as a wine bar type of guy while Rutherford was more of your public bar type. Crowe was also upset about comments in Rutherford's *NZ Truth* column that Crowe was not mixing with his team, even eating in a different room during the Tests. Yet, they managed to put those differences aside during several important partnerships during New Zealand's winning World Cup run, until it ended in their semi-final loss to Pakistan. More recently, the most obvious example is the situation that developed between Ross Taylor and Brendon McCullum when Taylor lost the captaincy to McCullum, a controversy that stirred up much negative publicity, especially for New Zealand Cricket and the way it handled the matter. While Taylor made himself unavailable for the subsequent tour to South Africa, he did rejoin the side and continues to make an invaluable contribution. Furthermore, Martin Guptill, who had sided with Taylor during the captaincy debacle, went on to be not only New Zealand's most successful batsman during the 2015 World Cup, but also the leading run scorer in the tournament with 547 runs while receiving two Man of the Match awards.

Jon Hotten wrote a piece on 'The myth of team togetherness' for Cricinfo in 2013 commenting on some of Andrew Strauss's thoughts about the need for togetherness. In brief, Hotten, when responding to Strauss's criticisms of Kevin Pietersen and Phil Tufnell for not meeting his theory, says: 'There have been hundreds of other oddballs, individualists and contrarians, because cricket, the most singular of team sports, not only attracts them, it practically demands them. The notion that a team be united is necessarily modern. In the era of gentlemen amateurs and salty pros, they didn't share a dressing room, let alone an ethos or a team song. In our new world, when even the slimmest of advantages is coveted, it has assumed a kind of critical mass. Anyone questioning its relevance is asking to be an outcast.' Yes, indeed!

Let's face it, most people in whatever area of life find it hard enough to get their own act together without being distracted and consumed by others' problems. Most would say good relationships within families is a different matter, where emotional ties are important, but far from essential when it involves international cricket. Many agree that becoming too comfortable at the international level is not a performance enhancer. Therefore, playing happy families is hardly a formula for players and teams to constantly challenge and extend themselves, nor develop the mental toughness needed to perform consistently well; in fact it's more likely that the opposite result will occur. Furthermore, what makes an organisation believe it can brainwash players in their twenties and thirties? A coach may be able to pass on some mental skills related to the game that he has found to be personally useful. But for any player with a serious mental condition, it is totally unrealistic to think that coaches, fitness trainers, managers or anyone other than a qualified psychiatrist is capable of dealing in such a specialised area. Much of the groundwork preparing players for the challenges that lie ahead should have been done at age-group levels, before the player has reached first-class cricket, let alone the international level.

In 2006, Ric Charlesworth, the NZC high performance manager, put forward a paper headed 'Cultural Transformation' which strongly expressed his observations of NZC at that time. Ric had an exceptional background: eight years as a cricketer for Western Australia, eight years as coach of the Hockeyroos, six with the Kookaburras, he attended four Olympics Games as a player, and was a politician as well as a qualified GP. He said: 'It does appear to me that there is a general approach which is best related in the statement that many are happy to play for New Zealand and see that as the ultimate achievement rather than becoming the world's best in their area of expertise. I believe this approach pervades almost every area of New Zealand Cricket from top to bottom. We are too ready to rationalize our performances with justifications and excuses. It also seems that in some ways we are not realistic about where we really stand in comparison to the rest of the world and are happy to make excuses and bluff rather than find solutions.'

I remember thinking, at last we have someone from the outside looking in with a significant background in sport, both as a player and a coach — someone who they might just listen to. His strongest background was in hockey, but eight years as a first-class cricketer with Western Australia was not to be sneezed at. I identified with much of what he was advocating. He was also mostly singing from the same hymn sheet as me when identifying the lack of work ethic among players and also their lack of a desire or commitment to face up to the realities necessary to excel. Players were also guilty of a lack of openness, honesty, a willingness to learn, accountability and personal responsibility. I had also noted that some players were becoming adept at protecting their own positions in the side. Initiatives to persuade the players to embrace the concept of personal responsibility and to respond to team requirements positively had so far proved to be largely ineffective. How realistic is it to expect that a few well-chosen words will significantly change entrenched practised behaviour, particularly when these habits had been accepted for so long?

Around that time, the All Blacks had apparently (if you believe what was being reported) mastered the concept of personal responsibility and responding positively to the requirements of the team. While rugby is a different beast to cricket and requires a greater degree of on-field trust and teamwork for success, it's intriguing that off-field strategies to enhance teamwork seemingly work better with them than cricketers. Some argue the reason for this is the personality difference between the two groups. I'm told the All Blacks sweep out and tidy up their dressing rooms wherever they play. Would New Zealand's cricketers be prepared to do the same? Would New Zealand's cricketers ever accept the 'no dickheads' rule that applies to the All Blacks? I would suggest some might, but generally very unlikely on both counts.

Leadership groups have seemingly proved to be very successful for the All Blacks, and maybe with some other sports, but there is a lot of evidence to say that the version of this concept developed by New Zealand Cricket has proven to be counterproductive for themselves and their employees. Their concept has certainly added further distractions for the players. The players' core objective of focusing on playing the game of cricket has been seriously corrupted. It has also succeeded in producing another layer of management within, the politics that go with it and a group (run by a small minority) that has become a law unto itself. This has occurred because of the substantial power it has been granted. Being permitted to influence contracts, selection and having a major say in the hiring and firing of support staff has become accepted practice — conflicts of interest don't seem to matter, nor employment law or process. This situation is an example of an employer being compliant with the demands of a designated group of employees. The chosen group has been successful in shifting compliance from itself onto the organisation as a whole — from its support staff to the board of NZC. As a result, the non-playing employees of the organisation are not treated with equal respect, emanating, I suspect, from player devotees on the board.

The shift to securing obedience and control of their employers has not happened overnight. The seeds were planted back in 1996 when the board of NZC supported the 'miscreant' (a word used by the CEO of NZC at the time) behaviour of two players, Cairns and Parore, signalling that they were 'bigger than the organisation'. The planting of these seeds has flourished since then, particularly with the powers granted to Daniel Vettori when he became captain, and peaking when the national body complied with the cravings of a captain (Brendon McCullum) with a cult personality in 2012–14. Input from captains, coaches and leadership groups is not the issue, it's the extent and breadth of their inclusiveness and decision-making powers that is so damaging, whereby the board is automatically compliant to the wishes of the players.

I recall when the team sports psychologist Gary Hermansson was part of the support team. One of his tasks was to chair the team leadership group in an effort to get them focused on improving their cricket, rather than exchanging information about T20 contracts, or who next they wanted to remove from their support staff.

New Zealand Rugby's leadership groups followed a very different path to cricket. Rugby did not fall into the same traps as cricket by including areas where obvious conflicts of interest existed, let alone relinquishing their own responsibilities. The leadership group concept was initially welcomed by their players. But it didn't take long before they became fed up with the time commitment and so many meetings. Even some of the more capable thinkers such as Anton Oliver enjoyed it initially, but soon preferred to put his energies into concentrating on playing the game. The highly-rated Carl Hayman took off to play overseas for the Newcastle Falcons in 2007, when he still had much to offer New Zealand rugby. Apart from the money, it was said he had also become frustrated with the time taken up with leadership meetings. Since then, a better time balance and more sensible terms of reference have been applied.

It's 23 years since the great upheaval of New Zealand Cricket after the drug tour of South Africa and dreadful home Centenary season, but what has been achieved in that time? A solitary Champions Trophy for the men's team back in 2000, and ongoing controversies that grow by the day in New Zealand sport. In addition to cricket, you can add Cycling NZ, Rowing NZ, Football NZ, Netball NZ, Hockey NZ and Rugby League. Problem-solving is not something New Zealand Cricket appears keen to face. A good starting point would be to admit and recognise that problems exist and need to be seriously attended to. Sweeping them under the carpet or hiding behind false information and by continuing to close ranks rather than searching for sustainable solutions is no way to act. They need to follow at least one of their stated tenets that they are open and transparent, otherwise we can expect the cyclical nature of controversy that surrounds the supposed showpiece of their game to continue.

Immediately following NZC's handling of the miscreant players' performance in the West Indies and the sacking of the on-tour management, more trouble appeared on the polluted horizon. Later that year (1996), the manager of the new Black Caps regime, John Graham, threatened to withdraw his services unless the newly-appointed coach, Australian Steve Rixon, received staffing help. After only a couple of meetings between the players and support staff, Graham said that 'he had already lost faith in the ability of the new coach to advance the team and he didn't wish to be part of that'. Ashley Ross, another Australian, was promptly promoted into becoming his assistant. Rixon had been 'spin' sold to all and sundry as a people's person, which is another way of saying 'a good man manager'. He went on to become known as a fielding coach and it was anticipated that he would establish the right culture. At the end of a three-year term, he was given a second term by which time the New Zealand team had been publicly labelled by Australia and England as the biggest 'sledgers' in world cricket. This is just another example of an administration compounding the original mistake in order to save face.

Over time, almost without exception, New Zealand Cricket has not been prepared to reprimand or support any attempts to bring destructive players into line if they are seen as established in the side, even though they may be causing more harm than good. Having been on the receiving end of such treatment by the board, for different reasons, I could argue that it is a dubious assumption that all players with good figures are indispensable. Closer scrutiny will show that some are likely to lose more games than they win. The selfish, destructive personality often uses the argument 'keep me happy, I'll play better and that will be good for the team'. What is more, we have tended to promote these players (who view themselves as bigger than the game) as role models and given them unwarranted status within our teams.

Personally, I've not been too concerned about the way individuals spend their time away from working hours (unless they break the law of the land), as long as their on-field performance is what's needed. One exception to that is having wives and families on tour, because of the additional unhelpful politics that generally occurs and the inevitable consuming distraction. Scheduling to provide gaps in between tours or maybe during T20 leagues is a better way to accommodate family time. I don't agree with the theory that one set of rules must apply to everyone after hours, although sometimes protocols set by the players themselves are likely to be stricter than what I would come up with. Handling the destructive, self-centred personality can be straightforward, just by making sure they are not given the licence to manipulate things for their own advantage, and to the detriment of the whole. Over the period of my time as a player, coach and selector at first-class and international level, there are no players that I would have said needed to be automatically dropped for their on-field or off-field behaviour. There were some who crossed the line to the point of needing to be sorted out, but I was mindful of not falling into the trap of setting or assuming the behaviours I set for myself (good and not so good) needed to be followed by others.

I've witnessed so many of the best players who have after-hours habits that wouldn't be described as something to be recommended. Tom Graveney, who was a very fine player, was a big beer drinker, and yet he was first down to breakfast, first into the nets before a day's play and a very valuable asset. In my mind, Graveney was never in the category of being a problem. It would be an interesting exercise to get a group of appropriate people together to give their views on how they would deal with fractious personalities and what weighting they would apply to an assortment of behaviours. Some of the more notable personalities in this category would be: Martin Crowe, Chris Cairns, Adam Parore, Jesse Ryder and Brendon McCullum. Of this group, Jesse Ryder has been the only one singled out as being unacceptable. The leading question is, why was Ryder singled out and not the others? Intriguingly, one of the two decision-makers in bringing about Ryder's fate was McCullum, one many would also put into the divisive category. My experience is that players in this category are more likely to be less tolerant of others. They appear to have a stronger desire to get their own way and are more prone to manoeuvring to have opponents of their behaviour eliminated. I'm sure those with a background in psychiatry are far better qualified than me to come up with more answers on this subject — I can only comment on my experiences.

When protocols are being established between players and management, some of the more contentious issues under this system might be how much alcohol is acceptable, should curfews exist and if so, to what extent? Interviews with the media can also be a contentious issue. Players are often given the freedom to say virtually whatever they like, whereas non-playing staff, who may be the target of their wrath, are muzzled. It would be interesting if both parties were permitted to air their grievances openly and be judged by the public shareholders of cricket. This would likely make both parties more measured and contemplative. Employment law may play a part, but to what extent should international sport call for a different set of rules? I expect it to be up to individual players, when protocols are being set, to defend a position with the group, which they believe has been successful for them, even though others might initially have a different view. But who would want to tell a Tom Graveney, particularly at the age of 40, that three pints of beer was the limit? The likes of a Jesse Ryder was viewed as having an alcohol problem and was allegedly prepared to sneak out after so-called bed time to satisfy his thirst. Attempts were made to curb his after-hours issues. He did get into some strife socially and was seriously physically assaulted on one occasion and injured himself on another — there may have been other occasions that I'm not privy to. These injuries did affect his availability, but it's hard to be critical of his on-field behaviour and performances when considering his stats. His playing record is superior to most that have played for New Zealand. In 18 Tests he averaged 40.93, in 48 ODIs he averaged 33.21 at a strike rate of 95 and a first-class average of 45. He had a very good pair of hands in the field and was useful enough bowling a few overs of medium pace. He's always carried a few extra pounds in weight, but so did the likes of Cowdrey, Botham, Bedi and many other successful players. As far as I'm aware, his on-field behaviour wasn't a notable problem. He wasn't a selfish player, or a back-stabber, and he didn't go squealing to the media with complaints about his team-mates or his support staff. The reports of Ryder's time playing for Essex appeared to be free from the same issues he had playing for New Zealand. Perhaps anonymity in England compared to New Zealand made the difference? His biggest problem was that his shortcomings were more public compared to some others, hence more difficult for his employer to conceal.

I used alcohol as a sedative to get to sleep when I toured the West Indies in 1972. On two or three occasions I had batted all day in very hot conditions and was not out overnight. I went on to score double hundreds the following day, so I could argue that alcohol had worked for me on those occasions. Would it have been better to have taken sleeping pills or just accepted less sleep because I couldn't switch off my brain? At the time I wasn't aware of relaxation techniques or hydrating, which might have been a better option. In those days, a drinking culture had become the norm, particularly in English county cricket, and I was part of that.

No guilty player is going to admit to being in the back-stabbing category or being a selfish player at the expense of others. They are the ones that do the most damage and this is where warnings from selectors, managers and coaches come into the equation. If a player doesn't heed warnings, then only at that point does the axe possibly need to fall. However, if the offending player knows they can manoeuvre a weak administration into supporting what generally becomes their blame game, all control is lost. Furthermore, when the coach is axed instead of the player, the bad man managers are surely the administration. Perhaps they should be taking on board a quote from Socrates when he said, 'The easiest and noblest way is not to be crushing others, but to be improving yourselves.' Unfortunately, too many administrations follow the path of least resistance, backed up by fixed ideas and preconceptions.

One of the programmes I experienced titled 'Leading Teams' (not as a player, fortunately, but as a selector) was partly based around players thinking of others first and how they could help their peers improve themselves through honesty sessions and the like. Very nice and caring. Leading Teams (an Aussie invention) aimed to, in their words, 'align teams by creating shared vision and behaviours that empower all members of the team to engage in open dialogue. We develop leaders who model and defend the behaviours that the team identifies as non-negotiable'. Its Performance Improvement Programme (PIP), which it said was a 'unique and visionary training methodology', covered five key areas: coaching and mentoring, effective leadership, aligning teams, personal development, and organisational development. Aligning teams involved understanding how culture and values affected team performance, analysing the current culture of the team, creating a desired vision and developing desired behaviour within the team.

It also involved peer performance assessment and it was this aspect that created the most controversy within the New Zealand team ranks. At the time, Craig McMillan, the recent batting coach, said that during the 2007 World Cup in the West Indies, five players would be assessed after each game. Every member of the team would give those being assessed a score between 1 and 10 for their performance. Management would keep the totals and use them for the end-of-year review process. McMillan felt there were two problems with the system. First, players would be given a score of 5 or 6 even if they performed poorly because other team members wanted to avoid conflict. The second problem was in regards to senior guys like captain Stephen Fleming — it seemed that no one wanted to give him any low scores. It was all because he was the captain. During a series of one-day matches in Australia in 2007, McMillan was one of two players selected for a peer review assessment, which involved other team members coming up with three words to best describe him. The group led by Stephen Fleming described McMillan as 'competitive', 'stubborn' and 'self-centred', which McMillan felt was unfair. I left the room despondent.

I thought Ken Rutherford's comments gave more realism to the subject. He said: 'This sort of assessment stuff doesn't impress me, especially at the end of a day. Look, there're blokes you are never going to get on with but it's amazing what a six-pack of Speight's and a talk with all the guys will achieve at the end of the day. I know it's old-fashioned but when you're in a team, guess what, you're in a team. You're all part of it and don't need idiots from fantasyland telling you to assess your mates. It's wacky and that's being kind.'

An open-door policy should also be encouraged, although getting players (or people generally) to walk through it when they might need to is a real problem — I doubt if this is just a New Zealand thing? One of the areas covered in the Leading Teams programme refers to encouraging team members to engage in open dialogue. But once again, timing is of the essence. Getting this variety of material being taught to the youngsters is when it is more likely to be absorbed and acted upon. We know only too well the reluctance to allocate and prioritise money to education at this level, not just in cricket, but right across society. In the meantime, although Rutherford's comments may sound too simplistic, more often than not they work better than a more theoretical approach. Having a drink in the dressing room at the end of a day's play among team members is still, I presume, standard practice. Another unpretentious system which worked well, particularly when on tour, was to rotate the rooming list. More often than not it would break the ice between two players in a positive way, players who previously didn't have much time for each other. Nothing much is lost, even if it didn't work. But so what? There's a job to be done, so get on with it regardless!

All of this stuff from the 'fantasylanders' is under the pretext, I suppose, of team-building. A curious approach to improving performance, when applied to international cricketers? Mother Teresa had her own act together enough to give worthwhile help to others, but there are precious few who are capable of that. More money flooding into the game was, and still is, providing make-work schemes for academics, consultants and outside businesses. It is also attracting opportunists manoeuvring into positions on boards.

Every team has a wide range of personalities (bravo to that), and to assume that their in-built and practised behaviours are going to change virtually overnight because someone else wants them to is unrealistic, no matter how well the various corrective measure programmes are presented. What motivates individuals to perform at their best varies greatly and as long as they don't continue to break codes of conduct and agreed protocols in executing whatever makes them tick, I say let them get on with it. To meddle in this regard may stifle a player's motivation to excel. I was under the impression that individual difference was to be encouraged. Do we want robots or genuine characters? Some players will have more personal and professional integrity than others. And what about technical skill? It seems that this only receives a cursory glance! Probably because there are fewer qualified people to evaluate it compared to all the non-essential people being *lined* up to cash in.

Setting and achieving professional standards involves recognising and curbing the behaviour of selfish players who undermine team performance on the field, and by applying sound selection policies and agreed protocols to deal with that. But I would query the need or value of most of these so-called team-building programmes.

Programmes to develop leadership skills have been around for decades and are still in vogue, covering a broad area of subjects. I'm all in favour of the area encouraging everyone to question and have the confidence to speak up. Nevertheless, there has to be an understanding that if your case doesn't win the day, you accept the decision and move on. Unfortunately, the willingness and acceptance of questioning and challenging the status quo is largely absent from our society — or at least discouraged. One significant example of a gagging approach occurred in August 2018 when of all places, a university (Massey in Auckland) Vice-Chancellor banned Don Brash from speaking even in anticipation of what he might say. Those that don't have the confidence to put forward an argument also need to understand, put up or shut up and no back-stabbing. In the teams I've been associated with, the reality is only a small minority of players (two or three others) have the desire to captain teams (at least in their minds), apart from perhaps Pakistan and Australia. Most prefer to concentrate on their own performance (a major challenge in itself), whether it be batting, bowling or fielding, and have little interest in field settings and who should be bowling from which end and for how long. There is a suggestion that it is an advantage for all the fielders to know what the bowler is trying to do. My response in respect to fielders' roles is they would be better off concentrating on their own performance. Simple things like whether they should be in closer to prevent the single, or deeper to help counteract the boundary and so on. One shouldn't overlook the reality that most bowlers don't have the ability to put the ball precisely where they want to anyway. Richard Hadlee was a fine bowler but even he couldn't put the ball on a particular spot as often as he would have wanted. He did it more often than most but that fact remains. Others that come to mind in this category are: Glenn McGrath, Dennis Lillie, Ewen Chatfield, Brian Statham, Derek Shackleton, Tom Cartwright, Derek Underwood, Bishan Bedi, Srinavas Venkataraghavan and Hedley Howarth.

In fact, there seems to be an exaggerated assumption of the skill levels of players in international cricket. A trained eye sees it very differently. Some players are just better than others but still well short of what is possible. Another perspective here would be to say that I could think of nothing more distracting and counterproductive (for both parties) than my batting colleague trying to give technical advice to me from the other end, or between overs. Tactical discussions, particularly during run chases, may be a different matter.

There is also a view that the more players (captains) you have on the field giving advice to the captain, the healthier it is, and that this makes for better decision-making. I'm far from convinced about this either. Captains usually have a number of strategic options open to them, so if too many, often conflicting, ideas are offered, this can undermine confidence. It can also create confusion and irritation, not only for the captain, but also for other players whose advice isn't taken up. As I see it, a better approach is for players with advice to go through the vice-captain (or senior pro), who can vet their suggestions and pass on what they think is worthwhile. This system not only controls the amount of advice, but also results in players being more considered with their opinions. It's not as though the captain is short of input on the field when you consider his ongoing contact with his bowlers and vice-captain. In all of this I can't help thinking, once again, that players are best to focus on doing their own jobs as well as possible and allow others to do theirs. Attempting to master the basics is a big enough challenge in itself for all concerned.

During the playing of the game of cricket, the vast majority of decisions stem from one player competing against another and is therefore the most singular of team sports, unlike the case in many other team sports. Generic comparisons continue to be made between cricket and rugby, particularly in New Zealand, when the reality is they are vastly different games. In rugby, for instance, a player is reliant on teammates moving into position to receive a pass, or players coming in very quickly behind another to protect him and the ball. Logically, rugby requires greater emphasis on physical strength and team strategies if a team is to combine and function well. Players' arousal levels also need to be much higher to cope with the extremely combative physical nature of the sport. Over time so-called motivational talk becomes repetitive and less convincing. In just about anything you can name, to gain higher levels of consistency, self-sufficiency and skill are vital components, never more so than in cricket. After all is said and done, there is no substitute for skill. I was fortunate in playing a skill-centred sport, where I only had to overcome 163 grams of leather, not 120 kilograms of raging muscle. Curiously, in discussions with a rugby union prop forward, he said, 'I would far sooner pack down in a scrum than face a fast bowler in cricket.' I felt like quipping, 'If the ball hits you, it's only on you for a moment, so how can it hurt you?' I stole that one from that 'tough bugger', Yorkshireman Brian Close.

Back in 2011, the Australians produced what was known as the 'Argus Review', which had a section on 'Improving the Australian team's culture'. Hindsight, albeit in 2018, suggests it wasn't especially effective. But the report was a prime example of a make-work scheme, making a mountain out of a molehill, by attempting to impose idealistic expectations on players whose personalities were already well ingrained. A more successful approach would be to simply enforce the agreed behaviours as written by the ICC and MCC — those written in London and Dubai, not Melbourne! The mountain I refer to made statements like 'a 360-degree feedback process is needed followed by adult conversations, senior players including the captain and vice-captain receiving mentoring by an external professional at least every six months'.

It talked about leading by example, role models, desired behaviours, opinion-shapers, trust and honesty, induction processes and so on. All this and more to get players job-ready and in between times I suppose they can practise and play the odd game. I thought you only had to drink Speight's to be the perfect man. This stuff might be better served shaping the character and obligations of administrations and boards who wouldn't have the distraction of having to play the sport.

Frankly, I don't see those culture improvement programmes making a skerrick of difference to the on-field performance of a player. They're more likely to irritate, and many of the best players I played alongside would tell the Argus lot and any others in the same game to bugger off. I suspect some of the current players share similar sentiments. The reality is that long-established, trained responses automatically kick in during the execution of the various skills. During the heat of the battle, the subconscious takes control, and making good on-field decisions, if anything, is more likely to be compromised by the attempted interference from others.

In the last couple of decades, the common belief has been that it is captains, coaches and, to a lesser degree, managers who are most responsible for creating the 'right culture'. It is expected that through their 'leadership' they can play a significant part in motivating players and establishing the right behaviours. It's as if it's believed cloning is possible and all the different personalities can be moulded to fit their theory of what will work best for everyone. Even if you subscribe to this dubious point of view, New Zealand Cricket's pre-Hesson era when they had four different national coaches in as many years suggested that if any organisation needed to change its culture, it was New Zealand Cricket itself. Allowing such a turnover of coaches caused enough disruption for the power to shift firmly in the direction of the captain and senior players. It's quite a shrewd move for them to make, if arresting power away from others is the objective. It also opens the gate to surrounding yourself with poodles. It is not unusual for current administrations to claim they are an improvement on their predecessors, but in NZC's case the fundamentals connected to running their elite team have not improved.

Buzz words and phrases like 'empowerment', 'ownership' and 'leadership' tend to be directed more towards the group rather than the individual, and yet much is made of the need for personal responsibility and accountability. Realistically, though, can team-mates/friends with vested interests and the like be expected and encouraged to act as judge and jury of their peers' actions? What makes us or them think they have the experience and knowledge to do it in the first place? There was a period when players became increasingly frustrated and tired of all the off-field demands on their time, much of which is spent attempting to do other people's work for them. It seems to me that more and more managements are opting out of their responsibilities, increasing the workload of others and, indirectly, their own workloads, although it could be argued that managing and coaching/advisory positions are more akin to facilitating and coordinating. But is this what is needed? The main problem is not so much that teams have been encouraged to run themselves, it's the additional powers of influence they have in other areas, such as selection, contracts, and the employment and sacking of those around them (support staff), that is creating the main cause for concern. I recall writing a piece around 2007 questioning whether once the novelty wears off, do the players really want to have so much control and is it sustainable? Regression in more recent times has made me revisit this view, because since then, the gold rush appears to have increased the temptation of self-interest for players to control as much as possible.

Even Gordon Tietjens (New Zealand's Sevens head coach from 1994 to 2016) chose to speak out about 'player power' when in August 2018 the New Zealand women's hockey coach Mark Hager was being publicly criticised by some of the players — I note that in January 2019 he departed the scene. Tietjens questioned whether players are gathering too much power in the modern sporting environment and also wondered whether what we might be witnessing was another example of the players asserting their increased clout. 'If you go back to when I coached the Sevens, I just felt we were empowering the players too much,' he said. 'Their focus should be solely on getting better at what they do and being focused on their game as an athlete.' Hear, hear. How much more damage will it take before sports organisations get their act together? The casualties are not just the support staff around teams; it can also include indirectly the perpetrators by encouraging them to take their eye off the ball.

Adrian Seconi in writing a piece for the *Otago Daily Times* went on to give another example: 'Empowering players did not appear to help Silver Ferns coach [Netball] Janine Southby. She stepped down last month after a Netball New Zealand review found the "team needed clearer direction, structure and boundaries, on and off the court".' Seconi went on to say, 'arguably she gave the players too much leeway and was then made a scapegoat.'

These are further examples of a blame mentality blindly winning the day. The initial setting of team protocols and the possible need to revisit them as things progress is a collective initiative between players and management and is not new. Thereafter I thought management was meant to oversee the application of them. Any reviews that might follow a perceived breakdown between parties become a major problem for sports organisations. Having enough knowledge of the subject on boards, or any consultants that might be employed, is mostly proving to be a challenge too far. And yet it should be a relatively simple process to establish where the breakdown has occurred and who has been responsible for it. Sacking innocent parties, due in most cases to a predetermined partiality for one of the parties, having locked in fixed ideas at an early stage, is not only a travesty of justice, but also a recipe for inciting repeats. There is also the likelihood of players having the backing of a players' association, whereas the coach and any other staff is either on their own or likely to have to fork out for legal representation.

It is widely accepted that players should be encouraged to be personally responsible for their game, take ownership of it, take the lead in their own preparation and be accountable for their performance. So why shouldn't this include their own actions, and why does so much time, effort and money go into undermining these principles? Nowadays, players are being presented on a platter all the comforts, pampering, and pastoral care given to a juvenile emperor. Under the guise of help, players are surrounded by people advising them about all and sundry, much of which is peripheral stuff. This discourages them from searching and finding their own answers. Instead, it cultivates a blame mentality, destabilising personal responsibility, self-analysis and learning. Aristotle said, 'I cannot teach anybody anything, I can only make them think.' At best you can suggest to a person some options to try, but they will only believe in what they have proved to themselves by doing.

The amount of time spent on team-building and ongoing advice from all and sundry around them becomes a major distraction. Ed Smith in his book *Luck* related the instance he experienced at the Kent County Cricket Club in 1999 when the players were given ringbinders full of documents headed 'Kent Cricket — World Class'. What the players were being presented with was a 'new era'. 'The age of ultra-professionalism had arrived. And professionalism, of course, above all demands control. 'No longer would anything be left to chance' (chance was an awful relic of amateurism). There would be specialists for everything — physiologists, psychologists, nutritionists, optometrists. One player quipped that the only -ologists not represented were gynaecologists. 'We also spent a great deal of time discussing how we would play, even how we would live. It was like living through a social experiment in social engineering. The team's previous problems and differences would be erased,' Smith said. 'The search would be for a "Core Covenant". Cricket is not an island in this applied thinking towards achieving successful outcomes and the search for mantras to employ in this process has become a genuine growth industry.'

It also appears that (for a whole host of possible reasons) many players regard themselves as the experts in cricketing matters and are closed off on this subject from learning from others, apart from, possibly, *observing* their peers. The necessary degree of humility needed for minds to be receptive to learning seems to be largely missing, although if anything there is more likely to be an openness to absorbing what the various -ologists say. Brendon McCullum is a good example of precisely this, by employing Kerry Schwalger, who stated his occupation as a 'Professional Neuro-Human Performance Specialist', spin doctor cum mental skills coach.

A survey carried out by Ric Charlesworth in 2006 revealed that 60% of the 20 contracted New Zealand players couldn't come up with the name of a coach who they thought could help them with their game. And not one of them named the serving coach. I doubt if those percentages have altered much since then. It is very unusual for players at the international level to ask for help — minions, yes. Minions are welcomed to give them throw-downs, hit catches or taking a glove at fielding practice. The time is overdue for professional players to arrange for their own (whatever you want to call them) coach/mentor/advisor. In fact, some have already gone down this path. It's nonsense to believe that coaches on tour with teams, particularly the two or three additional ones (batting, bowling and fielding coaches), are going to be used any more usefully than as minions. Today many of the top players play for several teams annually, each of whom have different coaches and support staff attached to them. So what influence is there likely to be with enforced fraternisation with so many different transitory personnel? It's as though those running the game have locked themselves into an ideology that was questionable in the beginning, let alone continuing with it in today's environment.

Where does 'The Coach' fit in to all of this, other than maybe organising practices, collating and passing on information and, according to the current captain (Kane Williamson), adding to the over-used expression called culture? In a piece written by Mark Geenty in the *Dominion Post* on 15 August 2018, he unknowingly added fuel to this fire when he wrote: 'The coach who was newly-appointed in August 2018 had a reality check of what he could expect before he even took on the main job. It wasn't the best start to a future captain-coach relationship, for Gary Stead and Kane Williamson. Last summer, Stead joined the Black Caps camp for a brief stint when batting coach Craig McMillan took some family time, as part of New Zealand Cricket's succession planning. Word later got around cricketing circles that something had irked the skipper. The story, recounted by several sources, was that Stead had tried to coach Williamson's batting and that wasn't well received. It was nowhere near the cricketing crime of the century, and provided an early lesson for Stead's future reference. Clearly the world's No 4-ranked test batsman does it his way, toiling the longest in the nets and summoning assistance from familiar faces when required.'

This begs the question, if the batting coach doesn't coach batting and the bowling coach receives the same treatment, presumably Stead as 'The Coach' will be wondering about his status. Earlier, when McCullum was captain, he stated that when it came to talking tactics with 'The Coach' (Mike Hesson), he got his way. The current captain, Williamson, has described the main role of the coaching position as 'adding to the culture'. So one could be forgiven for coming to the conclusion that all three coaching positions are principally about adding to the culture of the team! Sadly, the reality is, the coaches are largely overpaid lackeys. Ed Smith made a telling comment when he said, 'from the safety of retirement that he no longer had to worry about uncomfortable logic or painful truths'. I can subscribe to the fact that very few players were interested in receiving uncomfortable logic or painful truths, let alone asking for any advice. For some, keeping the blame game up their sleeve tended to be the preferred option. Unfortunately, weak administrations are susceptible to diverting blame away from players onto coaches and managers under the pretext of poor man management. Having been a victim of this behaviour, my advice would be, don't sit back and be as naïve as I was to think that employment contracts or process mattered, nor to anticipate integrity, decency and honesty to prevail.

The never-ending subject of man management rears its controversial head, generally when teams or some individuals are not performing well. Deflecting blame is as old as the hills and even though circumstances and environments can be worlds apart, it doesn't inhibit a spectrum of assumptions and hypotheses from all and sundry.

One of the most common assumptions for getting the best out of each player is the alleged neediness to treat every player differently according to their mental makeup. Sounds plausible and may be true in many circumstances, but to what extent is it as applicable to those playing international cricket? What makes unqualified people, in particular, think they can rapidly change another person's personality in the first place? Better to go with their flow as much as possible, because as with any adults, players will already have well-established personalities. But that doesn't mean all of their traits necessarily merit or justify encouragement. International cricket is a tough, unsympathetic environment, one which ideally requires fortitude, and emotional resilience. Why would it be in anyone's best interests to encourage traits that destabilise those principles? The acknowledgement and appreciation of adult conversations are essential.

I think it's reasonable to say that a calm rather than an aggressive, abusive approach should be standard practice. However, truth and reason remain a necessary obligation, particularly in preparation for the challenging inhospitable atmosphere facing every international cricketer once he steps onto the field of play. For a batsman, there are 11 opponents who want to evict him from the crease as soon as possible. For bowlers, opposing batsmen are looking mercilessly to destroy their efforts to succeed. Any expectation of empathy from your opponent is delusion.

It's easy enough to be popular with the soft, gentle character or the ultra-ego personality by voicing copious amounts of praise following some success or sympathising after failure. But the magnitude and significance of the praise conveyed should be interpreted by the receiver by taking into account the character of the person delivering it. In other words, a nod or a wink from one character may be more telling than an effusive response from another. It should be remembered that confidence comes from knowing, not pretending. It's like empathy; it works best when it serves truth, not fantasy. Ultimately, handling success ideally embraces humility, whereas performance setbacks and self-improvement require courage, not blame.

When Smith was a county captain, he had an analogy for describing man management, when he said: 'If a difficult and disruptive teammate went through a good spell, and someone congratulates you for "managing him well", what should you do? If a captain tells the truth — "I doubt I've had any influence on him at all because his behaviour is random and unpredictable" — then you risk reinforcing a correlation that doesn't exist. When the difficult player reverts to type, as you suspect he will, you'll be saddled with the blame for not managing him well.'

The same thing applies to a coach who suffers accusations of poor man management when the truth may well involve juvenile behaviour. A disruptive player is never going to realise that the blame game is unproductive until administrations make it clear that they will not be supportive of it. Instead, players as a whole should be encouraged to adopt a more mature approach by concentrating on extracting as much information as they can from coaches or whomever. It's true to say that a coach should get as much out of a player as possible, but accepting a player's actions that have become unacceptable and likely to be detrimental to the whole setup is a dereliction of duty. For disruptive juvenile behaviour to become less likely, more time and expertise needs to be invested in our emerging elite players. Capturing their attention at an earlier age, boosting their ability to question, and making learning an enjoyable experience, will also hasten their maturity towards adulthood. The timing of this preparation is more likely to prepare them for the variety of challenges ahead and be a better outcome for everyone concerned.

The main argument for the existence of 'The Coach' seems to be that someone needs to draw everything together. The question is what is he drawing together that players can't access themselves, and how much of it is necessary in the first instance? Statistical data taken throughout their matches (which are regularly covered by television) can be easily accessed by everyone. Much of it provides information that the players should already know, due to their own observations and analysis during the game. Players who are not prepared to critique their own performance generally don't like others (particularly coaches) doing it either. That personality may be more open to statistical data because it can be delivered in a less confronting manner preserving their ego. Often the stats only paint part of the true picture for those that can distinguish the difference between good and bad luck. Numerous other possibilities and circumstances are ever present, influencing results. Dropped catches, bowling into the wind, pitch conditions, state of the game, who they were bowling to, when and for how long etc. As for knowledge about their opponents, most players would have had the chance to scrutinise them during previous encounters. If it's a new opponent, a trained eye will soon pick up on what's needed. The main challenge still remains, which is having the skill to execute.

During match performance, it should be obvious for a bowler and his captain to know if he is over-pitching too often, having been driven successfully off the front foot countless times. Or the reverse, whereby too many back-foot options were offered. Whether the bowler's line was too wide of off-stump or too straight, and the options that provides for the batsman. It's not complicated! The ball-tracking information presented on television and mapping where each ball pitches is more of an entertainment tool for viewers than an educational device for players and coaches. The segmented breakdown of where each ball has pitched is recorded and presented in generalised categories of short, good and full of length. The placement of these categories does not factor in the variation of pitch conditions, the bowler's height at delivery, his pace and whether he's a swing seam or bounce bowler. They don't consider the height of the batsman, the preferred positioning of his feet, whether he prefers playing off the front or back foot, or he takes guard outside the crease nor the circumstances of the game situation.

Wagon wheels for individual batsmen (mapping their scoring shots) are also limiting because of conditions and circumstances. Undoubtedly, batsmen have distinctive tendencies, strengths and weaknesses. From patient to impatient, from good to bad judges of line and/or length, preferences related to playing off the front or back foot, or through the off- or on-side and so on. Certainly there is the opportunity to pre-plan a particular strategy against each batsman, but the significance of this claim tends to be overestimated. Sure a batsman might be known for having an uncontrollable urge to attempt a difficult shot unwisely early in his innings. It may be a favoured stroke, or even a strength, but it may be reckless for him to attempt it early in an innings before his hand-eye-feet coordination of judging pace, bounce, swing and seam have been programmed in. Examples of some of the more testing shots might be the hook, or an expansive drive through the covers from a wide swinging half-volley. The reality is that bowlers, even at Test level, are mostly human (even fast bowlers!), and therefore they are not able to land the ball on a sixpence. Predominantly, the line they should be endeavouring to bowl as often as possible is down the corridor of uncertainty, because inconsistency is still largely inevitable. In short, the corridor I'm referring to is a ball that hits the top of off-stump if it doesn't deviate after pitching. Any departure from this line is better to be towards the off-side to what is referred to as a fourth stump line. Getting the length right has to also be on target to complete the maximum amount of uncertainty for the batsman. A good length will depend upon pitch and atmospheric conditions and the batsman's preferred positioning of his feet. In general terms, the ideal length under good batting conditions is one that has the batsman in two minds as to whether to play forward or back. If the pitch is slow, a slightly fuller length is generally better, particularly when containment becomes the priority. When the ball is seaming or swinging, a fuller length becomes an attacking option — this length is known as the nicking length. This is also a situation when the positioning of a bowler's feet and point of delivery becomes even more important. On occasions like this, when bowling outswingers to a right-hander, the classically preferred option of getting in as close as possible to the stumps at delivery can become less effective. By delivering from wider in the crease, the swing can be reduced enough to take the outside edge rather than defeating it. The greater the movement, the fuller the length needs to be. It should be remembered that the ball only needs to deviate from the pitch enough to take the outside edge rather than going past it. Batsmen tend to respond to this fuller length in a less cautious manner, increasing the likelihood of a miscalculation. Naturally, any number of other aspects can come into play, but following core fundamentals is more often than not the wisest approach to follow. It's all about manoeuvring the percentages in your favour, even though luck will undoubtedly play its part as it always does. Nevertheless, patience is often a virtue.

Some coaches like to incorporate data mining and scouting into any plans that they might come up with. I view this as another area that should be of more interest to a cricket statistician and only a passing interest to someone within the game. Certainly, some historical evidence can be valuable, if you don't want to repeat the mistakes of the past. Sure when I was coach, I always considered some of it. However, coming up with historical evidence that represents a winning formula presents too many anomalies. In part, it relies on the belief that the majority of teams in the past have gone about playing the game in a similar and tactically superior way. Figures are produced (particularly for ODIs) presenting the notion that the ideal is to be no more than a given number of wickets down after a certain number of overs with at least so many runs on the board.

From time to time commentators repeat an assumption, based I presume on statistical data, which predicts in advance the batting team's final total. When ODIs began to appear on prime-time television, the late Richie Benaud is credited with starting one of these predictive assumptions, by suggesting that you could expect the score at 30 overs to double by the end of the innings. I suggest that most data mining is better suited to board and computer games, but of minimal value in the real world when humans are involved. To think of applying this information as a strong guide to how you play the game of cricket is too much of an unnecessary distraction. What really counts is responding to what is immediately in front of you and understanding that the diverse makeup of teams, the distinctive skills of individuals within them and the pitch and atmospheric conditions will be different from one game to the next.

Looking through historical venue data is interesting and may provide some insights into how a pitch might play, including par scores for a particular ground. But once again this information will be very limited compared to a trained eye and how it will play on that particular day. The groundsman may have become victim to unseasonal weather leading up to the match, hampering preparation, or it may even be a new groundsman. He may have been instructed to produce a different type of pitch to his normally preferred creation for a number of possible reasons, such as assisting the strengths of the home side as opposed to those of their opposition, or because a result pitch was needed or the reverse and so on. Customarily, New Zealand toured India immediately following the monsoon season in mid-September, at a time when I assume the pitches had less time to recover from the big wet, when the temperatures were still in the thirties and likely to still be humid.

In the 1970s, I recall discussions taking place during one of our tours in India about whether or not it was acceptable for the home nation to prepare pitches to advantage themselves. A view that came from the Indian perspective was, why not? We expect you to do likewise when we tour your country — I must say, that sounds plausible. One of the fascinations about cricket is experiencing a variety of conditions for players to challenge themselves, and for spectator entertainment. For more than 20 years within New Zealand, the Turf Culture Institute has been employed to assist with pitch and ground preparation. Although the results of its testing is designed to largely assist groundsmen, the core samples of the pitch taken during the preparation phase and particularly just before each game is information that can be used by captains and coaches. Bulk densities and moisture contents are of significant interest and can be particularly helpful at a home venue where your background knowledge has often been able to witness and interpret the results over time.

Par scores are a combination of what teams have done against other oppositions on the day, not this day, and it should always be remembered that a good total is simply as many as you can get. Judging and handling the present is challenging enough without attempting to apply the past, or second-guessing the future. The challenge for everyone is invariably to simplify and distil the essence of information, so as to enhance focus, not to cultivate assumption or confusion.

By their own admission, coaches find little if any time to coach. Serious coaching can happen on a one-to-one basis during any significant periods of down time. This seldom if ever happens with international players today because of all the other contract opportunities. Furthermore, players need to be open to coaching in the first place. Any willing players would still need to choose their own coach/mentor.

Advice on the peripheral stuff is dominating, sidelining what really counts. If the position of 'The Coach' remains on a full-time basis, he needs to be at least strong in the area of strategising with the captain and the captain needs to be open to it. In his book *Declared*, McCullum says, 'Hess's influence [was] telling. He's never been a forceful technical or tactical coach, but he [was] a great organiser.' He tells us that 'tactically' he and Hess worked 'well in combination' and 'normally' they'd 'end up sailing towards [McCullum's] point of view'. The evidence has been compelling for many years that coaches attached to the New Zealand team and probably international teams as a whole are just spare parts. When you put McCullum's statements alongside those of Kane Williamson earlier in this chapter not requiring advice on his batting from the coach, it adds further current weight to the discussion.

Personally, I view the coaching position (and only one coach, not three) as a part-time appointment and probably only for the first couple of years of a newly-appointed captain. Thereafter, the coach's time commitment can be reassessed. The coach's work needs to revolve around being the chief advisor to the captain and, of course, open to any questions that might arise from other players who should already have their own chosen mentor — it's possible, but unlikely, their mentor will be the team coach. The coach could come in a day in advance of a major game and leave the night after the game, following a possible debrief. If the tour schedule of games was tight and the team was touring a foreign country, it may require remaining with the team longer. However, T20 games could be dealt with through contact via Skype or FaceTime, if at all. This structure would also help to attract the best people to the position of coach — people who have had considerable experience in first-class and international cricket, ones that have had experience as captains and have considerable knowledge of the past and the present. Why would anyone with these skills want to be predetermined to functioning as a team lackey, when much of that stuff can be carried out by the manager or some locally hired lackeys/gofers for a fraction of the cost? Furthermore, why would a coach with the background I've just referred to want to work with a captain who was closed off to learning and why would a personality like that be selected as captain in the first instance? I remember asking Jerry Coney if he had considered operating as a coach in the way that he and I had in the 1980s. His immediate response was 'What would be the point if they're not going to listen?' I suppose the timing of my question may have had a lot to do with who was captaining New Zealand at the time.

For some time now, the position and status of coaches in cricket have been exposed for what they really represent and yet the reality continues to be ignored. A quote from the long-serving All Black coach Steve Hansen caught my eye on a comment he made about coaching the All Blacks. It was in a Marc Hinton piece on 24 September 2018, following the All Blacks' surprise loss to South Africa. Hansen said, 'I'm meant to be the teacher and they're meant to be the students'. I realise context is important, but at the time, I wondered if there were signs of a power shift in rugby, and some kinks appearing, even in the armoury of a celebrity coach in a genuine team game. It does bring a smile to my face when coach/teacher Hansen is referred to as 'Shag'.

In the month prior to Gary Stead's appointment, some of Kane Williamson's remarks made to journalist Andrew Voerman about the coaching position following Mike Hesson's resignation from his role with the New Zealand team in June 2018 were also quite telling. Veorman started off his piece by saying: 'Williamson and other senior players will be involved in the search for a new coach, but they won't be desperately looking for someone to tell them what to do, or to hold their hands as they chase World Cup glory, empowered by their former coach's inclusive leadership style. Williamson said, "There're so many other leaders in the playing group and in the support staff" and hopes their new coach will add to the environment. "That's where the focus is, and that's what you want from a coach — adding to the environment".'

He went on to say when referring to when Hesson and McCullum were together: 'They sort of created an environment where people felt a sense of comfort and they could then play in that selfless manner, which is so important.' He also added, 'backing players for long periods, where guys could actually come into the environment and not feel like one day they're here and the next day they're there.'

Following Stead's appointment, Ross Taylor was quoted as saying 'Gary is likely to be more hands on than Hess was'. That will be interesting, because the evidence would suggest that the coaching job over the past decade has become more of an amenable, compliance role.

My suggestion to Williamson is be very wary of what might be just around the corner and therefore think as much about the medium to longer term as you do about the present. It would also be advisable to research examples of appropriate historical evidence.

The strong inference appears to be that the recipe for success has arrived because, according to Voerman's research, 'the team has spent the best part of the past five years consistently performing at a level not seen since the 1980s.' I suggest that consistency is often used in relative terms and in New Zealand's case there has been a mixed bag of good, average and poor periods over several decades. In general, a report card should read 'Could do better'. I'm afraid sitting around purring like a pride of lions while digesting a kill doesn't convince me that the next feed is guaranteed. Much of this reminds me of another quote from Ed Smith, who said sport was full of 'abject misunderstandings of causes. In seeking to explain where things may have gone right or wrong there was a never-ending quest to identify the wrong causes and pin them to the wrong events'.

When I was spending time at the academy with the New Zealand Under-19 squad, I came across a young Williamson for the first time. At this stage, he was a couple of years younger than most of the group, and yet his talent still stood out. What impressed me most about him at that stage of his development was his willingness to openly seek advice, even when being mocked by others in the group. It would be interesting to know if his inquiring mind is still as resilient as it was back then?

The unanswered question is, who are all these leaders leading other than themselves? If it's leading themselves, then they are less likely to require others. If their peers are leading them, or the leadership group is attempting to, where does the group's hubris and conflicts of interest cease and the checks and balances begin? Why, in the first place, is it assumed that all the knowledge necessary can be found from within their small group? Furthermore, it doesn't stop boards from giving them additional powers of control.

Jane Cadzow in the *Sydney Morning Herald*'s *Good Weekend Magazine* painted a very different picture to the one generally represented in the sports pages. On this occasion it applied to Australian captain Steve Smith after the sandpaper ball-tampering episode, but it could have applied to most people who specialise in the narrowness of one subject. She sees Steve Smith as 'a man with a case of arrested development, someone who has been cosseted and coddled by professionalism, who has spent so much time in the bubble that he had no idea what to do when it burst.'

The difference an international sportsman experiences compared to other occupations is the amount of attention, money and so-called fame they receive at such an early age.

On 27 October 2018, Steve Waugh when commenting on the Cape Town ball-tampering scandal was quoted as saying 'the authorities let it happen'. He labelled Australia's attempts to sandpaper the ball as 'stupid' and 'ridiculous' and suggested the players had 'lost touch with reality' in an environment that had become fraught over the preceding few years. He went on to say the players were 'in a bit of a bubble and they are protected, you know they are insulated from a lot of things. They've got a lot of people around the side that protect them and tell them how good they are and how everything's fantastic and sometimes you can lose touch with reality.'

Cricket Australia (CA) commissioned The Ethics Centre to conduct a review of its organisation and the men's team, which was reported in the *Otago Daily Times* on 30 October 2018. The report started with CA being branded as 'arrogant' and 'controlling' and accused of treating its elite players like commodities, allowing 'alpha male' egos to develop a win-at-all-costs approach.

The players, who were involved in a bitter pay dispute with CA last year, felt they were treated as commodities, whose only value to the organisation was driving commercial success.

Here we go again, a blame mentality taking centre stage. The players were happy to pocket more money from the commercial coffers, and CA was content for the players to have the freedom and total control over how they presented themselves on the field of play. So it's pretty obvious who's controlling what. It's becoming more common for cricket boards to focus on controlling the income of money (not so much its spending) and neglecting the cricket side of governance. How much more evidence is required before it is conceded that the excessive degree of player power has to be reined in?

The evidence is overwhelming that the decline in standards initially has had as much to do with the cricket board's dereliction of duty by allowing player power to escalate to the point of self-destruction in Australia's case, but also to varying degrees with other countries, not least New Zealand.

The review also found the ball-tampering scandal was not an aberration and players were reluctant to challenge their team-mates' behaviour. 'People being driven by ego and an alpha male culture privileges combativeness over collaboration and discourages healthy, constructive disagreement,' the review said.

On-the-field sledging, which has been one of the major criticisms of the Australian cricket team, was also inherent in the team's culture, with certain individuals asked to 'play the mongrel'. I recall, probably 30 or more years ago, an Australian bat maker telling me 'you need a bit of mongrel in you to be any good'. In addition, he used the C word to supplement mongrel.

'A culture of disrespect for the opposition, as seen in the common practice of abusive sledging, runs through Australian domestic and international cricket, to a degree not practised by other nations,' the report said.

They could have more accurately included club and children's cricket too, from what I'm told. There is also a growing concern about the increase in sledging in the various grades throughout New Zealand.

As I've already alluded to in this chapter, the Australian history of violating the spirit of cricket has been going on for much longer than is being recognised in this latest review and is endemic in much of their spectator base. The simple answer to enhancing the integrity of the game of cricket is to apply the laws that already exist. We've been witnessing for far too long what happens when teams are left to run themselves without the necessary checks and balances, particularly when a team like Australia has become intoxicated with so much playing success over an extended period.

Cricket Australia has taken further steps with its ticket and entry conditions expressly prohibiting any sort of racist taunting, stating in part: 'I will not engage in any conduct (whether through the use of language, gestures or otherwise) which is likely to offend, insult, humiliate, intimidate, threaten, disparage or vilify any other person (including any player, match official, other official or other patron) on the basis of their gender, race, religion, culture, colour, sexual orientation, descent or national or ethnic origin.

'If I fail to comply with this condition, I may be refused admission to, or evicted from, the Venue by any Authorised Person without refund or compensation of any kind; and I must deliver up any and all Tickets that I have in my possession at the request of an Authorised Person.

'In addition, I acknowledge that the failure to comply with this condition may result in the imposition of other sanctions (such as being banned from the Venue in the future) and possible further action including criminal prosecution.'

For example, Indian captain Virat Kohli has been the subject of 'Kohli's a wanker' chants, although MCG authorities deemed that insufficient to take action. Maybe in this case there was an acceptance and understanding that MCG crowds wouldn't bother giving Kohli this much attention if he wasn't a threat, hence 'Kohli's a wanker' should be viewed as a compliment.

However, the racial nature of the 'Show us your visa' chants were seen in a dimmer light and Cricket Australia responded.

What enters my mind at this point is the challenges the likes of Paul Sheahan must have experienced when he was headmaster of Geelong College. Sheahan played in 31 Tests for Australia before retiring in 1973. Although I didn't get to know him personally, from all reports he was principled. How frustrating it must have been for him (and others like him) when pupils under his charge very likely viewed those playing cricket for Australia as important role models.

Williamson may be getting a relatively cushy ride with the skill and behaviour of the cricketers around him at present. A partisan media and a submissive administration are presently compliant, but the philosophy in operation sounds like it's too soft, not robust enough to withstand the inevitable hardships which the international game, and a changing personnel, will throw at them. In time this scheme will surely meet its nemesis; the corruption caused by excessive power from within will be permitted to raise its ugly head once again, because the door is being left ajar for the rise again of destructive personalities.

It's as though the skills of the game have taken second place to the amount of energy going into getting the players so-called 'job-ready' in other ways. Once again, the reality is, the fundamental work should have already been done 'before the horse has bolted'. By the time players reach first-class level their learning focus should be ready to switch onto in-depth observation, experiences through doing, improving decision-making, self-analysis and contact with their own mentor when necessary. I would argue that much of the work being carried out with the New Zealand team and, I suspect, other teams, would be more beneficial for the younger-age elite squads while they are still more open to change and learning. Still bright-eyed and bushy-tailed! I know I've made this point several times, but its relevance keeps popping up in various contexts because of its importance.

Imperative among these lessons is an understanding of what it means to be a professional. I note, the definition of professionalism is underpinned by a series of 'Core Values', such as: integrity and honesty — for trust to flourish there needs to be ethical, honourable, sound and incorruptible behaviour; humility — a sense of your own vulnerability opening up a positive approach to learning; leadership — making decisions, judgments and acting on them without dependency on others, being responsible, accountable and looking to solve problems, not apportion blame; attitude and desire — remembering that life is, say, 10% what happens to you and 90% how you react to it.

The description I've just outlined of the definition of professionalism does leave me with conflicting thoughts. Have I been drawn into mimicking and exaggerating the necessity for players to require so many tenets? Perhaps it's simpler, more effective and realistic, to encourage youngsters to just be open, honest and questioning with a strong desire to get better! To understand that there is no substitute for skill and mental fortitude, which only they have the power to find and deliver.

All of the attempts at cultural transformation and the flood of peripheral information seem to largely ignore the character and entrenched practised behaviour of players (and people generally) by the time they have reached the international playing level. To think that these players' behaviours and motivational stimulus are going to change overnight is unrealistic, no matter how well the various corrective measure programmes are presented. The makeup, personality and state of mind of players varies from bulletproof to depressed. Players within the same team are personally stimulated by a variety of motivations. They range from internal to external drivers; from self-fulfilment to doing it for others; to national pride; to statistics; to money; to self-interest and any combination of those. But hopefully they're all there for the same reason — team performance and personal fulfilment.

Why should anyone be surprised if money is the main driver when the chief learning style of today's society is to be a 'learning consumer'? Already players have got to where they are because of whom and what they are. For some, whom and what they are could have been significantly enhanced earlier in their development had they received a healthier education programme, geared to mature their approach for the challenges ahead. In my experience, attempts at a later stage of social engineering are a waste of money and are mostly consciously or unconsciously resisted, hence a waste of time or worse. Too much is made of the need to construct so-called team cultures. It would be far more effective for management and players to sit around the table before each series of matches and come up with some agreed protocols. Management is then responsible for the application of those protocols.

What should follow from that is a culture that grows naturally in line with the variety of personalities in the team. Most problems that arise should be dealt with by the players themselves or, if necessary, by management. As with most of the don'ts, they are only there to prevent rebellious behaviour. Any major issues may need to be directed towards the board, and the selectors may be brought into the equation. An open-door policy allows players to express concerns that may develop and if they want to take matters further they have the players' association to turn to. The real advantage in structuring things this way is that it accommodates checks and balances. Everyone gets their say (democratic principles), the best arguments irrespective of who presents them should prevail and then everyone can concentrate on doing their own designated jobs without unjustified distraction. For this system to operate successfully, it requires the board and the CEO to have substantial cricket knowledge and the integrity to match it. But before anything can change, there has to be an acceptance and agreement among all those involved in the running and functioning of NZC's showpiece that there are still numerous challenges to be confronted.

EIGHT
KILLING BOWLERS WITH KINDNESS

THE HYPOTHESIS CONSTANTLY BEING ECHOED IS THAT OVERUSE IS THE root cause of injury to bowlers, and particularly among the medium to fast-medium variety. However, my contention is bowlers are being 'killed with kindness', by being under-bowled rather than the opposite. Moving from Twenty20 leagues straight into Test matches certainly increases the risk of injury.

Fitness gurus today see physical fitness as being of paramount importance and yet bowlers are being wrapped up in cotton wool. Isn't this a contradiction? Is bowling that dangerous to physical health for adults? Doug Ackerly in his book *Front Foot* has some interesting things to say about the change in the no-ball rule (changing from drag markers for the back foot to the front foot rule) and its possible relevance to bowling injuries.

It's reached the point where teams are adding an extra bowler or expecting part-timers to share perceived overloading. Is there a next move allowing bowlers to have replacement fielders? They already have an endless supply of food and beverage (on ice) on the boundary at deep fine leg and third man, plus during any breaks in play. Batting low in the order can often result in spending as much as half the duration of a match sitting around with their feet up in the shade.

Before we know it the poor old batsmen will be angling for time off. If a batsman is having a successful match, are his psychological and physical workloads too demanding? Ah, I forgot — bowlers belong to the sweating trade and the batsmen are the 'posers' who don't even need to break into a sweat!

I'm not aware of other sportsmen and women putting themselves through only a fraction of the workloads their sports require in preparation for, and during, competition. For instance, athletes don't train for marathons by running 5–10 kilometres, nor do cyclists only train a couple of days a week nor cycle over much shorter distances than their races require, or get to put their feet up for half their event. I'm not claiming that the physical fitness levels required to play international cricket are within cooee of many sports, but I am saying, use it or lose it. A well-planned bowling fitness programme needs to have reached the levels required in advance of impending commitments. The workloads thereafter should retain the same intensity to reduce the risk of injury. When considering the gaps between Test matches, and even the rest periods during games, there is sufficient recovery time without the need to give bowlers matches off. To do so is more likely to undo some of the good work already carried out than anything else. Continuity of play is more likely to add to the endurance, stamina and psychological strength of not just bowlers, but all players. I'm not suggesting that players should be playing for the full 52 weeks in the year, but if fast bowlers, in particular, are going to pay attention to staying fit and healthy, they need to be vigilant in their preparation before returning from a break.

In the longer forms of cricket, bowlers, other than spinners, need to be prepared for 25–30 overs in a day's play and then be fit enough to repeat it the following day if necessary.

Researching comparisons of bowling workloads through the decades, I went back as far as the 1920s, and found the number of overs bowled by individuals today is far fewer than those bowled by their predecessors. In his book, Ackerly conducted a considerable amount of research confirming this result. He adds that the modern quickie is also probably sending down fewer deliveries in the nets. The assumption that an increase in the international playing programme of countries has resulted in bowlers' workloads having increased is simply not true. In fact, in the last decade or more we've seen a significant reduction of overs bowled by individuals. I think it is reasonable to suggest that this can be largely attributed to the prominence and greater influence exerted by physiotherapists, fitness trainers, biomechanists, a generally more indulgent society and players' associations pushing the notion of pastoral care. It has also become normalised to give players games off to so-call 'charge their batteries' — all very nice and caring, but I'd suggest it's not assisting bowlers' health, nor is it performance enhancing.

This action of time off is also applied to batsmen, particularly if they are having a lean run. I could think of nothing worse, unless it provides an opportunity for a player to get some runs at a lower level, or the player in question needs to be replaced. Otherwise what is being achieved, other than increasing the inevitable anxiety? There seems to be a snowballing number of acts that undermine mental strength, softening rather than hardening, evading rather than confronting.

In the 1920s, the likes of Maurice Tate bowled around 1500 overs in an English season, and another 600 if he toured with England in their winter. Ray Lindwall managed 1122 in 1952. In the early 1960s, Fred Trueman bowled around 1100 overs per county season alone. In 1969, Graham McKenzie bowled 1324 overs, the South African Mike Procter, when playing for Gloucestershire in the late 1970s, bowled 800–900 overs in county cricket and batted at number four in the order. In the 1981–82 season, Richard Hadlee bowled 1131 overs. In the 1998–99 season, the England seamers generally had higher workloads than other international players. For example, Andrew Caddick bowled 910 overs, Dean Headley 792. Courtney Walsh bowled 437 overs for the West Indies and another 600 overs for

Gloucestershire. Internationally, Sean Pollock bowled 515 and Glenn McGrath 740.

During this period the New Zealand seamers who bowled most overs were Shane O'Connor (533) and Chris Cairns (497). In the 2011 calendar year, Chris Martin bowled 358, Tim Southee 297 and Kyle Mills 257. At the time, even these workloads were considered to be excessive by New Zealand standards.

Further examples of some recent recognisable names and their average annual workloads are: Dale Steyn 477 overs, Morne Morkel 390, Peter Siddle 439, Ishant Sharma 454, and Stuart Broad 584.

In March 2012, I wrote that one of the reasons given for New Zealand selecting squads of 14 players for the home ODI and T20 series against Zimbabwe was to control bowling workloads. That made me suspicious, so I checked the amount of bowling the selected players had done between the second Test in Australia ending on 12 December 2011 and the start of the ODI series against Zimbabwe on 3 February.

The number of overs bowled by each of the players in the mix at that time during those 51 days was: Andrew Ellis 56, Kyle Mills 53, Michael Bates 46, Doug Bracewell 44, Tim Southee 43, and Jacob Oram 27.

Contradictions abound. Increasing workloads for bowlers in preparation for Tests is understandably said to be important. I agree. Why then were Bracewell and Southee both rested from three and two ODIs respectively to 'freshen up' for the upcoming three Tests against South Africa beginning on 7 March, when their workloads since 3 February were for Southee a combined 36 overs in the four of six ODIs he played in during that period, while Bracewell similarly in three games bowled 26 overs? Perhaps fortuitously, in their return to the Test arena, it may have helped that Southee was only required to bowl 10 overs in the first innings and Bracewell 16.2 overs, due to South Africa totalling a modest 238. The absence of thorough preparation was about to take another twist. Southee was dropped for the second Test against South

Africa after not taking a wicket in either innings and was sent back to play first-class cricket to rediscover his confidence and work on his action.

This is just another example of selectors either being cut out of the selection process or being misled by so-called experts specialising in other occupations.

In 2017, in assessing the workloads on Trent Boult and Tim Southee, I may have missed a handful of overs they bowled in some T20 league I haven't been able to track down, but their figures were:

Boult: (Tests) 211.4 overs, (ODIs) 144.2, (T20s) 21, (IPL) 24. Total overs = 401.

Southee: (Tests) 126.2, (ODIs) 125.2, (T20s) 10, (IPL) 10, (Natwest T20 Blast) 45. Total overs = 316.4.

Other possible causes of injuries to bowlers in relatively recent times could be attributed to the substantial increase in the modification of bowling actions. If a bowler is deemed to have a biomechanically 'at risk' action (often referred to as a mixed action), avoiding a refit will not be easy. My question — yet to receive a convincing answer — is, does current knowledge provide enough solid evidence to replace past practices, or is the degree of understanding still too experimental to be applied to international bowlers? County cricket in England with its extremely full programme over many decades was proof enough that uninterrupted play for all players had worked very successfully.

What are the risks of altering the action of a bowler who has over many years conditioned himself to deliver a cricket ball in a particular way, a way which may follow the path of least resistance for his body type? At what stage can an action be changed, and to what degree, before the risk of injury or further injury increases? What are the time-lines, workloads, strength and conditioning work applicable to bowling actions when making a change? How much is known about repairing and preparing the body to bowl? Jimmy Anderson at one point in his career was talked into altering his action, but following some setbacks he decided to return to his old one. The change was not only unsuccessful in preventing injury, but also reduced his swing and pace.

The jury still seems to be out on dealing with this whole issue. Some people are happy to go along with the view that in today's world, young people's lifestyles make them less physically capable. I suppose that's true of the general public, but with trained sportspeople spending much more time in the gym, I would lean more towards the view that today's society makes it more difficult for players to become as mentally strong as some past generations. Part of that can lead to looking for shortcuts, not being prepared to put in the hard yards.

Ackerly has tackled the whole question surrounding bowling actions and the associated impacts, causes and effects over time using numerous examples. A staff member of a recent touring England team told me the research they did showed that many successful bowlers from past decades had, by today's reckoning, dangerous 'at risk' actions. The conclusion was that by building up to and then keeping their high workloads up, any extra biomechanical strain on their bodies was counteracted by the added strengthening created by repetition. This being so, where does all the prominence of today's gym work lead to? Perhaps mostly superficial self-esteem when taking your shirt off in public!

NINE

NZC LOST IN POWER STRUGGLES

In early April 2014 after about a year spent in the wake of the turmoil caused by Taylorgate, I summarised some thoughts challenging the obvious conflicts that continued to play out at New Zealand Cricket and I present those thoughts here.

Recently, New Zealand has been performing well, very well on occasions, and that is good to see. We have some first-class performers, especially, but not exclusively, in one-day cricket. We have a fine crop of medium-fast bowlers, for instance, a couple of highly accomplished batsmen in the top order, and some very good hitters to back them up. With the right sort of governance, we could be consistently better more often, because players would have an improved chance to further develop their potential. Time after time over many years, NZC as a whole has been let down by the absence of good governance, in particular, the areas directly related to the performance and the wellbeing of its elite players — pampering is no solution. Too often I have witnessed policies that have undermined the progress of players and in some cases added to their tendency to self-destruct. Policies closely related to 'spoilt-child syndrome'. NZC's approach has been largely driven by the fear that players may make themselves unavailable. I offer some examples and a few thoughts on these further on.

It ought not to be necessary to preface what one has to say about the great and fascinating game of cricket with the above preamble. But as I see it, it is, because, given the nature of many who administer cricket and of those who play, follow, write and talk about the game, anything other than 'good news' and 'plumping' is often deemed 'negative' and too hard to handle. I found myself in agreement with some observations made recently by Professor Dean Helton — details of which I will refer to later.

My principal concern and interest in cricket all along has been, and remains, with looking at ways to refine and improve performance. In order to do that you need a group of people prepared to open their minds to debate and learning, to carefully observe, and have the knowledge and insight and experience needed to interpret what they see and hear. That means working at trying hard to differentiate between reality and illusion. It's too easy to get caught up in the moment, be it good or bad, get side-tracked, and lose perspective. It's essential that those in charge produce constructive, well-thought-through policies for the future, ones that are solidly founded in logic with guardianship of the game uppermost in their reckoning.

Cricket at the elite level in New Zealand continues to be marred by power struggles, posturing, excesses, self-interest, conflicts of interest, contradictions, and back-stabbing. There's much that's been neglectful in the running and the playing of the game. Recent attempts to salvage something from the wreckage have once again been largely thwarted by the incumbents and it looks like more of the same. The band keeps playing the same convenient tune about welcoming and engaging in robust, inclusive, transparent, open and honest debate. The reality is much of that is locked away in a tomb somewhere in the middle of the Sahara or perhaps closer to home in a spin doctor's cupboard. Questioning and legitimate dissent is viewed as disloyal, unpatriotic. Truths are too uncomfortable, too hard to handle. That's been the long and short of it for years.

Some senior players in particular are very supportive of this approach because it helps them to retain the power they have been given. I suppose the justification is why put the energy into changing or improving a system when it's far easier to use the existing one? It should not be surprising that coach and captain reviews are used to justify, promote and reinforce previous decisions not to examine or challenge them. As with many failures, they can often be traced back to the initial mistake. The assumption appears to be that as soon as significant money arrives at the door of a sport, the money-men, or those in associated occupations, are seen as the ones needed to run the game. History tells us they would be better served trying to sort out their own mess. The 2008 global financial crisis is a recent reminder of that. In my view, there is no substitute for people with a considerable knowledge of the sport to be the directors of it. At least they're far more likely to make decisions that not only have a better chance of working, but also result in, hopefully, more prudent spending. A common theme arising from judges in courts of law handing out sentences to directors of failed companies is that in the future, directors need to know more about the subject they are governing. This message seems to have escaped the attention of some consultants advising on the personnel and makeup of boards.

In May 2016, New Zealand Cricket decided to do a survey of its former international players and a questionnaire was sent out to all those qualified. I responded to the request to take part by saying that for a number of reasons I wouldn't participate. I did, however, write a letter to the members of the board of New Zealand Cricket saying I would sooner email them individually to express some of my fundamental concerns while also informing them of what I had observed, and experienced, over many years of constrained involvement in the organisation. I told them that by emailing them directly I could guarantee I would reach them while also emphasising I did not require the protection of anonymity as suggested in the survey. The board members at the time were: Stuart Heal (chairman), Geoff Allott, Greg Barclay, Neil Craig, Liz Dawson, Richard Hadlee, Don Mackinnon and Martin Snedden.

My letter to them, on 23 May, continued:

> I will not look in detail at all the concerns I have about many of the decisions made by NZC. Instead, I prefer to focus on what I have observed as the primary reasons for the ongoing failings that undermine NZC as a respected organisation. Take, for instance, power struggles, conflicts of interest, and self-protectionism. Such are not uncommon in our society, but in NZC's case, it's the extent of it that is so damaging. Time consumed in papering over these areas has resulted in the neglect of principled, dynamic thinking and a failure to welcome and engage in open dialogue and embrace soundly produced ideas.
>
> Over the decades that I worked for NZC in various roles, the papers I put forward for discussion were either ignored, or treated with disapproval. NZC has an unenviable record of hiring, firing (pay-outs) and of disillusioned staff leaving voluntarily. Apart from squandering considerable sums of money and losing some of its best talent, the integrity of the organisation continues to suffer. Those are some of the reasons why I applied to be on the board of NZC.
>
> A prime example of self-protection has been demonstrated by the current chairman who has been in the chair for about three years, having previously been a board member for five years. On taking over the chairmanship, he made public statements about one, his desire to talk to as many people as possible and two, utterances alluding to the need for the organisation to be open and accountable. Throughout this period, he has lived 30 minutes' drive away from my house in Wanaka. I'm still waiting for his call!
>
> In my view the questionnaire — though possibly well intended — is not much more than window-dressing. Until NZC stops being guarded, defensive and prejudiced and becomes strong enough to both

stand on principle, and is open to being critiqued, it will continue to be looked upon with distrust.

Yours faithfully,

Glenn Turner.

This resulted in a response from the chairman, Stuart Heal, on 24 May 2016:

Glenn,

Many thanks for your response to our ex-players questionnaire. Your candid views are appreciated at our board and will be discussed along with the other responses and feedback from the questionnaire. I would also like to point out that, despite being eligible for another term, I am not standing for re-election to the NZC board later this year thus creating a vacancy on the board. With that in mind maybe you might consider putting your name forward for consideration.

Kind Regards

Stuart Heal

The timing of this is important. I've invariably been, and am, a counter-puncher. For instance, this email was sent a considerable time after having been turned down in my attempts to become a board member. So one can't be accused of spoiling my pitch in advance. Having said that, many of the papers I had sent through over time challenging the *status quo* were likely to be viewed as doing exactly that! My email was, in part, to test the incumbent board's willingness, or otherwise, to open themselves up to engagement. It helped to eliminate any excuse that they are operating any differently to their predecessors. Heal's reply, although a fob-off, was at least a response of sorts. It was also strange for him to suggest I put my name forward for the board in the future when he must have known full well that I had already done so previously and been rejected. I even mentioned it in my note that I'd applied previously.

Nevertheless, when Richard Hadlee announced his retirement from the board in September 2017, I decided to once again test the workings of NZC. I phoned Sheffield, which was engaged by NZC to short-list Hadlee's replacement. Its representative was quick to tell me that NZC was looking for another accountant to support Neil Craig and that there was enough cricket knowledge already on the board.

My stance on these matters, as I said earlier, is to encourage more discussion/debate in areas where I feel these key aspects of advancement have been neglected in the rush to sell and promote cricket at the expense of questioning and challenging ideas.

Earlier on, I did manage a session with the CEO Justin Vaughan, who at the time responded to everything I had to say in total agreement. Naturally, I wanted at least some of my ideas to be discussed and challenged, but nothing was offered. None of his actions that followed represented what he had agreed with earlier. In hindsight, my conclusions were beware of he who is in total agreement, and he who is prepared to sacrifice principles for the sake of convenience; and when boards follow paths of least resistance, combined with fixed ideas and captains who believe that selection is their responsibility and entitlement.

This was borne out in an exchange I had with Vaughan in the wake of New Zealand's tour to India in 2010. I understood a review of the tour was to take place and queried him by email on 14 December. He replied within five minutes of getting my message: 'Currently ongoing. Very difficult process to get everyone in one place so doing a lot of one-on-one conversations. I'll give you a call tomorrow to get your thoughts.'

The next day I emailed Stephen Boock saying: 'Boocky, After speaking to you, I thought the intention was for this review to take place (if possible this week) with some of your group present?'

He replied, also promptly: 'Good morning. Yes, that's right. The tour review took place Monday. I was there with M Crowe on behalf of the new CC. Boocky.'

I replied to him a little later in the morning: 'And I thought Justin was genuinely trying to be inclusive and re-engage me in the process, silly me. It's not just a question of being promised one thing and then being excluded, it's the dishonesty that goes with it. I have made every effort to give Justin a chance to win back my trust, but this latest episode makes that impossible.'

Geoff Allott, who was director of cricket at the time, did tell me that my exclusion from the review was an oversight, but I knew there was a reluctance to involve me in player reviews because on a couple of previous occasions I had exposed some hard truths, which didn't appear to be welcomed. I thought this was what the process of review was supposed to be about. Everyone deserves that if improvement is the intention and certainly that is what I would want if I was in their shoes. A more cowardly approach of praise alone was seen as acceptable. What was more concerning were the attempts to mask a toxic culture of back-stabbing and dishonesty and the barriers the hierarchy was prepared to put up to conceal it. You challenged it at your peril, as I discovered.

Supporters get a lift when New Zealand performs well. There have been any number of examples of that and the surge in interest when that happens is good for the game. But, too often in New Zealand, good performances have been impossible to maintain at any sort of consistency. A smaller pool of players to choose from compared to our opponents are part of the reason for that, but not the only reason. We need to be smarter than our opponents, especially when we have players with the skills and abilities to achieve greater success, but that doesn't mean losing sight of the fundamentals. At the moment in Kane Williamson, Ross Taylor, Trent Boult and Tim Southee we have a group of players who stack up with any we have produced in New Zealand as the core around which to build a team. However, when players like these emerge, it is absolutely essential that a structure is in place to ensure they, and those chosen alongside them, are able to perform more consistently at their best.

NZC has quite a record of hiring and firing, not honouring contracts and payouts; a record of kicking staff sideways and entering into schemes that any trained eye would tell you wouldn't work from day one. For example, the adoption of the 'Leading Teams' scheme, a system devised by Australians and which had been rejected across the Tasman. That fiasco, which cost several hundred thousand dollars, was taken on board by New Zealand Cricket lock, stock and barrel to the extent that Australians were employed and one shifted to New Zealand to run it. It lasted too long before being dumped as another failure.

In relatively recent times, Saqlain Mushtaq (with a batting average of 14) was flown from London business class (and at an undisclosed fee) to teach the Black Caps batsmen how to pick and play the doosra. Sure, he will have been capable of helping them pick the doosra, but what was really needed was some help with playing spin — obviously not his forte. On the last tour to Sri Lanka, unsuccessful attempts were made to employ Muttiah Muralitharan (batting average of 11) to do something similar.

In the last few years there have been about as many changes to selection policies as there have been coaches. Administrations in the cricketing world (probably not just NZC) continue to adopt a primitive, ill-informed approach to interpreting good and bad performances and who is responsible for what. Their decisions tend to be dominated by expediency, sidelining reality.

England's disastrous Ashes tour in Australia in 2015 is a good example. Alastair Cook was quoted as saying 'I'm totally responsible as captain of the team.' It's a nice gesture, but he would have known that the coach would be first on the hit list. For starters, the team doesn't belong to either of them and, given the nature of cricket, what logical reason is there for them to shoulder the majority of blame for the team's results? The accountability for performance is the personal responsibility of each player and each should be judged individually. They form the parts that are ultimately responsible for the overall performance of the team. With respect to the captain, the difference there is that he needs to be judged mainly on two counts, one as a player and the other for his decision-making performance on the field of play. Likewise, the coach should be accountable for his role, which doesn't include being able to wave some mythical wand that controls every ball the players bowl or play. All the other marginal stuff that keeps being parroted *ad nauseam* and heralded as crucial in the support of the reasons for success or failure and where the buck should stop, is largely irrelevant drivel, masking and, mostly eliminating, what really counts.

Board members are the ones who have been sanctioned to preside over whatever it is they are governing: In the case of cricket, that surely means that CEOs, coaches, captains and players and any other staff members are ultimately servants of the organisation. Therefore, the board's performance and overarching accountability is to the cricket community as a whole. But once again, as with all the other positions in the organisation, the board's performance should only be judged by the success or otherwise of its functioning in carrying out its designated role, not (as is often the case) mainly, if not solely, by the team's on-field results be they good or bad. Ultimately, in teams (more so in cricket) it is still up to the individuals to deliver. I've witnessed the self-congratulatory puffery present around board members when the national team has success. I've already covered their performance in and around the 2015 CWC. But let's also look at their contribution to the 2019 CWC, or should I say lack of it!

Just before it started, the news broke that NZC was in serious financial strife, casting a shadow over the game's future. Its conflict of interest selection policy was once again exposed publicly when the convener of selection (and senior coach) was overruled by the captain regarding the selection of spinner Ish Sodhi over Todd Astle. Intriguingly, as it turned out, Sodhi was only selected for one game during the Cup even when other conditions suited spin. The board rightly arranged three practice matches against Australia in New Zealand and then proceeded to allow nine of its World Cup squad to take leave of absence to remain in India with the opportunity to collect more Indian Premier League (IPL) money. Maybe a generous gift to some of our players' bank accounts (those that were getting game time) and a charitable contribution to Australia's preparation—their players had been released from IPL duties. Wives, partners and families of the players were not only permitted extensive access during the Cup, the cash-strapped organisation provided an additional bus to transport them around the UK.

Invariably, when people from alien occupations invade foreign territory, they tend to abrogate their responsibilities by allowing others to make important decisions. In the case of cricket, the assumption has been made that the captain and players have all the knowledge and will perform better if they get what they want; therefore judging them is seen as unnecessary and unsupportive. It also appears to be perceived as unaccommodating for the board to overrule the wishes of the CEO.

I'm not alone in thinking that successive boards' approaches have, predictably, resulted in the players and CEO learning how best to make life more comfortable and less challenging. It's a very convenient and self-protective way for alien boards to operate, because, in most cases, the full range of arguments on cricketing matters are dodged, not welcomed or required to be presented. Even if they were, these boards are not capable of assessing the substance and accuracy of the arguments, or the minority of those among their number with some background in cricket are either not up to it or not able to persuade the majority. Understandably, the majority have a very limited appreciation of the realities of what goes on inside teams and the effect their decisions have on the politics, functioning and performance of teams. Their lack of in-depth cricket knowledge appears to be judged as being more than compensated for by other skills they may bring to the cricket boardroom table. Too often even those skills are somehow left behind in the corridors of another occupation. With 70 or so staff at head office, along with contracting work out to consultants, you would think that the need for a majority of aliens on boards would be unnecessary and counterproductive.

The new NZC board is still weighted heavily towards people without enough knowledge of cricket: effectively it is a five-two split and although the eighth member has some cricket knowledge, he should have to abstain (because of his conflict of interest with the captain) from just about every cricketing matter that relates to the Black Caps.

The panels that select the boards are largely made up of people who are also in the category of not knowing the subject well enough. Predictably, their sympathy and support will be with their own kind. Unfortunately, many who are successful in getting onto boards are captivated with the game and the players, which appears to be seen as adding weight to their suitability to govern. Being servants of the game is commendable, but problems begin when they are servants of the players. I would argue that decisions made from the heart are seldom what is required.

University of Canterbury psychology professor Deak Helton's research has unearthed some of the less obvious answers to these questions, other than accusations of self-interest, status, satisfying egos, and the like. It may provide some understanding as to why alien boards underperform, even in the areas they should know something about. Helton said that 'when watching sport (even more so when playing it), the brain can only do so many things at once and it starts to reduce activity in the parts that handle the higher cognitive processing — the internal thoughts, deeper thinking, reasoned planning, and the processing of negative emotions.' I suppose this gives some credence to the statement that sport is the opiate of the masses, but unfortunately it seems to extend to the boardroom.

Furthermore, it's not as though a number of the hierarchy at NZC were not involved when 'Taylorgate' reared its ugly head, or when the so-called 'Selection Pie Chart Scheme' was hatched by John Buchanan and sold to them. In the blink of an eye, John and his associate Kim Littlejohn were sidelined, the selection pie rejected and put out for the garbiologists to collect. Partway through his contract Buchanan, who was probably costing NZC more than any other administrative employee, joined Littlejohn and a plethora of former employees who were unceremoniously sent packing. Although I was not convinced about the value of Buchanan's 'Selection Pie Chart Scheme', he and Littlejohn were decent people and didn't deserve the treatment they received.

Their scheme drowned the art of selection in a sea of figures and fluffy estimations and demonstrated insufficient consideration for cricket knowledge and a trained eye. The Pie Chart divides selection into six parts, with a percentage weighting allocated to each area.

- Significant performance = 100s, 5 or more wickets in an innings, catches (35%)
- Consistent performance = averages, strike rates, contribution rates (25%)
- Contribution to team = what do they bring to the team, i.e. leadership, work ethic, mentoring ability (15%)
- Fielding = able to do required core skills to an acceptable standard (10%)
- Fitness = athlete meets the required fitness standard (10%)
- Selectors' intuition = gut feel as to whether the athlete will be able to perform at the required level (5%)

To assume that current players have all the knowledge is to presume that they have reached the pinnacle of their wisdom. It conveniently ignores what more experience and learning over time will contribute to their knowledge. It also avoids the value of history and how it can be applied to benefiting the present and the future. Furthermore, by giving players greater powers off-field (such as involvement in team selections, contracts and the employment and dismissal of support staff), it encourages additional in-house politicking, heightened jealousies and an increased degree of nepotism. Moreover, players' minds get distracted by these power struggles, and for some, entry into business ventures undermines their own ability to perform. The exceptional form and response of Ross Taylor (following his humiliating sacking from the captaincy) in the series against the West Indies and the ODIs against India is a good example of the improvements a player can make when he is freed from all of this nonsense and finds refuge by focusing on his own game. He has had to learn the hard way, that to rely on the support of others is a mistake, too unstable, too risky, makes for fragility.

Brendon McCullum's exceptional performances in the Tests (particularly against India) could be largely attributed to his determination to prove that he was still worth his place in the Test team. This came about in response to a lengthy period of failures and widespread questioning about his place in the Test side after he had given up wicket-keeping. His response adds further weight to the argument that humans are no different to animals in that they run faster when they are either very hungry or being chased.

To sum up, no team belongs to any one coach, captain or senior player. It should be made quite clear that they are in fact servants of the game and the organisation.

If boards fail to take control, be responsible and accountable for the guardianship of the game and its intrinsic values, the whole organisation suffers, not least the potential of the end result.

TEN

CRICKET JUST ANOTHER PRODUCT – FAST FOOD?

Alas, cricket's become just another 'product' like so much else. Some — perhaps many — cricket enthusiasts may find that irritating, but the reality is that the game is being as vigorously promoted and aggressively sold as a whole lot of inanimate objects. When society had fewer distractions and found more time to smell the roses and reflect, more people found the time to involve themselves in the longer forms of cricket. In many ways at that time, cricket mirrored societal behaviour more than any of the other sports that I'm conversant with. Today, England and Australia remain the only two cricketing countries continuing to support Test cricket in large numbers.

'Product' cricket is now attempting to move with the changing times. It may sound logical to some, but is it when it is increasingly undermining the values of the established game? The question is how smart is it to follow an ethos of servicing instant gratification, shorter concentration spans, feeding player greed and entitlement, when the replacement value system is built around reliance upon increasingly exorbitant sums of money for its existence?

The question of sustainability and at what cost immediately comes to mind when so-called progression is often closer to regression and, similarly, growth to decay. The main progress, growth argument for the proliferation of T20 cricket appears to centre on the need for more money to support the overall survival of cricket as we know it. And yet, first-class programmes have already been reduced and there is talk of shortening Tests to four days. In England they are about to start up a 100-ball game and although Test cricket is still well supported there, the main winners from that are the counties with Test grounds. Furthermore, the existence of 50-overs cricket has been under threat for some time. In my estimation it would be more accurate to apply regression or decay to the spread of the T20 product, undermining and degenerating, rather than supporting the survival of cricket as we know it, or has it already become as we knew it — does it matter? Is it realistic to expect the game to reject the worst of societal changes and still be viable as a professional game?

If you don't care much for the survival of endangered species, why would you angst over the old species of cricket if you think it has become a rodent? If so, what's wrong with bringing in a predator to eliminate the rodent? But is it a rodent and what are the ramifications of introducing a predator? It could become a bigger problem in the future. Remarkably quickly the old species can become extinct, a distant memory. Very quickly you don't know what you don't know, so missing it is not an issue. Perhaps amnesia can be a blessing for those of us who have been around for a while!

If there is a genuine desire to retain the intrinsic values of cricket, there surely must be a better approach than money at all costs, or surrendering to the old adage of 'knowing the cost of everything and the value of nothing'. Some better options than selling the soul of the game might be to reduce the number of matches on the international programme, cut some of the administration costs and reduce payments to players. The principle of less is more is being constantly sidelined right across society. Unfortunately, cricket is following the trend.

The 'growth' of the dairy industry in New Zealand is another example of so-called progress demonstrating unsustainable practices where money has also led to greed and entitlement. In their case entitlement to water and, in too many instances, an environmental disregard for ecological considerations all round. *Laissez faire* practices have impacted on their reputation and drawn more attention to critiquing the production of some foods and farming practices as a whole. Alternatives need to be found for all concerned, not least the livelihoods of farmers. Maybe in appropriate places the growing of hemp and the construction of the infrastructure necessary to take advantage of all the products this super plant produces is a helpful solution. In 2017, belatedly, dairy farmers' actions have been challenged at the parliamentary level even prior to the outbreak of the deadly disease *Mycoplasma bovis*. As significant polluters, the dairy industry has had some success in externalising the impact costs onto the taxpayer in New Zealand. It may be prudent to remember that although nature may bat last, it will have the final say! It had the final say at least for a day or two in Queenstown during the 2019 New Year's holiday break. I just happened to be there for a day to witness hordes of tourists sunning themselves on the shores of Queenstown Bay, having been directed not to enter New Zealand's pristine water due to the presence of *E coli*. What a place and timing to advertise New Zealand's clean green sales pitch to the rest of the world! Parallels can also be drawn between what has happened to Queenstown and cricket. Queenstown has become a clogged party town, attracting the younger folk to indulge themselves.

Nikki Macdonald (a journalist for stuff.co.nz) on 24 November 2018 wrote a piece that she had started a year earlier, investigating who uses our water, how much, and for what. Fifteen Local Government Official Information and Meetings Act requests and one Ombudsman's investigation later, she still didn't have reliable answers. She found that 'there was a critical shortage of good data, even though water takes of more than five litres had to be metered by 2016. You'd think it would be easy to get good data on how much water is being used, and by whom.' She added, 'You'd be wrong!'

There is an expression in New Zealand, 'She'll be right, mate'; in Australia, 'No worries, mate'; and in India, 'What to do.' Humanity as a whole appears to have a convenient habit of ignoring anything that might be awkward or troublesome — the inconvenient truth! Even for many of those who might believe the science urging humanity to change its polluting behaviour, it isn't enough to prevent them from assigning blame elsewhere. Those in small populated countries like New Zealand are quick to point the finger elsewhere; excusing and rationalising their behaviour by expressing irrelevancy in comparison to what the bigger populations are doing. Apparently, our inaction is vindicated, because it's up to them to change their ways, not us. Why did New Zealand bother to become the first country in the world to give women the vote when no one else was doing it? I thought we were proud of the fact and believed it was the right thing to do. Similarly, it would be right and honourable to lead the way environmentally or at least take responsibility for our own actions. New Zealand with all the advantages of a relatively small population in a supremely diverse and exquisite landscape will be severely compromised. The same attitude applies to our cricket. In both cases the misuse of entrusted power comes to mind.

The so-called developing countries, who are often those with the largest populations, argue that it's their turn to do what it takes to increase living standards for their middle and lower classes. The most convenient answer seems to be that advances in technology will resolve all. Probably the biggest curse of all is to continue down the path of increasing population growth, to feed the insatiable appetite of the current form of capitalism. We are arguably getting better at dealing with immediate dangers, but that's no defence when preventative measures are still being put on the back burner. To quote George Monbiot, 'tipping points are likely to remain invisible until we have passed them'.

Cricket is yet to implode to the degree of other examples, but don't feel too comfortable because cricket appears to also be heading down an unsustainable path. Similarly, we haven't yet experienced the full effects of global warming and climate change and the possible impact it might have on cricket itself. I may be clinging to straws when I suggest, the results of these crippling changes may contain and restrict the movement of societies where people may have more time to contemplate. Something similar may occur when automation replaces more and more jobs, when the state is driven down the path of paying a universal basic income. It is already under way in Finland where they are currently trialling it for unemployed Finns aged from 25 to 58 with a guaranteed monthly sum of 560 euros replacing their existing social benefits.

Who knows, society may experience a return to the popularity of the longer forms of cricket, but if at all, it would be much further down the track. At that time another new breed of players would also need to emerge with the skills to play the 'new modern game', which existed before the turn of this century!

What are some of the differences between the longest (Tests) and shortest (T20) forms of cricket that make the former worth saving? I've written enough about the core values and spirit of the game. They automatically become more relevant in the longer forms of the game. Tests also require stamina, perseverance, tactical planning and awareness, increased amounts of self-discipline, problem-solving and time for the true character of players to show through in a possible 30-hour, 450-over game.

The following is a brief attempt to look into the factors that define one game from the other. It may be helpful to use the analogy of witnessing the difference between observing a couple of fruit trees throughout their annual journey from the sap rising to the fruiting as compared to, at best, a fleeting glance.

It takes time for the winter cold to subside, making way for the onset of spring, signalling to the roots that it is time for the sap to rise. Soon the warmer temperatures increase enough for the budding and flowering to develop ready for pollination. This is when nature and luck can make its presence felt. Luck good or bad can arrive at any stage. Bee populations fluctuate from one year to the next. Overhead weather conditions play a pivotal role the moment the pollination period begins. The two trees alongside each other will be competing for water all along and the one with the strongest root system has the potential to bear more fruit. But the direction of the wind during pollination may not favour the stronger tree and only part of it may get pollinated. The temperatures during the development period of the fruit may be hotter or cooler than what is ideal. Hotter temperatures will ripen the fruit earlier, whereas colder temperatures will delay ripening. An early frost or a hailstorm may destroy all the fruit. Some years' weather conditions favour bountiful harvests but it is always intriguing to observe the nuances, the ebbs and flows along the way.

The comparison for spectators witnessing a T20 event is only seeing the fruit during the final stages of its journey, a mere snapshot of what could be possible. There are no guarantees of a bountiful harvest or its equivalent in cricket with either event. In the case of a successful Test match, the spectator rewards far outweigh those of a successful minuscule version such as with T20.

In cricket parlance, when defining some of the qualities missing from T20 matches, it's easier and, I hope, as effective to just refer to Tests and the plethora of competencies and awareness ideally needed to play it well. For starters, the ball has an added life of 60 overs. What that brings is an ongoing variety of options developing for batsmen, bowlers and captains as the condition of the ball changes. The chance to take a new ball or delay it at the end of 80 overs opens up another tactical option for the fielding team. Furthermore, field placements are less restricted compared to other limited-over forms of the game, which opens up additional opportunities for more tactical options.

The changing condition of the pitch has plenty of time to make its presence felt from one day to the next and certainly over five days as wear and tear develops. Sweating under the covers can occur during rain delays, freshening up the surface. Overhead weather conditions can also play its part delivering humidity for swing, changing light conditions, shifting wind intensity and direction, and variations in temperature from hot to cold. Players are generally under prolonged pressure due to the length of the game, testing their physical endurance and mental strength. A bowler might be asked to bowl 30 overs in a day and repeat it the following day. A batsman may be required to bat for 12 hours over two days — uncertainty is ever present. Tactical responses are forever changing from defending to attacking and just about everything in between. Sometimes, it's defending to save a game, attacking to win a game, or chasing and setting oppositions a target to chase. You compare that with what's offering in T20 other than saving time for other activities.

For other than the lure of money, what serious bowler would want to travel thousands of kilometres during an Indian Premier League to possibly bowl 50 overs in 30 or so spells, over a 40-day period, while batsmen thrash away at the other end? What satisfaction can a middle-order batsman get from being left with a handful of balls to play a so-called innings on a possible 14 occasions (assuming he bats in every game) over a 40-day period?

Let's flip the coin for a moment and search for a few other thoughts about T20 cricket from a more optimistic angle.

It doesn't matter which form of cricket you are playing or watching, it should be recognised that they all require categorised qualities and an emphasis on some skills more than others, but skills nevertheless. To compromise mastering core skills will invariably come back to haunt every player in all formats of the game.

In short, T20 batting should still be all about good balance, and shot selection. Good balance comes from the correct positioning of the head, which then assists good transference of weight and timing, and shot selection from making good decisions. What then needs to follow is holding good shape throughout the execution of the shot that comes from a solid base, a still head, and by not over-hitting.

Sadly, these core skills in T20 are too often being butchered by players. Players are either succumbing psychologically to the pressure cooker time frame of the game, or have an inability to execute well, or a combination of the two. The most successful innings are still played by applying 'classical cricket shots'. It's frustrating, and possibly amusing, to observe how occasionally a batsman's well-executed innings can, in the latter stages, change to ugly unsuccessful heaves.

The bowlers also seem to be struggling psychologically and too often their execution is poor. I suspect that this is as much to do with the influence of the longer forms of cricket, where they begin the play and batsmen mostly respond according to what is delivered. In T20, more often than not the roles are reversed, whereby the batsman at least attempts to begin the play by making an aggressive pre-emptive movement. In order to compensate for this distraction, bowlers find themselves making last-minute adjustments, causing inconsistency and a general lack of control. Additionally, bowlers will also attempt to anticipate a batsman's pre-ball positioning in advance to try to take back the initiative. The reality is, nevertheless, that most bowlers have less control than one would expect, even at first-class and international level. To confirm that, you only need to recall the days when bowl-offs at an undefended wicket decided the result of tied matches. Hitting the stumps proved embarrassingly difficult. Bowlers in this situation mostly bowled off a much reduced run-up in an attempt to cover up their blushes.

In brief, the bottom line is yorkers bowled at middle and leg stump are still the hardest ball to score from and defend. Precious few bowlers can do it, so they resort to bowling liquorice allsorts, under the pretext that all the variations of line, length and speed will be more effective. I think that would be more effective on another stage, 'singing a rolly bowly ball a penny a pitch'. While this sort of stuff is being dished up, why batsmen see the need to improvise so much and resort to ramping and reverse sweeps is a mystery to me, or is it in both cases simply a matter of a lack of accountability, due in part to it becoming normalised?

The risk of being bowled out within 20 overs and the apparent embarrassment that appears to be associated with it occasionally still creeps into the tactical approach of individuals and teams.

The bottom line for me is I still find T20 cricket ugly, almost unwatchable. I suppose I would need to be side-tracked enough by concern for the result to gain any pleasure from watching it. As I have already alluded to, it can be very difficult for players to play it well and most don't. Additionally, all the other limitations associated with such a massively-shortened version of cricket make it very hard to watch for anyone with an unbiased, educated eye. I imagine the main pleasure for fans of this invention comes more from the joy, belonging, unity and the appeal of partying in an atmosphere created by a large gathering of like-minded supporters of the same team. However, I do think that you can have a game of cricket in 50 overs per side.

Lo and behold just when we thought we had reached the climax of the whittled down form of the game involving teams (excluding double-wicket tournaments), along came a T10 league being played in the Middle East in November 2018. I suppose they needed to spend their black money somewhere. There was great excitement reported in a match played in Sharjah (UAE) between the Sindhis and the Rajputs. Batting first, in their 10 overs the Sindhis scored 94/6. This was chased down within a mere 4 overs by the Rajputs with the rotund wicket-keeper batsman Mohammad Shahzad scoring 74 off 16 balls at a strike rate of 462.50. Shahzad had been criticised for being overweight, but was quick to come to his own defence by saying those scoring high in the fitness tests couldn't hit sixes like him.

The engorgement of limited-over cricket among first-class teams has not been as recent as many might think. Fast-food cricket and quick highs have been around for a number of decades. History tells us that 65-over cricket involving first-class cricketers in England began in 1963, 40-over cricket in 1969, and 55-over cricket in 1972. One-Day Internationals (ODIs) started with 60-over games in 1971. The first inter-county T20 was played in England in 2003 and the inaugural ICC World T20 was played in South Africa in 2007.

Since then, cricket's ruling body has done its best to heighten the spectacle by altering the laws to make it easier to score more runs more quickly. Power plays, field placement restrictions, shorter boundaries and limiting the number of overs each bowler is permitted to bowl have all played their part. The balance between bat and ball is almost impossible to manufacture, because dismissing 10 batsmen within a mere 20 overs (although not impossible) is less likely. Batsmen may argue it's not just a game set up for them. Their longevity at the crease is severely compromised because of the extremely risky options they are forced into making. The potential of a few hefty blows disappearing 20 rows back into the stands is meagre compensation.

The bowlers might justifiably be thinking they are being used as cannon fodder for batsmen to show off their muscle while they also pilfer most of the emotional admiration from spectators. But bowlers still begin the play, regardless of the possible soft-shoe shuffling going on at the other end, so they have the initial power to determine what happens next. A disciplined, tightly-controlled approach would logically be the most sensible answer. Instead, what is often witnessed is a scattered confetti approach, performed under the guise of allegedly keeping the batsmen guessing. More to the point, I suspect it is merely attempts to conceal a lack of skill and mental fortitude. The other side of that coin is an unrealistic expectation that bowlers can find some consistency while bowling a limit of 4 overs in an innings in as many as three or four spells.

To counter that, batsmen might respond by uttering, what about the lack of balls we can justifiably face to play ourselves in? Oh well, never mind — if animals are expected to perform in circuses and are well feed, why not humans, I suppose!

Around the time of the 30 January 2018 IPL Auction, Heath Mills, chief executive of the New Zealand Cricket Players Association, told the *New Zealand Herald* when referring to the auction process, 'I think the whole system is archaic and deeply humiliating for the players, who are paraded like cattle for all the world to see.' A sceptic of T20 might suggest the Mills comment is in keeping with this form of the game and its benefactors. Mills was endorsing a tweet from Peter Clinton, a former chief executive of Wellington Cricket, who said: 'The IPL Auction is such an undignified, cruel and unnecessary employment practice. Ridiculous that it exists today, belongs in the medieval ages.' Mills went on to say: 'There's a lot of good things about the Indian Premier League and it's been great for cricket but I'd like to see it mirror the rest of professional sport in the way they engage athletes. Some players do exceptionally well out of it but the vast majority would like to see the system changed. They would like to negotiate with coaches and owners behind closed doors.'

Mills' criticism centred upon the players' lack of control over their own destiny. Under the auction system, they are commodities, available to the highest bidder, and have no input as to where they play. He said: 'The players enter the auction not knowing where they are going, who their team-mates are going be, who's managing them, who the owners are — no other sports league in the world engages players on that basis. We've seen some players play for five or six teams over the 10 years the league has been going. Coaches cannot build an affinity with players, they can't build a long-term culture. Players' associations around the world would like to see it change.'

Supporters seeking to identify with a club have also traditionally valued a mix of continuity and new signings, although the IPL's heavy turnover does not seem to have hampered its popularity, as it has become an irresistible part of the world cricketing calendar.

The league was founded by the Board of Control for Cricket in India (BCCI) in 2008. The IPL has an exclusive window in the ICC Future Tours Programme. The important question here is, was it a mistake to give the IPL so much relevance and to what extent has it undermined the world of cricket as a whole? Someone else can write their next book answering that question.

The reality is, even if player associations succeed in convincing the BCCI and the various franchise owners that players must be employed for more than one tournament, what will this actually achieve? It is quite common for international players to have four or more contracts annually with different teams and therefore as many coaches, who also have no guarantee of holding on to their positions. Even if you believe in the warm fluffy stuff of what coaches provide at this level, building affinity with players and establishing long-term cultures over a few weeks each year is unadorned fantasy.

What also springs to mind is how realistic is it for players or those representing them to be treated other than as commodities? Expecting big money, guaranteed selection for more than one tournament and effectively dictating to the owner the composition of their teams is unrealistic. The suggestion of the IPL being great for cricket is erroneous and more to do with self-interest than the good of the whole.

ELEVEN

GAME PLANS FOR ODIS

When serving my most recent stint as a New Zealand cricket selector, I believed that we should be doing everything possible to get the best out of our cricket resources, especially in preparation for significant events, and most often for Cricket World Cups. Part of this process was to prepare discussion papers aimed at provoking discussion towards achieving preparedness that would make New Zealand as competitive as possible. Sadly, I never got the feeling that my efforts were particularly welcome and left me feeling that New Zealand Cricket was doomed to continually attempting to reinvent the wheel when there was no need. The expertise has always been available in the country but too often it has been overlooked, whether local or foreign. With that in mind I have presented in this chapter four papers I made available to New Zealand Cricket. On 16 March 2006, I produced a discussion paper headed 'Raising the Bar or Settling for Mediocrity?' It was a year in advance of the Cricket World Cup due to begin in the West Indies on 13 March 2007. I followed this up with another paper, in October 2006, titled 'Game Plans for ODIs'. I decided to continue on with a short paper on 'Improvised Batsmanship' in January 2010, and 'Planning to Win the Next World Cup in 2015' in January 2012. My efforts were ignored.

My intention was to tease out the arguments by challenging some of the mantras that I believed were holding back the progress of our national team and, for that matter, other teams too. So what were, and remain (some still remain), some of the fallacies that handicap the potential of teams, and more often than not lessen their chances of winning games?

Raising the Bar or Settling for Mediocrity?

(March 2006)

As part of the build-up to the 2007 Cricket World Cup in the West Indies, I think the most significant thing that can happen is for a critical analysis (review) of our one-day game. Any other work that may be carried out will be largely wasted if our application is not maximised. The following is an attempt to start the ball rolling.

At a time when most cricketing countries are thinking about preparing for the next World Cup, a One-Day International is played between two of the top teams (Australia and South Africa) whereby a score of 434 has been successfully chased down. Most teams have probably realised the need to work out how they might muster up 300-plus, but so far they seem to be as reluctant as we are to face up to what needs to be done to achieve it. This new benchmark figure that has just been set in South Africa must surely be a major wake-up call for all concerned. It has taken the top team Australia to lead the way past 400, challenging their opposition to throw caution to the wind, break all their prejudices and pre-conceived notions. South Africa replied with a score well beyond their wildest dreams. They would need to have overcome all the theories that have in the past limited the possibility of such a score becoming reality.

If we are serious about progressing our game it may be helpful to be reminded about New Zealand's quarter-final match against Australia in the 1996 World Cup in India (Madras), when New Zealand made 286 batting first. Although this match is 10 years ago and two World Cups old, the strategy used gave us a shot at beating a side superior to our own. Not backing off our strategy helped us to psychologically overcome the poor start we made when we were 16/2 and 44/3, and at one point were within reach of scoring 320. At that time 250 was considered a good total. In fact, New Zealand beat England with 239 and the Aussies could only muster 241 in the final.

Unless selectors, management and in particular senior players are prepared to accept and action the approach required to break the shackles of limitation, teams will continue to under-achieve. For top-order batsmen to settle for strike rates in the low 70s is no longer good enough. Crowe, Greatbatch and Turner were achieving around that figure 20–30 years earlier when 220 was a good total, when far fewer field placement restrictions made scoring quickly more difficult, when outfields were generally slower, and boundaries longer. On a good day many are still limiting themselves to a strike rate in the low 80s. It should be obvious that even if everyone is having a good day and strikes at a rate of 85, the team total is still only going to be around 255 plus a few extras. The bottom line has to be that on a good day a top-order batsman needs to strike at 100-plus. In reality a successful batsman on a good day needs to strike at 120. For this to be possible, a number of pre-conceived prejudices that appear to have become mantras need to be overcome.

I've already mentioned in an earlier email some of those that paralyse the potential of a team. The following is an attempt to provide further explanation.

1) The need for a player to bat through the innings.

Immediately this places restrictions on a player, encouraging a conservative approach to a game that can't afford it. Furthermore, this runs contrary to the need to approach every delivery with a mind-set of attack first and only defend if necessary. Anchoring an innings from one end places enormous and unnecessary pressure on what then needs to be done at the other end. When 40-over cricket (John Player League) was first introduced in England in the late 1960s, sides used this approach, until teams became better at the game and realised it was a luxury they could ill afford. I remember Lancashire's Harry Pilling presumably being asked to adopt this role, even in 40-over matches. Sure, Harry's job also included turning over the strike to provide chances for some very good hitters at the other end, such as Clive Lloyd, Farokh Engineer and David Hughes. Undoubtedly, Lancashire were very successful in limited-over cricket in the '70s, but the luxury of this strategy soon became redundant. It became recognised that possibilities, opportunities and flair should be opened up from both ends, overcoming the fear of not batting out your allotted number of overs.

2) Go (attack) from one end.

This is aligned to 1) above. Once again a strategy aimed at conserving wickets, not prioritising runs.

3) Keep wickets in hand for the final overs (often last 10 overs).

Why conserve wicket resources for a final fling at the end when they could have been used more productively throughout the innings when opportunities arose? It's as though the main purpose of the innings is to make sure the team is not bowled out in less than the subscribed number of overs — a sense of saving face! A perfect recent example of just how ridiculous it is to follow an ongoing, ill-conceived theory was the first ODI against the West Indies at Wellington. New Zealand batting first reaching 224 from 39.2 overs before losing their second wicket — the so-called ideal scenario had arrived? In the remaining 10 overs and four balls they lost a further 7 wickets for the addition of only 64 runs.

4) The need to consolidate after the loss of wickets.

This applies where it is early or sometimes even late in the innings.

Consolidation is often perceived as a period when scoring runs is of little relevance and the major priority is not to lose another wicket. I'm not suggesting that losing wickets is ideal, but stagnation is not an option. So often this approach compounds the problem, allowing the opposition to continue its ascendancy. The most recent example of not falling into this trap was expressed by Ross Taylor in the final one-day international against the West Indies in Auckland. He arrived at the crease with New Zealand at 8 for 2 after 4.2 overs. He immediately took the initiative and momentum away from the West Indies by continuing to be aggressive (not reckless) scoring 32 from 29 balls. The worry now is his senior peers getting into his ear and convincing him this is not the way to approach that situation.

5) We only need X number of runs per over.

The danger with this is that once the figure has been achieved within the over, future scoring opportunities are put on hold. Conversely, if the run rate hasn't been achieved by late in the over, high-risk options are taken.

6) He's a good finisher so we don't want to use him too early.

Good finishers are generally facing the opening or faster bowlers in the 'death overs' when the field is at its most defensive and what is more, when the ball is likely to be reversing. Why is someone with that ability not used at more opportune times (e.g. during the power plays)? On a good day, so-called 'finishers' could be left with enough overs to start and finish the job!

7) We can't afford to lose more than X number of wickets by Y number of overs.

It's difficult enough dealing with the present let alone second-guessing the future.

Individual hundreds appear to be celebrated without scrutiny. So often the player in question wastes several valuable balls in the 90s focusing on a personal milestone at the expense of what is needed for the team. The strike rates of the three hundreds scored by New Zealanders in the recent two ODI series were Fulton (85), Vincent (87) and Astle (93). If Astle hadn't faced the last three balls of the innings, his strike rate would have been 81. Too often, a player scoring a hundred may well have lost the game for his side.

Pre-match talk can often centre on what a good score would be on 'this pitch' or in 'these conditions'. These are just other dumb distractions! The answer should be 'as many as you can get' and any pre-determination very likely only serves to inhibit.

Enough for the moment, I've merely made a start to get things under way. I hope some serious discussion can follow, because sadly in the past it's as though these sort of discussions have been in the too-hard basket. On reflection, it was probably considered to have come from the wrong source.

Update note: On further reflection, what I can say about the New Zealand team's focus in the 1996 quarter-final against Australia had been an emphasis on batting and how to score more runs. At that time, there was a greater acceptance of the reasoning behind the definition of 'attacking bowling'. Put succinctly, 'attacking bowling is tight bowling'. It came from knowing and understanding the value of restricting run scoring, by knowing that by restricting scoring opportunities in a 300-ball innings, batsmen were frequently forced into taking risky options.

Fundamentally, bowl dot balls and the wickets take care of themselves! Set good fields and bowl to them. Of course, a batsman can be nicked out with the new ball, but discipline and personal responsibility were high on bowlers' priority lists. In more recent times, many bowlers appear to be sucked into believing that the tactical answer to bowling is to dish up a mixed bag of generous goodies for even tail-end batsmen to enjoy. No need for batsmen to improvise, to try to make something out of nothing (although they still tend to do so) when donations are on their way. I wonder if this lack of discipline and accountability has been fostered since player power has become more influential.

I suspect it has been a long time since a New Zealand side has had as much depth in their ranks, and two batsmen ranked in the top 10

(Williamson at 6, Taylor at 9) and a bowler at number 3 (Boult). As long as the current crop of players conform to their annual contracts by being available for all of New Zealand's playing programme, and their bowlers are set intelligent fields, more good results are a distinct possibility.

Game Plans for ODIs

(October 2006)

There are two fundamental differences in the emphasis between limited-over games and non-limited-over games. When batting, a greater emphasis should be placed on scoring runs rather than conserving wickets. When bowling and fielding, the emphasis needs to be on restricting runs rather than searching for wickets. Perceived defensive bowling can automatically become attacking bowling by the pressure it creates on the batting team to score more quickly, therefore meeting both the objectives of conserving runs and getting wickets. The stark reality is that no wickets need be taken to win a game, it is solely the runs differential between the two competing sides that determines the result. In fact, a team could be bowled out in just about any number of overs less than the prescribed number and still have enough runs to win. Likewise, not a single wicket need be taken to win a game! In other words, runs override wickets lost or the number of overs batted. Generally speaking, wickets taken in the first half of an innings slows the progress of the batting side, but not always. It can be helpful to the fielding team for some opposition batsman to remain at the crease if they are stalling the progress of run making. Fundamentally, the overall approach should represent strategies aligned to winning games rather than hoping the opposition plays poorly enough to lose.

SOME GOOD EXAMPLES of the aforementioned views were played out in the 2019 CWC semi-final between New Zealand and India. Opening the bowling, Matt Henry's first 5 overs produced figures of 3 for 13, having snared 3 of the first 4 wickets to fall — a Man of the Match performance. In between times, Trent Boult had removed Virat Kohli, and India were reeling at 24/4. Henry's success came from getting the ball to swing from an immaculately tight off-stump line, on an ideal length to the right-handers. By consistently landing the ball in the right area, he restricted run scoring and took wickets at the same time. In this instance his wickets were not due to forcing the batsman to take risks to up the run rate (that comes later with my next example), because against accurate new ball bowling the batsmen were forced into survival mode. Importantly, Henry didn't go searching for wickets with wasted or loose deliveries that would have opened up easier scoring opportunities.

After the collapse, the partnership that followed between Rishabh Pant and Hardik Pandya reinforced the mistake of being too cautious about retaining their wicket with little attention to scoring runs. When they came together, the run rate was 2.4, and 13 overs later when Pant was dismissed it had only increased to 3.1. When Pandya lost his wicket in the thirty-first over (India at 92/6), the run rate had stayed at about the same, 3.1. When Ravindra Jadeja joined Dhoni, India still wanted 147 and the asking rate had blown out to 7.8 runs per over. India had left themselves too much to do, and even Jadeja's 77 from 59 balls couldn't get them home.

So what had gone wrong and what had gone right during this period of play? New Zealand's first change bowler Lockie Ferguson bowled 6 overs for 13 runs and Santner came on and bowled a maiden over to Pandya followed by four dot balls to Pant who felt the pressure to score and proceeded to slog out to de Grandhomme stationed at Cow Corner. Santner wasn't getting any turn to speak of, but was very accurate, and with the pressure mounting Pant had opted for a high-risk option. Pandya followed Pant 7 overs and four balls later in precisely the same manner. By then Santner had bowled 6 overs 2/7. This was a prime example of tight bowling becoming attacking wicket-taking bowling — no need to bowl any magic balls.

We were also witnessing further examples of the effects of T20 batting where the art of collecting runs has been largely exchanged for boundary hitting at all costs. Unlike 50-over cricket that requires a wider range of skills, not just block slogging.

The following is a continuation of what I'd written in 2006 about 'Game Plans for ODIs' before I added in these thoughts from the 2019 CWC.

The abovementioned fundamentals are solid guiding principles when establishing and following game plans. They appear so simple and logical, easy to follow and yet so often they are ignored or sidelined at the expense of more comfortable and accommodating actions. It is often seen as unnecessary, too hard or uncomfortable for players and teams to make changes to their game, particularly if the status quo is relatively successful or most individuals' positions are secure. However, international sport should not be comfortable for those involved, not if the boundaries are to be constantly challenged and extended. The suggested changes being put forward in this piece are relatively easy to adopt because they do not involve the time-consuming process of technical change. It's all about doing more with what you already possess.

The most significant and immediate improvement that can be made to everyone's game (to varying degrees) is to have a better understanding and acceptance of the importance of accurate decision-making. There are some very simple applications which will allow players to apply the skills they already possess for greater reward. More focused thought processes during match performance is critical. The objective is to cancel out negative influences and free up practised memory to take control of decisions and their execution. Research has shown (with a selection of elite athletes in a variety of sports) that just prior to game performance, brain activity is very active, however during the execution of the performance, brain activity hardly registers. A further requirement for immediate improvement is a solid understanding of your own game, and how to approach it. Consistency comes with repeating a successful method and becoming good at it. A good understanding of the game, at least by the decision-makers, is also very helpful in knowing when to use the talents of each individual helping them to go about playing their practised game. Only then will the shackles of limitation be broken.

Pre-conceived theories about planning in advance the way you want the team's innings to be constructed is a mistake (e.g. setting run targets when batting or bowling). This seriously risks denying or ignoring the opposition's performance and automatically creates unnecessary restrictions and barriers. An innings should be allowed to evolve, able to take on its own dynamics, free from pre-conceptions. A consistently dynamic approach to the game by its players opens up limitless and unrestricted possibilities. With this in mind, when batting, a good score is as many as you can get, and when bowling, a good performance is restricting the opposition to as few runs as possible.

Batting first (setting a total)

The full focus of batsmen (without distraction) should be on playing up to their line of competence (maximum ability) in response to the playing conditions (pitch, overhead and field placements) and reacting (with a clear mind) positively to each and every delivery bowled. Put another way, you do the best you can with each and every ball.

Fundamentally, the approach is to think attack first, defend second and look to do something with every ball bowled. It is a proactive approach in terms of being aggressive and looking to dominate the opposition. It is important for each individual to understand their game, its application and the confidence that goes with it. It is then a case of repeating this approach consistently so that one becomes very good at it.

The batting resources of a team need to be carefully managed, in order to match the natural skills of the player to the situation. Asking the player to change their natural/practised game to meet a situation unsuited to their game should be avoided whenever possible. Other than in the case of a pinch hitter, who may well manoeuvre his feet into positions to try to dominate (attempting to make something out of nothing), most batsmen need to respond consistently to what is delivered — bearing in mind the field placements. Literally the response needs to be ball-by-ball rather than following some pre-determined plan ignoring the immediate reality of what is or isn't possible in dealing with that ball.

Ideally, the same players need to be consistently opening the batting. One or two others with the appropriate skills need to be consistently batting at 3 and 4 while the field restrictions are still in place. It must be remembered that decisions on where players are positioned in the batting order represents what is good for the team, not what satisfies the possible whim of the player. As a rule of thumb, the most effective batsmen for the prevailing circumstances should be at the crease with as many overs remaining as possible and they must be encouraged to execute their most valued game.

Batting second (chasing a total)

Largely the strategy remains the same as for batting first, particularly if chasing a sizeable total. If chasing a more modest total, the batting order and approach in the field restriction overs (currently 20) should remain the same. Thereafter, the batting order should be in response to what is required to be done. This doesn't mean that any of the batsmen change their practised game; it merely means that those chosen to do the job required are more likely to have tighter techniques.

The danger in chasing small totals is falling for the old adage of 'if we bat out our overs we will have scored the runs necessary to win'. I have witnessed it so often (and even believed it when I played) when individuals and teams make hard work of chasing small totals, even to the point of losing games, because of their changed, overly cautious/negative approach. To break from the certainty and confidence of a practised batting plan is counterproductive. To be defending balls that are normally put away is simply allowing negative influences in (thought processes) and to become distracted by focusing on the end goal. The critical element of dealing with each ball on its merits has been sidelined and decision-making compromised. The chances are that shot execution also suffers due to poor positioning of the feet and a lack of balance. The fundamental and established mind-set of attack first, defend second, being aggressive and looking to do something with every ball, is also lost. Moreover, the change of approach towards conserving wickets generally fails due to self-inflicted attacks of negativity.

Bowling first

For a time the popular view was to focus on conserving runs, but more recently the pendulum has swung very much towards taking wickets. As mentioned at the beginning of this piece, the reality is that no wickets need be taken to win games and that attempting to take wickets should not be done at the expense of runs. My contention is that tight bowling should be the top priority as it automatically applies pressure in a 300-ball innings, forcing batsmen into error as they attempt to make something out of nothing. Attacking bowling is tight bowling; bowl dot balls and the wickets take care of themselves at least as often and at a reduced strike rate.

Team totals have increased markedly over recent years and although this can be attributed to a number of factors, a cavalier approach to bowling and an emphasis on taking wickets, at just about any cost, has certainly contributed to it. The ability of batsmen to attack has improved, along with a greater eagerness to play the big shot. In the process, the ability and/or willingness to defend have deteriorated. This surely then raises the question, what is attacking bowling, particularly in the context of limited-over games? How can it be considered more attacking to dish up balls that provide more attacking options, under the pretence of forcing a mistake? Isn't it more attacking to force the batsmen into attacking deliveries they should be defending and at the same time conserving runs? If batsmen are not very good at defending, why shouldn't the focus be on getting them to defend as often as possible, or forcing them into the high-risk attacking shot? It should be remembered that the bowler begins the play; he can make it easy or difficult for the batsmen. It is much easier for a bowler to take a less-disciplined approach by bowling a mixture of deliveries varying in line and length, whereby consistency can be conveniently ignored. I suspect a lack of accountability in this area is largely responsible for the drop in standards.

There appears to be an obsession about the speed of bowlers, the assumption being the faster the better! This judgment tends to support the mantra 'we need bowlers who can bowl wicket-taking deliveries'. In the meantime, large totals are being scored! Additional pace may satisfy a macho instinct, but does it restrict run-scoring opportunities or take more wickets? My answer is, only if it is well directed. Quite simply it's all about where the bowler puts the ball and what he does with it. A ball pitching on the right length with the line down 'the corridor of uncertainty' often doesn't need to deviate to take the edge through to the keeper.

Another curious statement, in order to be critical of less-than-fast bowlers, is to say that 'they bowl along the wicket (pitch) as opposed to into it'. I suppose the attempt is to argue that the delivery skids from the pitch getting less bounce and grip and is therefore easier to play. Surely the condition of the surface of the pitch and the angle (or height) that the delivery is propelled into the pitch must play a major part in determining this result. However, Mr Malinga manages well enough bowling 'along the pitch'.

There is little doubt that if a bowler is too predictable, a batsman prepared to use his feet can take advantage of a one-dimensional bowler. It is important for all bowlers irrespective of kilometres per hour to be able to swing or seam the ball, to have a good change of pace and the ability to get the ball into the blockhole when needed. It applies just as much to a faster bowler. The assumption seems to be that because the faster bowlers are more physically threatening, their effectiveness is greater. This may be so against less-capable batsmen, however, most teams now have very few non-batsmen. The chances are a quicker ball travels faster off the bat (deflections etc.) and can be harder to defend.

As with the batting order, strictly pre-determining which overs each bowler will bowl risks not matching the natural skills of the bowler to the situation. A common mistake too is to insist on a bowler no matter who it is, bowling his full quota of overs, even though he is having a bad day. As with opening batsmen who need to get accustomed to facing the new ball, two bowlers need to be trained in using the new ball. Likewise, I see no good reason why two slow bowlers are not trained up and viewed as a real option to bowl blockhole deliveries in the so-called slog overs.

Although a number of teams are predictable in their approach, nothing should be assumed or taken for granted. Tactically it is important to respond very quickly to the moment and whatever it brings! It may arise whereby a batsman starts all out hitting in the twenty-fifth over. So-called death-over bowling may immediately need to be called upon with the appropriate field settings and the best-equipped bowler to handle the situation. The batsman might be Andrew Symonds, whereby the smartest response would be to get the ball into the blockhole, giving him one run down to long-on, on the first ball of the over! Another situation could be that death-over bowling never eventuates, because the batting team has lost most of their wickets and so on.

When it comes to field settings, the assumption once again seems to be weighted in favour of an anticipated wickets-first, runs-second approach. By positioning and/or retaining close catchers in those positions for longer, it is anticipated that this represents attacking and therefore more wickets will result. Needless to say, these positions seldom result in run saving or taking wickets.

I carried out some research on the combined dismissals of the Otago players and their opposition in the championship matches for the 2003/04 season. I wanted to test the assumptions I had made about the value of having fieldsmen in the various positions. Although it did not cover one-dayers, there are more fielders and for longer periods of time in catching positions in four-day cricket, adding more rather than less weight to the argument. Of the 207 dismissals recorded, 67.16% including run-outs were attributed to just two players, the bowler and the wicketkeeper (bowled 18.36%; LBW 18.36%; WK 23.19%; RO 4.35%; C&B 2.9%). If first slip is added in, a further 6.76% can be added to the 67.16%. It would be interesting for this type of statistical analysis to be continually updated to keep pace with the changing times. My figures are not derived from a large sample and not at the Test level of competition. There will also be a great deal of variability as to the number of players retained in catching positions and for how long.

It may be argued that the psychological aspect of having close-in fieldsmen creates problems for the batsmen. It is far more likely that a good player welcomes it (particularly once he has become established at the crease), because it takes a number of players out of commission in terms of run prevention. In fact one of the most attacking fielders for a very good player is more likely to be strategically positioned on the boundary, reducing the value of a favoured stroke from 4 to 1. No good player likes losing too much of the strike, nor being prevented from dominating the bowling. If this is occurring, he will take greater risks in attempting to assert his dominance. I'm not suggesting that while the good player is getting started it should be made easy for him to get under way with a deeply set field from the outset. In fact there is a strong argument to have an extra fielder in close for an edge early in his innings when he is most vulnerable. The better the player, the more justified these fielding positions are. To place fielders in other than run-saving positions for lesser batsmen generally provides them with runs they don't deserve, and what is more they are just as likely to get caught by fieldsmen in run-saving positions as they are in the slips or gully. It should always be remembered that the majority of batsmen are dismissed in ways always available to the fielding side, namely, bowled, LBW and caught by the wicketkeeper.

In conclusion, I would add that I'm not suggesting that anyone play beyond their level of competence. What I am asking for is for individuals, and the team as a whole, to use what they already possess, more resourcefully.

Looking at the players we already have batting-wise, we have a number of players that on their day are capable of striking at 100 plus. In particular: Astle, Styris, McCullum, Taylor, Vincent, Oram, Fulton, Franklin, Adams, Vettori. The first seven are all capable of scoring centuries at the above strike rate. All of the seven plus Franklin and Adams can hit it over the fence in front of the wicket. Vettori with his unorthodox batting seems to find the gaps often enough to score quickly and is also very good at turning over the strike. He could be used very effectively against spinners using his ability to sweep and late cut. Taylor is capable of taking a spinner apart and could also be used along with Vettori in this capacity. Taylor needs to be encouraged to practise and apply this skill. Fleming has shown that he can be a 6-hitter in front of the wicket but is seldom prepared to do so. He prefers to hit it through the field and can score at a decent clip. Jamie How has the potential to hit big, but still appears to be locked into pulls and hooks as his big shots. Hamish Marshall has been less capable than the others, but hopefully his recent performances and experience in county cricket will show through.

We have too many bowlers bowling four balls. What I'm not sure about is to what extent this can be attributed to their approach versus their ability or in fact their willingness to practise the required skills often enough.

Improvised Batmanship

(January 2010)

According to my *Oxford Reference Dictionary*, to improvise is 'to compose, to construct from materials not intended for the purpose'. On this occasion, I think this word does bear some relationship to what the batsman is attempting to achieve at the crease while improvising. He is moving around or changing his position at the crease in an effort to advantage himself in playing an attacking stroke. The assumption being that the ball being bowled is not going to be in his preferred areas for an aggressive play.

Some might argue that it is pre-empting and does therefore run contrary to the perceived wisdom that each ball should be treated on its merits. Although it is true to say that the risk factor increases and the purity of decision-making is compromised somewhat with an improvised approach, if executed well, the rewards can be greater and justified. Nevertheless, the practical application of improvising needs to be skilfully applied, minimising the added risk factor and increasing the rewards.

In their application, the fundamentals of sound batsmanship need not and should not be compromised, namely, striking from a solid base, keeping the head very still on contact, with good balance and transfer of weight. Any pre-emptive decisions must allow for a series of shot options to remain open. To commit solely to one shot in advance is an extremely high-risk approach. A common mistake is to over-hit, resulting in a loss of timing and therefore poor execution. It is vital not to move too far in any direction, because any loss of contact with the stumps obviously limits the ability to defend them (although not when progressing towards the ball) and increases the likelihood of poor execution. Additionally, when moving excessively sideways, the ability to make contact with balls judged to be in play is reduced. Every batsman will have preferred boundary shots (some more than others), but if the ball is not in the right areas to execute them, they must have bail-out options. It is obviously still important to remain at the crease, and bail-out shots can still produce runs.

I don't subscribe to the view that ramping or pre-conceived sweeps or paddles can be justified. Nor the argument that there are not enough gaps in the field, hence the need to play an extremely low-percentage shot in order to shift a fielder. That excuse is often used even after a fielder has been shifted. I'm fully aware of some very successful players who do from time to time introduce these 'shots', but it says more about their personalities than forming an argument in support of it. I will concede that those with limited ability probably need to develop an unorthodox approach to batting in order to increase their value. Nevertheless, opponents will quickly catch on to their unique range of shots and lessen their effectiveness. I don't see this type of player being in the top six in the batting order — certainly not one who relies heavily on luck.

Planning to Win the Next World Cup in 2015

(January 2012)

John Wright and Ross Taylor have both made strong statements about the significance of Test cricket and its importance to New Zealand. John Buchanan, on the other hand, said when he first arrived that the national team's focus over the next four years is going to be on limited-over cricket. Buchanan's reasoning is that New Zealand has shown more ability in one-day cricket than in Tests. That's true; the evidence is there for all to see. The temptation is, therefore, to pick up on what appears to be the easier option for immediate improvement in results.

The recent Test win against higher-ranked Australia will, in the eyes of some, raise questions as to where the focus should lie, and why. It's hard to fathom just what concentrating on one form of the game and not another means. Does it mean fewer resources being put into Test cricket, adjusting the timing of the Test programme to accommodate additional one-day and T20 stuff for whomever, or maybe encouraging players to take their holidays during Tests, or what?

My belief is that, initially, players develop more by concentrating on the longer forms of the game. How? Because it gives them more playing time, therefore less pressure in which to develop and hone their core skills.

If Tests are not the priority, it's a bit confusing when NZC gives a handsome 12-month retainer to one player who is only available for Test matches, and another 12-month retainer to one who is available for all forms of the game, but is only likely to be selected for Test cricket.

But if one-dayers are to be our priority, to give ourselves the best chance of winning the next 2015 World Cup planning needs to begin with the upcoming Zimbabwe series. Most of the initiatives should point towards players working on finding their A game and practising it relentlessly until they become consistently good at applying it. Furthermore, players should not rely on, or be distracted by, anyone else in achieving that goal. You can bet your bottom dollar that there will be many staff changes between now and 2015 (if recent history is anything to go by), and every man and his dog will be putting their oar in along the way. My advice to players is choose your counsel carefully, open your mind to learning and be personally responsible for your own development and performance.

There's a need for selection to work towards choosing emerging players in order to find out who has the required talent to be persevered with. This work should start immediately. At the same time it would be prudent to look at the current crop of players with a view to assessing which of them are most likely to be good enough to retain their places in the team through to and including the World Cup in 2015.

In the last two World Cups, the reality has been that selections, player preparation and their approach tactically to games have been more about saving face (putting in a respectable performance) than aggressively going out to win games. The fear of losing badly has tended to dominate thinking and consequently winning has too often relied on opponents having a bad day. South Africa did exactly that against New Zealand in the 2011 Cricket World Cup, allowing New Zealand to progress through to the semi-final stage. Set a modest total of 221, South Africa could only muster 172 in reply.

Leading into the World Cup, New Zealand's results on the subcontinent were so bad (0-4 against Bangladesh and 0-5 against India) that a last-minute panic resulted in major changes to the support personnel. At this point it was understandable that John Wright, the new crew and all those with an interest in the national team were going to be happy with a semi-final berth no matter how it was achieved.

The decision should be made earlier rather than later as to whether we see continuing to reach semi-finals as our ultimate goal. If we are not happy with that and are serious about giving ourselves the best chance of winning the next World Cup, we had better start preparing now. Whether World Cups warrant so much importance is another matter. But currently, they are given all-important status.

When comparing the batting statistics of the winning team, India, with our own in the last World Cup, it's clear just how much we need to improve to be serious contenders for the top prize in the future.

As part of formulating that view, I have compared the batting statistics of the first five batsmen for both New Zealand and India against just the top teams. I included Bangladesh in the top grouping because they had beaten New Zealand 4-0 in a series just prior to the World Cup. I didn't, however, include Zimbabwe for obvious reasons.

New Zealand statistics against Australia, Pakistan, South Africa, and Sri Lanka twice, read: McCullum 5 innings, 53 runs, 10.60 average, 94.60 strike rate; Guptill 5-120-24-56.33; Ryder 5-146-36.50-69.85; Taylor 5-250-62.50-76.21; Styris 5-107-21.40-73.79.

The Indian statistics include two more games than New Zealand because they had Bangladesh in their group and they played the final. Their matches include England, South Africa, West Indies, Australia, Bangladesh, Pakistan and Sri Lanka. Tendulkar 7-417-59.37-93.49; Sehwag 7-336-56-119.57; Gambhir 7-355-50.71-84.72; Kholi 7-236-39.33-87.4; Yuvraj Singh 7-261-65.25-95.95.

TWELVE
THE TRUE ROLE OF CRICKET CAPTAINS

CAPTAINCY STYLES HAVE GONE THROUGH SOME INTERESTING PHASES over the past couple of decades from Stephen Fleming to Daniel Vettori, Ross Taylor, Brendon McCullum and Kane Williamson all having very different approaches to the role. Through that period, what has become noticeable is the growth of the captains' powers to control all and sundry, not least selection.

In today's so-called professional era, I believe the position of captaincy is ridiculously over-inflated. I'm very sceptical of many of the claims made about the importance of a captain's role off the field and the influence they are perceived to have over the players' way of thinking. Unfortunately, what has been forgotten is that the captain is an employee of, and should be answerable to, NZC. I believe a captain is also answerable to the players under his stewardship, through providing each player with opportunities to excel. It also needs to be recognised that the eight support staff that travel with the team could all be regarded in their own fields as captains, whose work is coordinated by the manager and coach. Having the captain too involved in the hiring and possible firing of the support staff of the team is fundamentally flawed. The decision to give him, and to some extent the leadership group, so much power has effectively taken most of the decision-making inside the ranks of the team with little hope of that power being apportioned responsibly. It undermines the effectiveness and credibility of the support personnel and while contributing to diminishing true accountability, it has the potential to increase conflicts of interest and diverting players from their core role of playing the game. There have been occasions when as a result of exposure to this sort of all-encompassing know-it-all leadership approach, players were returning to their provinces and wilfully destabilising the systems put in place by the provincial coach because they knew better. One egotistical player during a brief return even went so far as to have a coach sacked. By undermining the efforts at the lower level, these players among other things were interfering with the basic structure of the game and meddling with emerging players' attitudes and general development and minimising in many cases the benefits of some good work already in progress. The corollary of that may well be the cause for some players emerging at international level through this structure suddenly thinking they didn't need to keep learning — they already knew it all. Well, there's only ever been one place that has led and sadly it has been evidenced in some of the performances witnessed through the years involving New Zealand sides.

New Zealand went through a bad patch about 10 years ago when the coaching revolving door got the speed wobbles. John Bracewell, Andy Moles, Mark Greatbatch and John Wright all had stints in the coaching role; Moles and Greatbatch got fired, while Wright walked away dissatisfied with the structure NZC put in place. What all this instability created was a capacity for blame being directed at the coach, a handy excuse for under-performing players, and greater power being claimed by captains. What got lost in the process was the accountability of the captain for the success or failure of his performance. I still don't think the issue has been resolved, because much of this has become accepted as normal practice. The power bestowed on the captain has put a stop to the revolving door of coaches, simply because their status has become one of obedience.

The playing captain's job should be largely to decide bowling changes and to set the fields following planning discussions with the bowlers and the coach and to make on-field strategic decisions. Batting positions in the order should normally be agreed to in consultation with the coach and the selectors. Obviously, there will be times, mostly during limited-over games, when more flexibility is necessary, especially in respect to positions in the batting order. Nevertheless, good planning should have covered most of the various scenarios that can develop as an innings progresses. This also applies to bowling orders and field placements. It's my view that every international side should have more than one captain, skilled up ready to do the job at a moment's notice.

There have been occasions when it appeared the captain was expected to allegedly play a major part in moulding and developing the team culture, creating a dedicated, mentally tough, personally responsible group of well-adjusted players who respected the spirit of cricket, supported each other, faithfully followed game plans and were loyal to the jersey and the nation. Phew, I'm, exhausted just thinking about it let alone writing it. What is supposed to follow are players who develop the trust and respect for each other that would automatically produce a winning formula. Having mastered all of that, it's assumed this approach will overcome any lack of skill necessary to execute in the middle.

So what are some of the qualities and requirements that make a good captain?

- First and foremost to make good on-field decisions and give the team the best chance of winning.
- Be responsible in providing each player with opportunities to excel, taking into account the strategy needed for the team's success.

- Good tactical awareness, the confidence to make decisions without dependency on others. He must nevertheless be prepared to take advice (avoiding aloofness) and have a positive approach to learning.
- He needs to be responsible, accountable and look to solve problems, not apportion blame.
- Demonstrate respect for his colleagues and members of NZC's support staff.
- Have the strength to be honest, ethical and incorruptible, hence strengthening the development of trust.
- Value and respect 'the spirit of cricket'.

Notably, before the official announcement of the team for the 2019 Cricket World Cup, reports were published that Williamson had overruled selection convener Gavin Larsen and coach Gary Stead in the choice of leg-spinner Ish Sodhi ahead of Todd Astle. Regrettable in the first instance, it demonstrates nothing has changed in recent history over selection conflicts of interest. But, secondly, it revealed to Astle that Williamson didn't have as much faith in him, which if Sodhi had been injured and Astle was called up, could have been interesting. Meanwhile, Sodhi was then aware that he didn't have the full confidence of the selection convener and the coach. Will the lessons never be learned?

One of the pitfalls captains must be wary of is falling victim to preferring to go with players who have been part of the team for long periods, irrespective of their form at the moment, or their ability. Succession planning is a vital ingredient of continuity in the game and it means that somewhere along the line new blood has to be introduced, even if that drops the experience ratio available for the captain to call on. Without acknowledging this, a captain will eventually find himself in an unstable situation with respect for him diminishing among the players.

Another fault that can occur is for incumbent captains being unwilling to accept advice on how captaincy may be improved. There is much to be gained from candid expression. An exchange of observations and ideas is stimulating, necessary and helpful. This is not new. It is a core element of battlefield command and has been for generations. It's claimed to happen in successful business places. It is the same with sports teams, especially in cricket, where individual skills come together in an overall team performance to produce results. I remember John Wright commenting once that discussions like this between selectors, coaches and captains should be encouraged and seen as normal practice. The fact is that New Zealand Test teams are cyclical in their success. Our lack of depth compared to other cricket nations means we have to maximise our abilities when a core group of players comes along. We need to have strategies that will give the side every opportunity to push hard for wins when chances arise. There is an art to succeeding in Test matches, even more than in ODIs.

There have been times when I have felt that captains have been given too much say in how the team is run. This can distract players in the side to the point where they have more to think about than the actual playing of the game. When transparency in the team is glazed over as the result of potential conflicts of interest and different statements being made to different people, it has a negative effect on those players. It is unprofessional and damaging and should be avoided.

To my thinking an annual assessment of the captain should be standard practice, just as all other areas of the game should be analysed for the betterment of all. The role of the captain should be reassessed and I believe there should be a formula put in place to provide captains, and potential captains, with education in at least The Art of On-Field Captaincy. Once again there are plenty of people who could contribute to such a scheme. There are former cricket captains who could contribute. The New Zealand Sports Foundation back in the 1990s ran a captain's course for leaders of the day and it provided concrete evidence that captains in many sports were totally ill-prepared for the leadership role that was, in most instances, thrust upon them. They were just expected to get on with the job and cope with the pressures, even while trying to deal with their own game. The days when a former New Zealand captain Barry Sinclair could be told while having a cup of tea after completing his warm-up on the first morning of a Test, that he needed to go out and make the toss because he was going to captain the side because the intended captain had broken down, should be long gone. Then there was the instance in the 1992 World Cup semi-final when halfway through the game John Wright was thrust into assuming the captaincy after skipper Martin Crowe was injured and unable to field. Such a scheme would go a long way towards preventing reinventing the wheel every time a new appointment is made.

But before getting involved in such a venture, it would be essential that captains have an open mind to the learning associated. As I have mentioned earlier, it is far too easy for younger people to claim the game has changed and that older people don't understand the modern game. Yet, the game will outlive us all and we need to be aware that while much has changed, much has also remained the same and acquiring wisdom is still central to understanding how the game can be played. This would be up to the game's administrators to ensure that their captain(s) knew what was expected of them and they would be accountable to the board for their efforts. It is interesting to hear World Cup-winning All Blacks rugby coach Steve Hansen acknowledge the benefits of the High Performance Sport NZ course that he did, so if he can do that in coaching, why shouldn't our sports captains be able to do likewise? Those with decades of experience behind them, and who have a background of captaincy, are keenly aware of the numerous options available to a captain given the wide range of circumstances that develop during a game. A good student of the game will look to make decisions that give the best percentage chance of success. I understand and accept that opinions will often vary as to what the best decisions are in specific circumstances.

After the different styles of Vettori, Taylor (all too briefly) and McCullum, Williamson should have the time to push the reset button on how captaincy should be perceived in New Zealand. Although it is still relatively early days in his reign, on-field we have already witnessed major shifts in his tactical approach to the positioning of fielders and the deployment of his bowlers. Williamson's more logical, less wacky approach means he has put his faith in the conventional theory of working with proven probabilities. A reckless gambling methodology is not his way. And I'm pretty sure he knows that with more time and experience he will become even more astute in respect of when to make bowling changes and alterations to field settings, and knowing more about when to defend and when to attack. There will often be some tactical norms that develop over time which need to be challenged. One that stands out currently with most, if not all, captains in international cricket is a reluctance to having a more attacking approach with field placements when an opposition has been set a virtually impossible number of runs for victory. Even when victory becomes all the more obvious the reluctance to change course frequently remains. A good example of this is when Australia set New Zealand 486 in the Boxing Day Test in 2019.

We already know his on-field demeanour will be less eye-catching, and appears more considered. He's not a show pony! Hopefully, this doesn't work against him to the degree that it did for Taylor. Fortunately, Williamson took over the captaincy at a time when he is less likely to be faced with others from within the ranks manoeuvring to unseat him. That will come later! I hope that Williamson doesn't go down the path of employing a 'spin doctor' and that he puts his faith in truth. I also hope he doesn't get sucked into the sort of media training that focuses on learning which popular buttons to push. Although his predecessor was very successful in that regard, Williamson is less likely to carry it off and why should he want to anyway? Williamson comes across as someone willing to break the trend, someone hopeful of gaining people's confidence through straight and honest dialogue that can be trusted. That would be welcomed by many, of that I'm sure.

As a captain I doubt that Williamson's example will be characterised by recklessness on and off the field. Hopefully over time he can persuade the PR machine to stop feeding the public the feel-good 'total team unity' (TTU) and 'happy family' lines and the prattle about 'culture' and the 'environment' causing one to reach for the mute button.

Players will do the right thing by the team if they have personal integrity or when knowing that if they don't, they are putting their selection on the line. Some will have more or less integrity than others, as is the case with any group of people. To believe that it's possible to get everyone in a team to pull in the one direction is to ignore character differences and the nature of human beings.

Don't expect Williamson to haphazardly make declarations that are likely to cost you a series or order a capitulation in a run chase which surrenders the opportunity to win a series. Don't anticipate him batting in a manner which resorts to self-indulgence, but expect him to genuinely put team first.

There will be some obvious differences in his approach and successes as a batsman as compared to his predecessor. The comparisons are poles apart. If Williamson's form continues down the same path, he will average a Test hundred every 6.3 innings compared to McCullum's 13.9. His Test average will be 9.45 runs higher and his strike rate (SR) 16.51 lower. His ODI average will be 16.59 higher and his SR 12.37 lower. In T20s, his average will be 1.13 lower and his SR 11.92 lower.

Williamson is unlikely to eclipse the SR records of McCullum (although they are still very good), largely because the game situations will not arise often enough for him to justify self-indulgence over team first. The figures above unquestionably show that Williamson's worth as a batsman is significantly more valuable in Tests and ODIs. McCullum's stats in T20 cricket are superior and accordingly his bank balance will be much larger!

McCullum's timing as captain couldn't have been better with the rise of Southee, Boult and Williamson along with an international class player in Taylor. Comprehensive home and away series losses to Australia at the end of McCullum's reign demonstrated how important it will be for Williamson to get New Zealand's opening bowling attack back firing on all cylinders. Cruelly, captains are too often judged only on the successes or failures of their teams. Will Williamson have as much public appeal as McCullum? Probably not with the younger set or those that prefer a fast-food outlet to a silver-service restaurant, or a pop concert over an orchestral concert. Whose example would I prefer my grandchildren to follow? No prizes for answering that!

THIRTEEN
ANOTHER FLAWED SELECTION SYSTEM

THE STRUCTURE AND MAKEUP OF CRICKET'S NATIONAL SELECTION panels continues to service self-interest, and I've yet to come across any reasoned or sufficiently convincing arguments for any of the applied systems that have been adopted over the past couple of decades since the game became professional in New Zealand. This is another example of the way in which our cricket administrations have failed to keep pace with the rapidly changing cricket environment. I'd suggest that efforts to come up with sound, reasoned solutions in respect to selection policies continue to be stalled by biased, outdated, superficial arguments in support of pre-determined decisions which ignore appropriate guardianship of the game, let alone addressing conflicts of interest. The supposition is that the head coach and captain's roles are the most important and therefore they should be given control of as much as possible. Having had considerable experience in all three positions, I believe these roles are all important and should work cooperatively towards the same goal of producing a successful team. As I said earlier, what tends to prevent this from happening is the erroneous view that the blame for poor team results should rest on the shoulders of one person. The result, often, is to inflate the entitlement of one individual to take over control of more than one role, lessening the prospect of meaningful contributions from the others. This entitlement reached a peak during Daniel Vettori's reign, supported by the chief executive Justin Vaughan and presumably the Players Association. Vettori made no secret of who he believed should be running the ship. His conviction was that he should get the team he wanted and if he failed he should be sacked. He manoeuvred selections to suit himself and the only sackings were coaches and selectors.

So what existed before the end of the century for New Zealand cricketers and what has changed since then for the need to revisit selection policies? Once the game moved from an amateur game to where those playing at the highest level for New Zealand could make a living from it, professional considerations needed to be introduced. Rotating the power of selection between coach and captain and a combination of the two during the amateur days was understandable, even with a couple of other part-time selectors in the background. In those days, far less international cricket was being played by New Zealand teams, allowing the coach time to view domestic first-class cricket, which was also on a much reduced scale. It wasn't until the 2000/01 domestic season that first-class games increased from 5 to 10 matches. Today, the coach may have the day-to-day knowledge of the incumbent established players, but there are too many other good reasons why controlling selection compromises him and the captain, not least serving conflicts of interest.

So what are the stronger arguments for a fully independent selection panel? In my view it should be a given that everyone should be encouraged to focus on their own task while still working cooperatively. Control of selection needs to be removed from inside the team's camp, avoiding incestuous gains taking hold. Otherwise, the door is opened to greater than normal levels of division, jealousy, distractions, strains on friendships and, at times, even a bit of looking after your mate at the expense of others. A good example of some of this was the fiasco surrounding the selection of Daniel Vettori's successor as captain, which dragged on for months. The delays were a public relations disaster and created divisions and jealousies within the team, since they were given grounds to believe the decision was theirs to make. There's nothing to suggest that this will not occur again in the future.

When the head coach is also a selector, and the dominant one at that, players are less likely to confide in him because by admitting to any weaknesses, they fear that may lead to their non-selection. In this regard I recall that a previous Australian Head Coach, Tim Nielsen, in an interview with Cricinfo, stated that 'players who have lost a bit of confidence in their game are more willing to talk to someone who isn't a huge influence on decision-making'. Nielsen, at the time, wasn't on the selection panel. He recognised that selectors are better not to be subjected to the politics of the team and the temptations arising from that.

If the selectors are exposed in this way, the incumbent players automatically have the day-to-day ear of the coach/selector, with the opportunity to promote their cause. This in-house advantage is not available to all the other first-class provincial players who have the right to be considered for selection every time the national team is chosen. There is no stipulation that the 12 to 15 players selected for home or overseas tours must be sourced from within the 20 contracted to NZC. Injuries and selections to fit all three different formats will from time to time necessitate selecting from outside the 20. Here it is worth remembering that today, head coaches of international cricket teams seldom, if ever, have the time or inclination to watch provincial cricket.

Playing XIs are often chosen on a game-by-game basis. That's understandable to a degree, but it usually means little consideration is given to succession planning in the cause of the overall development of the national team. What the existing system has also provided is more security for a few of the more senior, well-positioned players. Consequently, it has made it harder for up-and-coming players to get into the national side, and building more depth. Furthermore, if one or two do manage to get into the 15-man squad, their chances of getting game time is often controlled by vested interests from within.

In August 2018, Geoffrey Boycott in a piece for Cricinfo supported the view of having one independent selection panel when he said Ed Smith or James Taylor would be going on tour that winter to Sri Lanka and West Indies. 'But, on tour, the captain and coach pick the team. If Ed and James are only observers, then they are not much use and may as well watch the Tests on television at home and save the expense.

'It would be more important and helpful to English cricket if they took charge of team selection on tour as they do at the moment in England. We need to have continuity, with the selectors in charge of selection at home and away.

'I am a big believer in the chairman taking selection totally out of the captain's hands. There is no favouritism that way and we all know who is in charge of selection and where the buck stops. So far, Ed has done well, so carry on and do not give it back to the captain and coach when we go away.'

It's hard to keep up with the goings-on in cricket, the examples of flawed policies, or at least the application of them keep flowing — at some stage I'll have to draw a line under this book. Shane Warne recently published a book called *No Spin*, where he has a fly at his old captain Steve Waugh for being the one responsible for leaving him out of the fourth Test match in Antigua in the West Indies in 1999. I won't bore you with Warne's reaction other than to say it was predictable. At least this venom aimed at his captain could have been directed (if he'd been dropped) at those other independent bastards! It's just another example of what can happen when in-house conflicts of interest take hold.

It appears that selection policies are left to the whim of who has the strongest personalities and a lack of knowledge from the decision-makers. Certainly the success of any policy functioning well is still dependent on the people involved, but the least that can be done is to implement a soundly reasoned policy.

It is a mistake to think that the same criteria for selecting franchised teams (as in the case of a number of other sports) should be followed when selecting international cricket line-ups, because franchises are restricted and committed to a much smaller pool of players. In more recent times provincial coaches have been officially asked to be involved in talent scouting the provincial scene, but it is fantasy to think it will cover what is needed. I'm all for consulting provincial coaches. There's nothing new in that; it is normal practice. But asking them to act in an official talent identification role will create more problems than it will solve. Having been given selection criteria to follow, they will then be expected, I presume, to put forward their national teams. The expectation is that checks and balances will sort out any prejudices or bugs in the workings of this system.

Let's look at a few of the bugs and problem areas that immediately come to mind.

Of the six provincial coaches, there will likely be a range of experience between them. From new to coaching first-class teams, to new on the scene in New Zealand, to having been off the scene for some time and so on.

- As would be expected, in terms of expertise, most coaches are stronger in one area of the game.
- Some will naturally push harder for their own players than others.
- Some will be more convinced than others to follow the new selection criteria and there will be wide-ranging differences in their abilities to interpret what they see and are being asked to assess.
- I suspect most will find it an unwelcome addition to their workloads.
- To ask coaches in effect to analyse the abilities of players in three forms of the game and to all intents and purposes 15 other provincial teams is totally unrealistic.
- I can foresee players even more inclined to involve themselves in the politics of pushing their case for selection with their provincial coaches.

- I can forecast players feeling their case is not being pushed hard enough by their provincial coach if they aren't selected.
- I can foresee coaches becoming irritated by the pressure exerted upon them from all and sundry concerning New Zealand selections.
- After a period of time I can predict provincial coaches becoming disillusioned when their preferences appear to be continually ignored.
- I can foresee coaches just going through the motions of the system, hoping it will go away sooner rather than later.

My experiences with provincial coaches, and having been one myself, prompt me to ask, why would they want it? What's wrong with a system whereby a national selector simply asks a few well-chosen questions about a player or two? The provincial coaches may receive a few additional helpful measures they can apply to their own players, but they could benefit from this without needing to be burdened by lobbying for international selections.

No matter how this experiment is being dressed up, to all intents and purposes the head coach of the national team is making most of the decisions on selection. Maybe he's number two in the pecking order if the skipper is in control, as in the case of Vettori and McCullum and perhaps now Williamson, since he has come up through a system whereby it has become normalised. Who said dictatorships can only exist alongside Middle Eastern regimes and more recently in the United States of America? Attempting to correct one mistake with another is, I suppose, predictable when you don't recognise or concede to the first mistake. In the case of Daniel Vettori, New Zealand Cricket had already read my report outlining what can happen when you allow the captain to dominate selection. My paper wasn't even acknowledged. However, for a very brief period of time it looked as though the chief executive Justin Vaughan had agreed to a 'fully independent selection panel', but before it had a chance to operate it was scrapped for a return to the autocratic in-house model with no discussion or reasons given. I did question myself several times as to why I continued to accept being a 'Claytons selector'. My rationalisation was about hanging on to the hope of some questioning, or at least to be included in discussions. Once again my suspicions were that power plays were at work in the background dominating a weak administration. A case of, I don't want to know what you think, I only want you to know what I think. With that in mind the selection panel at the time of myself, Mark Greatbatch and Lance Cairns prepared the following paper on the subject of selection.

WHAT ARE the reasons for the National Selection Panel naming the playing XI?

Because an independent panel can more effectively apply succession planning by being more aware and mindful of the importance of medium to longer term objectives and goals; and by being less emotionally involved and distracted by matters of the moment and therefore having a more objective assessment of the situation.

- So that they can be held wholly accountable, for selection.
- Because they are independent and removed from the *teams'* family, friendships, mateship, favours, nepotism and the internal politics prevalent within teams.
- Because they are independent when deciding who gets the match fees (money).
- Because it allows those from within the New Zealand camp (players and management etc.) to be protected from blame, accusation and recriminations that stem from selection decisions.
- Because they are less susceptible to passing on personal information, *or possibly misinformation*, discussed around the selection table.
- Because after 11 consecutive losses in 2010 there was a need to alter the practice of continuing the policy of selecting the

same line-up when it was necessary to accept there was a need to take the opportunity to develop players who were entitled to expect they should be given a chance to show they could be better than some incumbents.
- Following the series loss to Pakistan, the question has to be asked, what was achieved over the period of the last 16 ODIs to develop the future performance of the team? We would suggest very little.

To what extent is it reasonable for the selection panel to influence the batting and bowling guidelines?

Some thoughts and observations:

- With the new structure of a 'Fully Independent Selection Panel', hopefully it will encourage much greater communication and cooperation between captain, coach and selectors, so that any questioning of someone else's area of responsibility is approached with an open mind and solutions sought without prejudice.
- Generally players are selected to perform specific roles and therefore if they are not used in fulfilling these roles, their future selection is being put at risk.
- Players are in most cases selected as belonging to certain categories and this can still allow for some flexibility. The categories are the two opening batsmen (who would normally be set), numbers 3 and 4, the middle order of 5, 6, and 7 and the rest. Within these four categories the captain and coach can have the power to move players around according to their preference, although in longer forms of the game number 7 (often filled by an all-rounder) is less likely to have the skill set of either number 5 or 6. In limited-over games, the opening batsmen are set, and more often than not 3 and 4, but thereafter the captain and coach need the freedom to move players around in response to the game situation as it unfolds.

- The bowling order is less fixed, apart from who opens the bowling. Nevertheless, in the longer forms of the game, it would be expected that your seam/swing/fast bowlers would be given the first use of the ball ahead of the spinners or part-time bowlers. Once again there needs to be much more flexibility with bowling orders in the limited-over formats of the game.
- The Australian National Selection Panel (NSP) selects players for specific positions, but the final positions are decided by the captain after consultation with the NSP. The NSP members have stated that they will become more active in this area in the future.
- The England NSP selects players for specific positions, but it accepts that the odd player offers options which it welcomes.

How does selection function during home and away games?

The selection panel should take the lead from the coach (if he still exists) as to when he wants the naming of the 11 to be made. A selector should be at the ground the day before the game anyway, so that the naming of the 11 or 12 can be made the night before the match, if required. Sometimes there is a preference to wait until the morning of the match so as to further assess the playing conditions, or perhaps the fitness of a player. The selector at the ground should be in contact with the other selectors so that the whole panel is still fully involved in the decision. With today's technology, selectors are able to watch every ball bowled in their own homes no matter what part of the world the team is playing in.

It needs to be formalised within the selectors' brief to make the final decision on the players who should or shouldn't be rested during or between series, along with players' availability to play for their provinces. The Australian panel makes the decision on who is rested with the appropriate personnel being consulted as you would expect.

Naming the captain

The captain is still supposed to be named before each tour but over time it would seem that our captains have tended to take their position for granted; this should no longer be taken for granted. With an increase in the number of games and different formats being played at the international level, together with players picking up other contracts, this means that a one-captain-fits-all policy is outdated. Other countries have already recognised this fact.

The England NSP regards the communication between it and the players, as to what its expectations of them are, is paramount.

Notes:

In light of all the previously stated arguments, it is counterproductive to have another separate selection panel operating when the team is on tour.

For the last 15 years or more, NZC has largely followed a policy of serving the ever-increasing insatiable appetites of a growing group of players. The assumption has been that these players were and are indispensable. Even for those that believe this, the truth is that only a handful of New Zealand players over the past 40 years have been in the elite category internationally. Some of our better-performed players are ending their international careers a year or two earlier than might have been expected, lured by the emergence of T20 leagues. The perceived threat of losing players has led to selection policies and contracts that ensure the retention of some players unreservedly. These policies have corrupted competition for positions and too often stalled player development and curtailed opportunities to build playing depth. A selection policy that lacks player accountability is also unlikely to bring the best out of the players when they know their positions are safe irrespective of their performance and their obligations to justify 12-month contracts.

An excuse for continuing to select in some cases 'the tried and failed' comes about through the convenient assumption that we don't have other players worthy of further consideration. A consistent and methodical approach to selection coupled with a captain prepared to develop players has the best chance of finding and growing our talent base. Furthermore, it will address the shortcomings associated with revolving door selections, by giving players time to demonstrate their worth. Clinging on to parts of the previously failed system will not allow a fully independent selection panel to be wholly functional.

The home series against Pakistan — when Vettori, Oram and Ryder all missed games through injury — demonstrated the importance of developing playing depth.

The new 'Fully Independent Selection Panel' system and how it is to operate needs to be conveyed to everyone concerned so that all can focus on their own responsibilities.

Once the lines of demarcation between the various positions of responsibility are resolved and applied, it will become operationally much easier for all concerned to function, not least who answers what questions publicly.

It will also be more difficult for the media to misrepresent, speculate and generally punch holes in a system that has more clarity and logic to it.

The main arguments used by captains and coaches to justify why they should control the selection of the 11 players is that they say they know if a player is netting well or in a good 'head space'. Irrespective of the accuracy of these assessments or predictions, they go nowhere near outweighing all the other reasons for why the captain and coach should not be burdened by selection matters.

Recommendations:

- The fully independent selection panel selects the playing 11.
- That there is only one selection panel and therefore a second (on tour) panel becomes inappropriate.
- A selector (called the duty selector) travels with the team

overseas and this duty can be shared among the panel. The same should be applied during a home series.
- That players are used in the roles and categories they have been selected for as outlined in the document under the heading 'To what extent is it reasonable for the selection panel to influence the batting and bowling guidelines?'.
- It needs to be formalised even though it is currently within the selectors' brief to make final decisions on the players who should or shouldn't be rested, along with the players' availability to play for their provinces.
- To formalise that the captain is named prior to each series.
- That selectors are entitled to communicate their expectations to players. One of the reasons for this is the demand from the Players Association that any player being dropped must be given reasons. Unless selection is controlled by 'The Selection Panel', why would they be expected to give reasoned explanations to a dropped player when the enforced actions of others may have been the ones largely responsible?

Glenn Turner, Mark Greatbatch, Lance Cairns

IN HINDSIGHT, there are good reasons to believe that the degree of influence in selection and player contract matters made available to the Players Association by NZC has played a significant part in retaining the powers of selection inside the players' camp. This might also explain the decision to suddenly withdraw my services from selection without discussion or reasons given. It wouldn't be the first time that lapdogs are caught out, unwilling or unable to justify the will of others!

FOURTEEN
THE CONTRACT SYSTEM — WHO WINS?

IN JANUARY 2012, I PUT DOWN SOME THOUGHTS ABOUT THE CONTRACT system that had been created around that time.

You have to hand it to them; the senior players have got their full-time, or are they part-time, employers by the 'short and curlies'. For the past four years or so, senior players have been discussing whether or not to sign year-long contracts with NZC. It probably didn't enter their minds that NZC would give them 12-month contracts and allow some of them to take up separate individual contracts and with very few restrictions. Not surprisingly, some players have found the opportunity to gold prospect in other countries irresistible.

Recently, the former South African batsman Barry Richards referred to the present as 'the day of the individual contractor'. He cited the West Indian Chris Gayle as an example of a player who doesn't want to be tied to his country for 12 months. Gayle is playing for the Sydney Sixers in the Big Bash, the Dolphins in South Africa, the IPL and somewhere in the UK, too. He could almost be seen to be negotiating match by match who he's playing for.

Interestingly, Richards became an 'independent contractor' out of necessity when South Africa was boycotted during the apartheid era. For him, it was either that or not play at all.

What appears to have gone largely unnoticed in New Zealand is that NZC has been allowing some players to act as individual contractors. They are selling themselves to whomever, virtually whenever, while at the same time NZC is giving them 12-month retainers.

Why? It stems from the threat of losing senior players and the perceived need to retain them at all costs. This compromises New Zealand's international programme and robs some players fully committed to NZC of their chance to receive retainers. I would have thought the 80-odd provincial players — paid-up members of the Players Association — would expect to be represented and treated with more consideration and respect. What it has done, though, is enable an additional couple of New Zealand players to receive IPL contracts because of their availability to fulfil a complete IPL programme. Other countries have not been prepared to compromise their international programmes in the same way.

It's a remarkable feat for a handful of players to have manoeuvred themselves into a position whereby they have already succeeded in having a Test match against Australia cancelled to make way for a bigger IPL contract. Arriving late to international tours; delaying having injuries operated on and rehabilitation work done during NZC's playing programme to accommodate other contract opportunities; accepting other playing contracts during agreed holiday breaks between themselves and NZC; being excused (rested) from fulfilling the requirement to be available for domestic cricket duties when not playing for New Zealand.

In my view it would be simpler, fairer and better by awarding contracts for each competition. The senior players' fears of losing out financially would be unfounded because if they are high in the pecking order in all three competitions, their overall income would remain about the same.

Of course, one can see why some would prefer that the status quo remained, as it would help a few protect six-figure retainers while minimising their commitment to NZC. One can see the attraction in being freed up to secure lucrative offshore contracts, which could result in them amassing seven-figure sums. Alternatively, the option could be to just sit around while the plebeians do the day-to-day stuff. No prizes for working out where the power lies in cricket today and I thought boards were at least in the background to govern?

I believe players have every right to pick and choose what they are available for, but to get away with double dipping is at best unethical and shows disregard for guardianship of the game. Surely there is enough legal knowledge on the board to put that right.

The main disadvantage of players contracting themselves out to foreign employers these days is that mostly it involves playing T20 cricket. For players to be serious about improving their game, there are periods when a decent amount of time can be gainfully spent away from the pressures of competition, working on improving their skills. The opportunity costs in the short term will be of concern to most, but improved players may literally cash in more substantially in time. Incidentally, they might even score more runs and take more wickets for New Zealand too.

For those misinformed about my background with NZC, first as a player and ever since, there was no professional cricket then in New Zealand and we were given a pittance per day in expenses (barely enough to buy a couple of bottles of beer in India). The reason I didn't play for New Zealand for a period had very little to do with money and all to do with being treated like a second-class citizen. Personally I have experienced very little change in that over the past three decades. When I played, I didn't give my wicket away easily and I suppose nothing much has changed since.

FIFTEEN

NEGLECT LEADS TO POWER CORRUPTING

THE WORLD OF CRICKET HAS A LOT TO BE CONCERNED ABOUT WHEN IT comes to match fixing and the opportunities the game presents for spot fixing and spread betting. There are no simple answers to these problems, nevertheless, administrations need to seriously continue to review the way they operate before they can legitimately conclude that they are doing as much as possible to prevent corruption within their jurisdiction.

A good starting point is for them to genuinely open themselves up to debate, challenging themselves and the status quo, looking at possible causes and their effect. They need to recognise, accept and apply core values, understand and anticipate human susceptibility in order to accurately anticipate, identify and solve problems. I have previously given examples in this book of where core values have not been followed and the damage caused.

It is widely accepted that one of these core susceptible human behaviours is that 'power corrupts and absolute power corrupts absolutely'. This famous quote is attributed to Lord Acton in 1887 and prior to that in the seventeenth century others came up with similar observations. William Pitt, for instance, when addressing the House of Lords in 1770 said 'unlimited power is apt to corrupt the minds of those who possess it'. Roman emperors declared themselves as gods and even Napoleon declared himself an emperor.

Today in India, Sachin Tendulkar is seen by many Indians as a living god. Sadly, he found it necessary to assure them that he wasn't a living god. There will have been historical times when money took on godly status and many people today believe money has leapfrogged God into the number one position. In the Hindu religion, they have a goddess of wealth and prosperity (Lakshmi), but she is not one of the Trinity of Brahma, Vishnu and Shiva.

Lord Acton's quote is still used widely today, signifying that human behaviour has changed very little over time. I think it is reasonable to deduce, therefore, that those in possession of excessive amounts of power (whether it be gained through money, position or status) are more susceptible to bribery and corruption. The question that then needs to be answered is, have the players in cricket been given excessive amounts of power? My experience in the case of New Zealand cricketers is an unequivocal yes, on all three counts, and I suspect it applies to most of the world of cricket.

I have personally experienced and witnessed numerous examples of the abuse of power by administrations in the '60s and '70s, and a similar degree of abuse by players from the mid-'90s to the present day. The 'me generation' has certainly been encouraged to cut loose.

So what are some of these examples?

On this occasion, I prefer to focus on the present rather than repeating historical happenings from the '60s and '70s.

In more recent times, improvements in technology have created an explosion in the number of televised cricket matches being broadcast around the world. This has created an unhealthy degree of hype and propaganda about the significance of the game and in particular its participants. As a result the bundles of cash and the excessive attention given to cricketers today, and the humility and ability of players to balance their newly-found fame, is constantly being tested. The gold rush has also resulted in and attracted a plethora of support personnel into the game. They are often keen not only to please but sometimes to pamper. Combine this with the fact that they are paid much less than the players, is it a surprise that the egos of young vulnerable inexperienced minds are given a further boost?

With the increased status of the game, boards have become top-heavy with people who have very little knowledge of the subject and who come mostly from alien backgrounds. These boards have largely abdicated their responsibilities by allowing players to dictate too many of the important decisions. They appear comfortable in allowing the tail to wag the dog. Once this occurs, debate and challenging ideas is snuffed out, by assigning decisions to vested interests, scuppering sound argument. In other words, it is not what is presented, but rather more who has presented it.

When a working dog has first rights over the food, he will likely gorge himself, unworried about what might be left for others, and sometimes finding himself wanting more. No need to perform on the hill, much easier to cosy up to their masters to extract more tucker, and better still, if they can choose who their masters are.

Too much control of selection has been taken inside the leaders of the pack, led by the top dog. It has become commonplace for players to be quoted in the media about selection matters. It is not uncommon for current captains and other players to publicly state how long they will stay in the job. I have witnessed the assumed rights of players strongly influencing the sacking of support staff. Many instances exist of players being permitted to publicly denigrate the performance of other staff members. When Graham Gooch lost the England batting coach's job, the captain, Alastair Cook, was the one who made the phone call to Gooch and answered questions from the media.

Annual contracts (retainers) and the priority order given to them are also heavily influenced by the top dogs. The top dogs take as much of the food going around as possible while others are left with the scraps.

They seem to be content in the knowledge that they can gorge themselves from additional pots of food while they continue to feed on their fixed annual supply. As a member of the support staff, you had better hope the pack is successful if you are to retain your job because blame and the players' axe is likely to be heading your way.

This is precisely where the game of cricket is in New Zealand today. It has been and will continue to be a recipe for underachievement and dereliction of duty and short term focused. There is no doubt in my mind, and I suspect in the minds of those who have been around long enough to compare, that the 'spirit of cricket' as outlined in *The Laws of Cricket* has deteriorated on a more consistent basis. The pendulum of power has swung from one extreme to the other in a relatively short space of time, having not left a semblance of equilibrium in its wake. Today there's a gulf, not only between administrations and players, but between sportsmanship and unethical standards.

A number of parallels can be drawn between the trends in wider society and where cricket finds itself today. Some would say it's not surprising, it's to be expected. Others want more, expect more, and hope that at least in sport more commendable values can be retained. To encourage a narcissistic mentality, materialism, money, image and fame is not a formula for success. Endorsing hard work, self-control and an open mind to learning isn't asking for too much, is it?

Wouldn't it be something if boards, players' associations and chief executives put the integrity and guardianship of the game ahead of themselves, players and money? The power of that would be something!

AFTERWORD

CRICKET'S FUTURE IN A CHANGING NEWS WORLD

The media world is at the forefront of technological change. It is stating the obvious to say that media, and newspapers especially, have been drastically reduced in what cricket, and indeed what sport, they cover nowadays. When Glenn Turner started out in cricket, it would be reasonable to expect that a top Test match in New Zealand, against England or Australia, would have writers from the *New Zealand Herald*, *Auckland Star*, *Dominion*, *Evening Post*, *Press* and *Christchurch Star* in attendance. The *Sunday Times*, *Sunday News* and *NZ Truth* would also be along for some of the time, and depending on the venue there might be local writers in attendance, along with the NZPA journalist covering the game for all the papers unable to attend. That's not to forget the vast numbers from overseas competing with each other through their various outlets. Nowadays there would be two, one from the *Herald* (NZME) group and another from Stuff Limited, previously known as Fairfax, and perhaps a few more from overseas outlets. That is a significant reduction in subjective comment on the national side. It also leaves the media far easier to manipulate by way of availability for comment of players, coaches or administrators. In every instance, and markedly so as the result of Stuff's decision to do away with regional sports reporters, the coverage of cricket at the level below international, and, more importantly, first-class level, and down to club level, is now non-existent for all intents and purposes. Yes, there is a smattering of material produced by NZC by way of press release on the first-class games. But there is no room for the local profile of a player who does well, or to explain the nuances of how a game is shaping. There is little avenue for the opinion writer to lend his or her view, based on having been at the coalface and understanding the issues.

Instead, it is usually only when controversy attends itself to the sport that every man and his dog takes to social media, or talkback radio, to vent his opinion. Most often that opinion is ill-considered and frequently lacking in *gravitas* while often overstepping the bounds of fair comment. What should be of concern, although it is to be suspected that it has never crossed the mind of many administrators, is that cricket especially, like its American cousin baseball, is a game that has grown up around the written word. The classic games, the colourful characters, the controversies and the great teams have all been described in the newspapers of every cricket hamlet in the world. Through the ages of the game, and the style presentations of newspapers, those views have been represented by the likes of: Sir Neville Cardus, Jack Fingleton, Bill O'Reilly, C.B. Fry, Denzil Batchelor, R.C. Robertson-Glasgow, Ray Robinson, E.W. Swanton, A.G. Moyes, Richie Benaud, R.S. Whitington, E.M. Wellings and more recently Christopher Martin-Jenkins, Phil Tresidder, Gideon Haigh, R.T. 'Dick' Brittenden, Tony Cozier, Don Cameron, Dicky Rutnagur, Henry Blofeld, and many more. Not many of their papers survive nowadays and, regrettably, nor do many of the institutions they represented. That's not to forget the classical writers who have contributed to the game's literature such as: C.L.R. James, Sir Arthur Conan Doyle, Sir James Barrie, Geoffrey Moorhouse, John Arlott et al.

Critics could say that clubs have their own ability to put their play online for anyone with a computer to read. But given the plethora of media outlets and other material online, who is going to plough through the various websites to gain the details of a local game? There was a time when newspaper reporters provided a key public service in recording club cricket and the same applied to the first-class game. Not everyone could attend those games but if scoreboards were ever left out of newspapers there was generally hell to pay. That process allowed journalists to learn to work with their contacts, to sense what news might be of interest and what needed to be exposed. There became an element of respect that the journalist had done the hard yards and if there was an opinion expressed then there was a basis for that opinion. But then the news model changed and unless there was some scandal or material to drive people to read material on newspaper websites, the powers that be were not interested. Nor was there institutional respect for those responsible for providing assessment of the game. If there were no quotes in stories they wouldn't be published. Journalists were expected to follow up whispered scoops, most of which ended having run out of gas a long way down a one-way street. Not everyone making comment, under the modern scheme, has done the groundwork and their opinion is less worthy — reflective as it is of the need for immediate, as opposed to considered, comment. Thus was broken the compact between reader and publisher. If the community link was broken, and this applied not only in cricket or sport, but in many other aspects of life, why bother to support a newspaper if it wasn't going to support you?

Similarly, when Glenn Turner starting playing cricket there was ball-by-ball commentary available on what was called Sports Roundup on the YC network of the New Zealand Broadcasting Corporation. This meant that for seven hours a day commentators at various venues around the country could have something like revolving 20-minute stints describing first-class games or, if there was action at one ground, a quick switch to get the details of a fallen wicket could be made. It produced compelling radio that echoed around backyards of New Zealand, on car radios and when the action truly hotted up, sometimes in offices, throughout the summer. But with the corporatisation of radio and television, Sports Roundup had to make way for Radio Sport, a station that needed significant financial input from NZC to keep it viable during its early days. However, the need for advertising to drive the station resulted in a diminution of commentary time with the cheap option of talkback call-ins becoming flavour of the day. It wasn't long before commentary disappeared completely from the domestic game. This had its own effect. Those first-class commentaries provided a chance for emerging commentators to cut their teeth in coping with the demands of live presentation, the need to fill gaps in play with meaningful utterances and not flights of fancy. Sadly, the ability to talk with ease on a variety of issues relative to the game during rain breaks has been lost due to the need to cater to the advertising dollar, so it's back to the studio we go. Now, NZC and the company broadcasting Test matches have been unable to reach an agreement on radio rights, so it appears Test commentary is doomed. That situation was made even less likely when NZME canned Radio Sport during the coronavirus pandemic. As a result, nothing is certain when some form of normality returns to everyday life. For those with an ear to the past, podcasts from the recorded files still make for evocative, if retrospective, listening. But they provide a reminder of the true value of the art of commentary. At least the ability to tune in through the internet to BBC cricket radio coverage maintains some contact with that style.

Television followed the cable model with SKY Television securing the rights, effectively taking the game out of the homes of those who could not afford to pay the fee required. While ratings were never an issue in a non-competitive market, the powers at SKY decided they needed 'entertainment' in their commentary, 'star factor' if you like, rather than the subjective, non-aligned approach that was provided when free-to-air television held the rights. This has increased the cheerleading formula involving the use of former players with no journalism or broadcasting training, who have the minimum background to make subjective criticism of aspects of play, a factor compounded by the liaison between the stakeholder, NZC, and the rights holder SKY, which requires a minimum of criticism. The Australian Channel 9 example is often quoted with former player Richie Benaud leading the former players used as their commentators. However, the difference was Benaud was trained in both newspaper and television journalism and his comments carried so much more weight as a consequence. Interestingly, so too were the outstanding British commentators John Arlott, Henry Blofeld and Christopher Martin-Jenkins. Jonathan Agnew was another, who did his share of journalism work after his playing career was over and before picking up the microphone. But, increasingly, it is the public, the game's shareholders, who are being short-changed. What do administrators have to fear from constructive criticism?

The added concern with the television situation is its tenuous hold on the game through competitive bidding for rights. SKY has lost the coverage rights for cricket to the streaming service provided by SPARK. Undoubtedly, the prize has gone to the highest bidder with potentially greater consequences for the game. It is not beyond reason that future steps could see the coverage taken up by an overseas entity with little concern for the game itself in New Zealand. Throughout all the funding processes, the very body supposed to represent the game and its 'stakeholders', NZC, is becoming more and more dependent on the rights dollar at the expense of the goodwill of the public it is supposed to be catering for. Stretching those two pillars much further is potentially calamitous. Again, the post-pandemic period is going to be very interesting from a television perspective as well as radio.

It is also all very well to say that there are websites that provide more cricket coverage, of all sorts, from around the world. But not everyone has access to websites. Apart from that a website is only as good as the content going into it. For example, Cricinfo used to run a New Zealand branch. Its coverage was New Zealand-centric. This did produce one interesting clash between the chief executive of NZC at the time Christopher Doig, and myself as editor of the site which provided content for NZC's website under contract. On the final day of a Test at Eden Park against Pakistan, New Zealand had been one wicket down overnight, chasing a total of 432 to win — an improbable target. But the side was skittled in less than an hour as Mohammad Sami cut loose with New Zealand losing nine wickets for 26 runs — an interesting irony given 26 was the lowest score in Test cricket set on the same ground in 1955 by New Zealand. The story posted on the site reflected the pitiful effort by New Zealand. Half an hour after it was posted Doig was on the phone saying there shouldn't be a story like that on the site. My response to him was what did he suggest? There was nothing to hide the fact that New Zealand had failed miserably. Did he want the reading public to understand that they would get the truth on his website or a soft touch that wasn't prepared to acknowledge the truth when it was impossible to avoid? It was pointed out to him that only a year or two earlier Doig had said to the writer when working on a newspaper that two of his players who opted out of a tour of the West Indies were 'miscreants'. If that wasn't a negative criticism of his product what was? His response was that he had no answer to that. The story remained on the site and, in the way of the media world, was replaced by other stories following up on what had gone wrong with the usual assessment by coaches and players. But Cricinfo did offer more than newspapers were able to offer across the board, without the regionalism and parochialism that was typical in the newspaper climate of the day. Its stories were New Zealand-based not only at international level but on the first-class scene with regular material being run from the major associations and about players other than those occupying the upper levels of the game. But when foreign ownership decided to retrench, offices like New Zealand, South Africa and the West Indies were easy to dispense with, while coverage was then done out of India. That, however, could only ever rely on existing news outlets being rewritten, or international coverage of the New Zealand team on tour.

That fact is, the media available to cover cricket has diminished significantly and so has the coverage. The decline in news content is unsustainable and could go a long way in reducing the appeal of the game in the longer term.

Nothing can ever remain the same. But it has to be said that a reduction in fourth estate coverage of the game can only diminish its significance. That will be of comfort to players, and it has to be said that the last united media outrage unleashed on the game in New Zealand was during the players' strike of 2002. The media's role as an independent force was graphically demonstrated on that occasion but it proved the last great blast of the power of the media. How some of the administrative gaffes of the last 15 years might have been handled differently had there been media with teeth involved it can only be wondered. The players won't mind that situation, they never do. When they are playing the game the consequences of off-field matters are of no concern to them. They live in a vacuum where everything is done for them — they are told when to be awake, when to report to meetings and what time they need to catch the bus. Self-sufficiency, an important element of playing success in any sport, is reduced under those circumstances. Compare that to participants in individual sports who have to make their way to the other side of the world to compete out of New Zealand's season. If they were not self-sufficient they would be broken before they ever managed to achieve success. For cricketers that arranged day-to-day lifestyle makes the outside world of little importance to them until their careers are complete. But there again is a danger, players beginning to think they are at the centre of the coverage equation. They are but bit players in a much longer running enterprise; the game has always been greater than them. They talk in the manner of the All Blacks in saying they are only caretakers of the positions they hold in the team. But how much do those players actually know of the game, and the legacy they say they are caring for? With all that in mind the question is, how much longer will there be a game to savour?

Lynn McConnell

March 2020

ABOUT THE AUTHORS

GLENN TURNER played 41 Tests and 41 ODIs during a career in which he became the only New Zealander to score 100 (103) first-class centuries. In his career of 455 games for New Zealand, Worcestershire in England and Otago and Northern Districts in New Zealand, he scored 2991 Test runs at 44.64 and 34,346 first-class runs at 49.70. He also played in 195 one-day matches. He captained New Zealand, Worcestershire, Otago, Northern Districts and International Wanderers teams. He laid the foundations that enabled future New Zealand players to pursue professional careers. He was twice coach to the national team, including the only Test series victory on Australian soil in 1985, and to World Cups in 1987 and 1996. He also had several stints coaching Otago and was a national selector for 15 years. *Cricket's Global Warming* is his fifth book.

LYNN MCCONNELL is an Auckland-based editor and writer who has written 24 books including the best-selling autobiographies of Ewen Chatfield and All Black Mils Muliaina and the *New Zealand Encyclopedia of Cricket*. He wrote New Zealand's first 50 test victories in *The First Fifty*. He co-wrote *Behind the Silver Fern* with Tony Johnson and the acclaimed *Galatas 1941: Courage in*

Vain and *Conquerors of Time*, the story of Jack Lovelock's 1936 1500m gold medal win at the Berlin Olympic Games. A former sports editor of *The Southland Times* and *The Evening Post*, he was New Zealand editor of Cricinfo.com and senior editor of sportal.co.nz.

🄵 facebook.com/cricketincrisis

OTHER BOOKS BY THE AUTHORS

GLENN TURNER

Lifting the Covers, with Brian Turner (1998)

Opening up, with Brian Turner (1987)

Glenn Turner's Century of Centuries, with Ray Cairns (1983)

My Way (1975)

LYNN McCONNELL

Behind the Silver Fern, with Tony Johnson (2016)

Playing Rugby League with Benji Marshall (2014)

Conquerors of Time (2009)

Mils Muliaina: Living the Dream (2009)

Galatas 1941: Courage in Vain (2006)

The First Fifty (2003)

Gavin Larsen's World Cup Cricket Diary, with Gavin Larsen (1999)

The Shell New Zealand Cricket Encyclopedia, with Ian Smith (1993)

Chats, with Ewen Chatfield (1988)

www.ingramcontent.com/pod-product-compliance
Lightning Source LLC
Chambersburg PA
CBHW021941290426
44108CB00012B/921